Shopping Tourism, Retailing, and Leisure

ASPECTS OF TOURISM
Series Editors: Professor Chris Cooper, *University of Queensland, Australia*
Dr C. Michael Hall, *University of Otago, Dunedin, New Zealand*
Dr Dallen Timothy, *Arizona State University, Tempe, USA*

Aspects of Tourism is an innovative, multifaceted series which will comprise authoritative reference handbooks on global tourism regions, research volumes, texts and monographs. It is designed to provide readers with the latest thinking on tourism world-wide and in so doing will push back the frontiers of tourism knowledge. The series will also introduce a new generation of international tourism authors, writing on leading edge topics. The volumes will be readable and user-friendly, providing accessible sources for further research. The list will be underpinned by an annual authoritative tourism research volume. Books in the series will be commissioned that probe the relationship between tourism and cognate subject areas such as strategy, development, retailing, sport and environmental studies. The publisher and series editors welcome proposals from writers with projects on these topics.

Other Books in the Series
Progressing Tourism Research
  Bill Faulkner, edited by Liz Fredline, Leo Jago and Chris Cooper
Managing Educational Tourism
  Brent W. Ritchie
Recreational Tourism: Demand and Impacts
  Chris Ryan
Coastal Mass Tourism: Diversification and Sustainable Development in Southern Europe
  Bill Bramwell (ed.)
Sport Tourism Development
  Thomas Hinch and James Higham
Sport Tourism: Interrelationships, Impact and Issues
  Brent Ritchie and Daryl Adair (eds)
Tourism, Mobility and Second Homes
  C. Michael Hall and Dieter Müller
Strategic Management for Tourism Communities: Bridging the Gaps
  Peter E. Murphy and Ann E. Murphy
Oceania: A Tourism Handbook
  Chris Cooper and C. Michael Hall (eds)
Tourism Marketing: A Collaborative Approach
  Alan Fyall and Brian Garrod
Music and Tourism: On the Road Again
  Chris Gibson and John Connell
Tourism Development: Issues for a Vulnerable Industry
  Julio Aramberri and Richard Butler (eds)
Nature-Based Tourism in Peripheral Areas: Development or Disaster?
  C. Michael Hall and Stephen Boyd (eds)
Tourism, Recreation and Climate Change
  C. Michael Hall and James Higham (eds)

For more details of these or any other of our publications, please contact:
Channel View Publications, Frankfurt Lodge, Clevedon Hall,
Victoria Road, Clevedon, BS21 7HH, England
http://www.channelviewpublications.com

ASPECTS OF TOURISM 23

Series Editors: Chris Cooper (*University of Queensland, Australia*),
C. Michael Hall (*University of Otago, New Zealand*)
and Dallen Timothy (*Arizona State University, USA*)

Shopping Tourism, Retailing, and Leisure

Dallen J. Timothy

CHANNEL VIEW PUBLICATIONS
Clevedon • Buffalo • Toronto

This book is dedicated to the memory of my sister,
Denise B. Reninger (1956–2003), who loved to shop!
Her courage made us more courageous.
In her weakness, she gave us strength.
In her suffering, she comforted us.
And in her faith, she gave us hope.

Library of Congress Cataloging in Publication Data
Timothy, Dallen J.
Shopping Tourism, Retailing and Leisure/Dallen J. Timothy.
Aspects of Tourism: 23.
Includes bibliographical references and index.
1. Tourism. 2. Retail trade. I. Title. II. Series.
G155.A1T56 2005
381'.1–dc22   2004017707

British Library Cataloguing in Publication Data
A catalogue entry for this book is available from the British Library.

ISBN 1-873150-60-1 (hbk)
ISBN 1-873150-59-8 (pbk)

Channel View Publications
An imprint of Multilingual Matters Ltd

UK: Frankfurt Lodge, Clevedon Hall, Victoria Road, Clevedon BS21 7SJ.
USA: 2250 Military Road, Tonawanda, NY 14150, USA.
Canada: 5201 Dufferin Street, North York, Ontario, Canada M3H 5T8.

Copyright © 2005 Dallen J. Timothy.

Typeset by Archetype-IT Ltd (http://www.archetype-it.com).
Printed and bound in Great Britain by the Cromwell Press.

Contents

Preface

The seeds of this book began to sprout in the late 1960s and early 1970s with my first unpleasant memories of shopping with my mother. As a child, I despised shopping with her, or anyone for that matter. It was boring, tedious, and so drawn out that I simply did not want to go, unless it involved a toy store of course but that was a rare occasion. During my teenage years and early adulthood, my contempt for shopping continued, especially where clothing and household items were concerned. Today, however, my needs and lifestyle have changed. As a result, I have come to enjoy the hedonic side of purchasing food, handicrafts during vacation time, farm animals, tools and other outdoor accoutrements, and antiques. Anything else is just not my style (clothes!). While these personal observations have directly influenced my line of thinking, time spent in shopping malls at home and traveling the world for work and pleasure have drawn me to examine people in shopping habitats and set me thinking on a more academic level about the leisure, or enjoyable, side of this consumptive behavior more broadly. Thus, from direct experience and extensive field work, a realization of the crucial role of shopping as a leisure activity and as a major component of the tourist experience began to shape the thinking for this volume and eventually led to its completion.

Most research on shopping has an applied focus, dealing with various aspects of customer satisfaction, retail store management, merchandising, distribution chain management and marketing. The less applied, social science side of shopping research is still in a rather nascent phase, although scholars from several academic areas have begun to appreciate the social, cultural, spatial, and political implications of shopping at the store, center, and community levels. Although somewhat tentative and cautious, a few authors began noting the possibility that there might be some semblance of leisure in shopping as early as the 1950s and 1960s, although the notion did not really take off with strength or serious conviction until the 1980s as consumer behavior specialists began to realize more courageously that people did not only shop out of economic necessity; rather, some actually enjoyed it and might have shopped for its ludic and social involvement.

Since that time, the notion of hedonic shopping has become the focus of much debate in the consumer science, psychology, retail management, and sociology literatures.

In the realm of leisure and tourism sciences, however, only a few scholars have attempted to tackle the notion of shopping as a legitimate area of study. Their work has proved its value over and over again and, as of the late 1990s, more people started jumping on the shopping research wagon, for the role of shopping, which is the most pervasive of all tourist activities, could no longer be ignored in tourism and recreation studies. Nonetheless, there are still some deep rifts in our understanding of the dynamics of shopping in the leisure and tourism contexts. Based upon this realization and the experiences noted earlier, this book was set in motion. The purpose of this tome is to put together what is known about leisure and tourist shopping into a framework and body of knowledge that will be of use to scholars and students who are interested in this long-neglected area of study and to retail industry managers who wish to understand better the dynamics of this important retail phenomenon and how they might better tap its economic dividends.

Dallen J. Timothy
Gilbert, Arizona, USA
January 2004

Acknowledgements

The author and publisher would like to thank the following for permission to reproduce figures and tables in the text: Elsevier Science for permission to reproduce Figures 4.2, 6.2 and Tables 6.6, 6.7, 7.1; Henry Stewart Publications for permission to reproduce Table 6.3; The Canadian Association of Geographers for permission to reproduce Table 4.2 and Figure 3.2; and New York University, Leonard N. Stern School of Business for permission to reproduce Figure 3.3. Every effort was made to obtain permissions, but in some instances there was no response by publishers or we have been unable to trace the owners of copyright material. We would appreciate any information that would enable us to do so.

Many people have played crucial direct and indirect roles in the completion of this book. First, I wish to thank Carol, Kendall, Olivia, Aaron, and Spencer for their support and kind understanding during the preparation of this book. Their patience is immeasurable and they must know they are more important than any of Dad's work! I am also indebted to Dave, Connie, Justin, Brandon, and Jesse for their important help on the farm, allowing me more time to complete this project.

Second, Mike, Marjukka, Sami, Tommi, and all the other extraordinary people of Channel View Publications deserve a very big thank you for being supportive, thoughtful, patient, and empathetic during a very difficult and trying time. Michael Hall and Chris Cooper were supportive of the book from the beginning and their understanding and genuine collegiality are deeply appreciated.

Finally, colleagues and friends with whom I have shopped have made a difference in the way I see shopping as a leisure endeavor. Many thanks go to Stephen Boyd, Tim Coles, Ross Dowling, David Duval, Michael Hall, Kevin Hannam, Dimitri Ioannides, Alan Lew, Richard Prentice, Bruce Prideaux, Petri Raivo, Victor Teye, and Cevat Tosun, who have demonstrated an erudite expertise in the complicated art of shopping (mostly bargain-hunting) and guided me to many interesting stores along the way.

Chapter 1

Leisure Consumption, Shopping, and Tourism

Get me out of this irritating natural stuff and back to the mall!

This 1999 comment by a female tourist in Volcano National Park, Hawaii, overheard by Lori Otterstrom, an acquaintance of the author, is very enlightening. It emphasizes the depth and breadth of relationships between tourism, mass consumption, and shopping. For this tourist, an essential trip to the mall while on holiday in Hawaii was interrupted briefly by an undesirable side-trip to a natural site. The following question seems to be posed: Why would anyone want to experience nature in Hawaii, when there is shopping to be done? There is little doubt that, once back in 'civilization', this tourist's shopping activities resumed. Thus, in the midst of the grandeur of a natural wonder, the desire for a transition from symbolic consumption (of nature) to a more concrete form of consumption (of goods) was pronounced. While visiting the natural attraction was indeed a form of symbolic consumption, it was not the most important form for this woman.

All types of tourism and tourist activities are, in one way or another, a form of consumption but it is the consumptive activity of shopping that is of most concern in this book. This introductory chapter sets the stage for understanding the relationships between shopping, consumption, and leisure/tourism from a conceptual viewpoint. It reviews the notion of consumption as the foundation of the relationships between tourism, leisure, and shopping and outlines the book's content. It also provides an overview model of the treatment of the subject of shopping tourism, retailing, and leisure.

Consumption

In medieval times, the notion of consumption differed considerably from to what it is today. For the majority of the earth's population, consumption was based on need and everyday survival, while for a small

1

handful of landlords and nobility, it centered on excess, spectacle, and status. The 18th century, however, brought about the initial stages of industrialization, and consumer capitalism soon followed. An increased domestic consumer market was thus created, and in response, new merchandise and wider product choices were introduced (Friedman, 1994). This early consumer revolution allowed an increasing number of people to purchase wider varieties of household goods, clothing, and body adornments in an increasingly broad array of retail venues (Coles, 1999b). Heavier industrialization during the 19th century spread greater wealth to more people and sectors of society, as industrial capitalism began to pervade the social economics of Western Europe and North America. With affluence came changes in patterns of consumption. It began to play a more central role in people's lives, providing opportunities to set themselves apart from other social status groups. Owing to their new-found wealth, the emerging middle and upper classes of North America began to imitate the lifestyles of European and British elites (Bocock, 1993: 14–15). In the economic works of Keynes, the propensity to consume was seen as a product of increased income, although not necessarily at the same rate, thus allowing the middle and upper classes to accumulate wealth (Friedman, 1994). Veblen (1934) studied this social class in the 1890s in the United States and it was from these observations he developed his theory of 'the leisure class'. Patterning their lives after how they thought the European aristocracy lived, the richer classes of the late 19th century practiced methods of consumption that typically precluded the involvement of the working and lower middle classes. Eating expensive food, drinking costly wines, wearing fine clothing and jewelry, and purchasing fine furniture for their stately homes became central to the lives of the leisure class of the 1800s (Bocock, 1993; Campbell, 1994; Davis, 1966a, 1966b; Satterthwaite, 2001), ushering in the age of mass consumption (Miller, 1987, 2001). In this way, according to Satterthwaite (2001: 8), rarities became commonplace.

In the late 19th century, caught up in the rush of this burgeoning class of consumers, cities like Paris, London, Berlin, Chicago, and New York expanded their transportation networks, enhanced their urban infrastructures, and built large department stores in their booming centers (Bocock, 1993; Coles, 1999a; Edwards, 2000; Miller, 1987). By the middle of the 20th century, mass consumption had spread throughout Europe and North America among all but the very poorest groups in society. As products became more diverse and variations in size and quality expanded, consumption was no longer the exclusive province of the upper class: even the working class, employed in menial jobs, joined the throngs of mass consumers, although patterns of consumption were still underscored by class distinctions (Bocock, 1993).

Consumption has been a key force in the development and sustainability of modern capitalism (Appleby, 1993; Preteceille & Terrail, 1985). 'Consumerism, that is the active ideology that the meaning of life is to be found in buying things and pre-packaged experiences, pervades modern capitalism' (Bocock, 1993: 50). As utility theory of demand suggests, people purchase what they want and producers manufacture what is demanded (Friedman, 1994). Modern mass consumption is based almost entirely on desires rather than needs and thus, at its very core, consumption is as much social and cultural as it is economic.

Miller *et al.* (1998: 3–7) summarize the history of the study of consumption, breaking it down into five stages of development. The first stage was characterized by a recognition of the new landscape of consumption, marked most notably by the development of supermarkets, retail warehouses, and shopping malls. Researchers also became interested in consumption because it was in opposition to traditional views of production (e.g. Marxism), which were seen as inadequate in explaining the decline of production-based working classes and the emergence of consumption-oriented middle classes. Likewise, consumption was seen as a way of bringing cultural studies and humanities further along in the social sciences.

Stage 2 is notable because, at this time, the study of consumption became independent and a recognized subject worthy of scholarly attention in several disciplines. It rose in popularity also because of its now-accepted role as a medium for the subjective construction of self and social identity. Additional activities, such as festivals, collecting, and catalogue shopping, became legitimized as new forms of consumption. Consumption was recognized as a vital attribute of modernity and its study became increasingly tied to place and space.

Research on the subject grew considerably in the third stage, with attention being paid more closely to production and distribution, rather than just consumption. This new trend began to examine the important roles of store salespeople, merchants, and other members of the workforce in the process of consumption. This period was also concerned with the meaning of subjectivity in that most works had previously too easily assigned consumer objects to specific groups of subjects owing to the overuse of social categories like class and status. Thus, the subjective meanings and values assigned to objects and subjects were seen as being inaccurate and too conforming.

The fourth stage addressed primarily the history of consumption and how the mass consumer societies developed and the retail growth that accompanied it from the late 1800s. Finally, the issue of place and space characterizes much of the research during the latest phase. In particular, place and space are seen as important elements in the formation of consumer identities. Researchers are now beginning to deconstruct the notions that space creates consumption and consumption creates place.

Based on the recognition of these important elements of consumption, several academic disciplines (i.e. sociology, anthropology, economics, politics, psychology, and geography) grasped the subject as a worthwhile and serious topic of study – each bringing its own unique perspective into the realm of consumption research.

Social and anthropological perspectives

Challenging the traditional economic views of consumption, with the recognition that it is, in fact, not merely an economic activity but also a social and cultural one, sociologists and anthropologists became interested early on (in the 1800s) in the ways in which consumption manifests in society and in various cultural contexts. Most of the sociological literature indicates that the consumption of commodities is based more on their socially conditioned meaning than on their functional use (Brown, 1992; Friedman, 1994; Newby, 1993). Veblen (1934) recognized this (originally in 1899) in his discourse on the symbolic meanings behind consumption. This line of thinking stems from history as described earlier, wherein levels and degrees of consumption were a sign of social status and class distinction. Thus, consumerism became connected to social identity and self-image with considerable implications for social inequality and individualism (Edwards, 2000; Miller, 1987; Starkey, 1989). Consumption does not just benefit from objects or services but, rather, it is the act of consuming objects itself that is a sign of personal and social identity; the image projected by the object is usually more important than its usefulness (Baudrillard, 1988). In the contemporary context,

> This certainly is the basis on which many cars are marketed and purchased, and certainly for many, it is a prime consideration when buying clothes. It is the need to identify and acquire these images that shifts some shopping activity into the leisure domain. (Newby, 1993: 212)

According to Solomon (1992), this is because consumers base their social reality on product symbolism and what it portrays to others.

Also of concern has been the effect of social relations on consumption patterns or influences of the social reference group (e.g. class, gender, age, friends, ethnicity, family) (McCracken, 1987; Miller, 1998). Shields (1992:

110) notes the importance of this and suggests that shopping and consumption have 'become a communal activity, even a form of social solidarity'. Anthropological perspectives have tended to focus on material culture and its various uses (Campbell, 1991), as well as the cultural significance of consumable commodities. Cultural artifacts and celebrations as commodities to be promoted and consumed by various groups and the resultant changes in their forms and functions are of considerable interest to cultural theorists (e.g. Cohen, 1988a; Graburn, 1976, 1984).

Spatial and ecological perspectives

The spatial dynamics of consumption were recognized in the 1930s by German geographer Walter Christaller, who developed Central Place Theory to describe the retail hierarchy of cities and towns. He theorized that the size and spacing of towns and villages were a result of people's consumptive behavior. In studying settlements in southern Germany, Christaller found that there were many small communities, which offered limited services and were located relatively short distances from each other. Larger towns, however, were fewer in number and located further apart. In today's terms, basic services (e.g. grocery store or petrol station) are said to be of a lower order, while specialized services (e.g. electronics shops, universities, etc.) are said to be of a higher order. Christaller concluded that a town with higher-order services implies that there are lower-order services around it but not necessarily *vice versa*. Settlements that provide lower-order services, he called 'low-order settlements'. These, he argued, were more plentiful and closer together than high-order towns, which are fewer and farther between (Christaller, 1966). While many of the basic elements of his theory still hold true today, variables such as population size, cost of travel, physical geography, and technology necessarily have created disparities in his model from place to place in intervening years. Following Christaller's early work, geographers became engrossed in retail location analysis and physical planning, which had important practical implications for the retail business community when it came to issues of scale, hinterland or service area, and size and layout.

The processes of suburbanization and counter-urbanization were instigated in part at least and extended through various forms of consumption (e.g. car ownership and highway development). Naturally, these movement patterns were of interest to retail geographers, as they sought to understand the role that consumption played in those movements and the ways in which these modern changes transformed consumption patterns (Bromley & Thomas, 1993; Lowe & Rigley, 1996). As Sack (1992: 2) noted, retail establishments, such as malls and department stores, are not only places where goods and services are consumed, they are also places that are spatially arranged to promote consumption.

In more recent times, spatial scientists have become interested in the social spatialization of retail places, consumers' use of retail space, and the implications of retail scale (Coles, 1999a; Guy, 1998; Shields, 1989; 1992; Snepenger *et al.*, 2003). Correspondingly, geographers have started deconstructing the processes involved in the creation of landscapes of consumption (Goss, 1992; Sack, 1998), for consumption is not only about products: it is also about consuming places, spaces and time – not just at the point of purchase but also in the production and distribution of goods and services. Consumption 'creates spaces and transforms places' (Sack, 1992: 25) with social meanings and collective identities. Sack (1992: 1) argues that 'places created by and for mass consumption are fundamental to our making sense of the modern world . . . and to our power as agents in the world'.

One thread of geographical inquiry is the relationship(s) between humans and the earth. The ecological viewpoint concerns the impacts that occur as a result of mass consumption. Cars, the must-have embodiment of mass consumption in most western societies, for instance, have acknowledgeable impacts on air and water quality. They are seen as expending natural resources (e.g. oil) too rapidly and indiscriminately. The negative effects of consumption on the environment and its subcomponents (e.g. forests, oceans, etc.) are a major ecological concern. Modern mass consumption is also notorious for the production of billions of tons of waste and pollution every year, which has to be disposed of or dissipated somewhere (Princen *et al.*, 2002; Sack, 1992).

Psychological interests

Consumer psychology is a well-developed and respected area of study. Its main emphasis has been on understanding the consumer experience and relationships with various products and retail venues. This approach to the study of consumption has probably been most utilized by the retail sector in an effort to understand consumer behaviors, expectations, and desires. Traditional studies have sought to reveal the influence of store design, atmosphere, and environment on customer satisfaction and choice (Donovan *et al.*, 1994; Downs, 1970; Jones & Simmons, 1987a, 1987b; O'Neill & Jasper, 1992; Sherman *et al.*, 1997; Solomon, 1992). Many other works have attempted to identify the motivations and decision-making processes behind different forms of consumption (Bellenger *et al.*, 1977; Hirschman, 1984; Westbrook & Black, 1985), as well as the emotions, moods, and subjective experiences that affect consumptive performances (Hirschman, 1980; 1986; Hirschman & Solomon, 1984; Sherman *et al.*, 1997).

More recent research on the psychology of consumption has tended toward the symbolic significance of material objects and concepts about self (Campbell, 1991; McKracken, 1987). Issues such as lifestyle and life cycle, sexuality, the body, fashion, and materialism have recently been spotlighted in psychological research on mass and individual consumption (McCracken, 1987; Solomon, 1992).

Historical and political views

Historians have long looked to pre-industrial societies for an understanding of (post)modern mass consumption before, during, and after industrialization (Campbell, 1991). Because consumption has been viewed with various political undertones, political historians have an interest in class issues of consumption as well, specifically in terms of power, empowerment, and choice. The ways consumption was/is used as a political instrument and how it assists various groups in legitimizing claims to power is a genuine concern among political theorists (McCracken, 1987). Perhaps the most notable is its uses as a tool for maintaining status and class position and, more recently, a justification for economic exploitation through production (Edwards, 2000).

While these short synopses cannot underscore the depth and range of thinking about consumption from each disciplinary perspective, they do highlight some of the major issues of concern that have a conceptual bearing on this book. All of these disciplinary perspectives contribute to our understanding of tourism and leisure as forms of consumption.

Consumption, Leisure, and Tourism

The antecedents (e.g. Marxism) to contemporary thought on capitalism focused on production and the role it played in a modernizing free-market society. Much thinking in the 18th and 19th centuries was geared toward production and work as being fundamental to people's lives and to their very sense of identity, and it was from this perspective that class distinctions were viewed (Bocock, 1993). Today's notion of leisure hardly existed at that time: work was the essence of life and was done as a means of survival. However, toward the end of the 19th century, with the spread of wealth among the burgeoning middle and upper classes, the spotlight moved from production to consumption. Class distinctions were recognized by consumption patterns rather than production, and consumption became defined as leisure – the conceptual opposite of the notion of production or work (Edwards, 2000: 3). According to Bocock (1993), this transformation marked the change from modernity into postmodernity because it entailed a social paradigm shift from production and work to consumption and leisure. In postmodern capitalist societies, therefore, leisure is the essence of life and work is done as a means of achieving leisure. Thus, the leisure class of today is defined by mass consumption and, more specifically, the consumption of commodities and services, such as travel, sports, arts, and the cinema (Balkan & Rutz, 1999; Dimanche & Samdahl, 1994; Edwards, 2000).

This shift to postmodernity and the rise of the leisure class raised significant issues related to the crossover between consumption and identity. Miller's (1987, 1998) work demonstrates the importance of mass consumption as a significant experiential framework by which individuals and societies relate to the material world. Most recent work on consumption and identity rejects the traditional view of consumption as a simple and straightforward act of purchasing, contending instead that consumption is a social process through which people identify with products in complex ways (Jackson & Holbrook, 1995; Miller *et al.*, 1998). Likewise, traditional views of identity tended to be fixed and singular in nature but, today, scholars have begun to recognize that identities are dynamic and manifold (Giddens, 1991; Jackson & Holbrook, 1995; Lash & Friedman, 1992).

Miller *et al.* (1998) argue that the family is the core context for self-development and identity, and others have concluded that broader social contexts and reference groups assist in constructing identities (Pearce *et al.*, 1996) through variables such as ethnicity, gender, class, and sexual orientation. From a gender perspective, consumption, in general, and product purchases, in particular, have long defined self and social identity. Women, for example, have traditionally been viewed as shopping enthusiasts. Today, however, activity- and product-based identities are not as fixed as they used to be, especially with increasing levels of shopping being done by men. Likewise, as noted earlier in this chapter, class identity has long been distinguished by material possessions and the ability to consume, whereas today class distinctions are not as clear owing to product diversification, price competitiveness, and other variables which have created conditions where people on the lower economic rungs of society are now able to afford higher levels of material consumption. The relationships between consumption and identity, then, are diverse and manifest in the context of materialism, place, and socialization processes.

Since its inception as an important area of social science research, leisure has been defined in three primary ways. First, it is commonly identified as a type of activity. Hiking, bowling, river rafting, playing football, reading, stamp-collecting, and cooking may all be considered forms of leisure from this perspective. Second, leisure may also be seen as a measure of time – time that is free from obligations such as work, taking care of the home, oneself, and family. Finally, leisure is often seen as a state of mind or a specific experience, resulting in feelings of satisfaction, excitement, fun, and belonging. However, leisure, in many cases, may be a combination of any or all of these elements (Barnett, 1995; Csikszentmihalyi, 1981; Jackson & Burton, 1999; Iso-Ahola, 1980; Mannell & Kleiber, 1997). Thus, leisure pervades many aspects of modern living. It is an important component of lifestyle and plays a major part in quality of life (Mannell & Kleiber, 1997).

Tourism is certainly one of the most important targets of modern-day consumption and is generally viewed as an extreme form of leisure. Pleasure travel, for example, takes place in leisure time, is a recreational activity, and occurs within the framework of a leisure state of mind. By extension, then, tourism may be seen as a form of leisure consumption (Walvin, 1992).

The act of consuming in general and specifically in leisure can be seen from two perspectives. First is the actual activity of consuming tangible products by ingesting (e.g. eating and drinking) or by using in a physical way (e.g. buying new shoes and clothes). Second, consumption also refers to utilizing services or items that will not be physically expended. This includes listening to music, watching a movie, taking a walk, and staying at a hotel. This second type is commonly known as symbolic consumption (Dimanche & Samdahl, 1994; Edwards, 2000; Urry, 1995). Thus, the act of travel not only includes physical consumption (e.g. dining out), it also includes purchasing air tickets, hotel nights, and guiding services, which fall more clearly under the purview of the second type of consumption.

Urry (1995: 132–33) noted several key concepts in understanding tourism as a form of consumption of spaces and services:

- As noted earlier, leisure tourism is the antithesis of organized and regulated work. It is a manifestation of how leisure and work are organized on separate ends of a social spectrum in modern societies. Work, as opposed to travel and leisure, is organized within particular places and occurs during regularized periods of time.
- Tourism involves a movement of people to destinations. This obviously entails movement through space and a period of stay in the destination.
- The tourist experience takes place in locations outside tourists' home environment, away from their residences and work. Periods at the destination are short term and there is an intention to return home following the visit.
- The places consumed by tourists are for purposes not directly associated with work and, in most cases, they offer some distinctive contrasts with work.

- A large portion of the population of developed countries engages in tourism and new social forms develop to cope with the mass character of tourism.
- Places are selected as destinations because of the perceived pleasures they will provide. People anticipate visiting certain destinations because of the images they have developed through various media, day-dreaming, and fantasies.
- The tourist 'gaze' is directed to landscapes that are different from tourists' everyday and routine experiences. Places are viewed because they are out-of-the-ordinary and provide visual elements not usually found in everyday life. Photographs are taken and postcards bought in an effort to relive, reproduce, and recapture the visual experience.
- The gaze is made up of signs. Tourism involves the collection of these signs and tourists travel the world in search of signs that mark place identities. For instance, tourists want to see the signs that indicate the Frenchness of France, typical Italian landscapes in Italy, and Oriental market scenes in Asia.
- Finally, tourism professionals attempt to reproduce new objects for tourist consumption. The objects are located in a complex hierarchy which depends on the interchange and competition between various capitalist and state interests involved in their provision.

Timothy (1998) discussed similar issues in his assessment of place collecting, which occurs when destinations are visited and perhaps enumerated. Often there is a desire to visit other places for competitive reasons. Seeking admiration from others, acceptance, and being able to boast of great travels sometimes motivates people to collect places. Stamps in a passport, souvenirs from unusual places, and postcards are physical manifestations of this phenomenon (Brown, 1992; Wallendorf & Arnould, 1988). Some people cross borders to be able to claim they have been in a foreign country. Others travel to many places so they can boast of numbers and widespread adventures. Finally, some individuals collect/consume places for the sole purpose of impressing others by their choice of destinations, including places that are on the global periphery or which have traditionally been off limits.

Shopping as leisure and tourism consumption

While there are obviously many forms of consumption, including leisure and tourism, shopping and retailing are the clear linchpins of consumption and the emblems of consumer society. The primary goal of retailing is to encourage people to shop and purchase merchandise and services. Many variables come into play in the retail mix or the environment that induce purchasing behavior. Among the most important principles involved in successful retailing are shop location, good value, range and quality of merchandise, and physical design (Downs, 1970). These store- and merchandise-related attributes do not act alone but work in conjunction with high-quality staff and customer controls to appeal to leisure and tourist shoppers and created satisfied customers, thereby possibly inducing them to spend more money, consume more merchandise, and return more often.

According to Edwards (2000: 106), the whole notion of mass consumption depends completely on the continuation of shopping and retail. Shopping opportunities are everywhere and, according to Underhill (1999: 31), 'you almost have to make an effort to avoid shopping today'. Bacon's (1991, 1992, 1993) research shows that nearly 20% of all travel journeys are to shop, second only to work. Owing to the leisure nature of consumption, shopping denotes significantly more than just the activity of buying a commodity at the actual point of purchase. Indeed, actually acquiring items through purchasing transactions is 'but a small part; shopping for goods remains a social activity built around social exchange as well as simple commodity exchange' (Miller *et al.*, 1998: 14).

Thus, 'shopping, even for everyday items, has now almost entirely lost its status as an activity and become simply an experience. It has lost a materiality and become a cultural event' (Humphrey, 1998: 114, cited in Edwards, 2000). Edwards (2000: 117–19) proposed several assertions that support these claims. First, the notion of the changing nature of shopping is that shopping is increasingly a leisure activity – not just a part of everyday survival (Babin *et al.*, 1994; Holbrook & Hirschman, 1982; Jansen, 1989; Jansen-Verbeke, 1987; Jones, 1999). This can be seen in the light of increasing leisure time, higher standards of living, and shops that encourage people to browse. Second, as noted earlier, shopping, consumption, and materialism are generally now seen as major influences in the creation of identity (Miller, 1987; Miller *et al.*, 1998). People are ever more defined by virtue of their consumption patterns, the products they buy, their possessions, and the socioeconomic class to which their consumptive behavior belongs (Starkey, 1989). Thus, shopping must now be seen as an individual and subjective activity, rather than a socially objective one, existing within a framework of functional reality. The third assertion deals with the meanings and associations connected with certain commodities (or travel destinations) that may not be intrinsically connected to them. In many cases, the symbolic meanings of items have surpassed their utilitarian value (Baudrillard, 1988; Bourdieu, 1984; Solomon, 1992; Starkey, 1989). The fourth contention is that the process and experience of shopping are guided and molded by a wide range of unconscious desires, wishes, and dreams that may or may not be fulfilled. Finally, shopping is principally a subjective experience of image-processing and value interpretation, which is socially constructed. Edwards notes that, given the large variety of products available, consumer choice is no longer a simple, rational calculation of utility. Indeed, it becomes an issue of wants *versus* needs, because relatively few products being sold today have basic human survival (needs) as their core functional value.

What becomes clear from this discussion is that shopping cannot be classified into a single, undifferentiated category (Newby, 1993). There are clearly as many forms of shopping as there are motivations to shop. For many people, shopping is a tiresome and functional task that must be done to meet personal and familial needs. This condition is accentuated by high prices, crowded shops, ineffective communications, rude or unhelpful salespeople, limited time, bad weather, lack of product variety, and, according to some observers, gender, social group affiliation, and age. On the flip side, shopping may be viewed as a fun, entertaining, or leisure activity from which hedonic or ludic pleasures can be realized. Shopping is typically seen as leisure owing to social affiliations, its function as a form of escape and sensory stimulation, its time frame, product variety, special bargains, and attractive retail environments (Bussey, 1987; Gratton & Taylor, 1987; Sargent, 1985; Tauber, 1995; Wakefield & Baker, 1998). Even grocery shopping may be seen as a form of leisure as people become more involved in the art of cooking and as product variety and store environment create retail atmospheres that are conducive to pleasurable experiences (Wade, 1985).

The status of recreational shopping as a serious area of study in the social sciences has improved considerably in recent years. Shopping now is seen beyond the traditional utilitarian perspective to include scholarly views that it be an intrinsically motivated phenomenon involving activities that produce experiences enjoyed for their own sake (Bloch *et al.*, 1991). Shopping's hedonic characteristics make it an addictive activity for many consumers, just like drugs, gambling, and drinking, because of its ability to change how one feels in a powerful and speedy manner (Baker, 2000).

It has been established that tourism is an important form of leisure behavior. It has also been noted that shopping is an important leisure activity. By extension, then, shopping and tourism naturally have common linkages. Although shopping as a tourist activity has not received attention in the literature commensurate with its significance, it is one of the most common motivations for cross-border travel and is nearly always noted as the principal and most common activity undertaken by tourists. Based on the retail, shopping, leisure, and tourism literatures, Figure 1.1 highlights several intrinsic and extrinsic variables that work together to make the

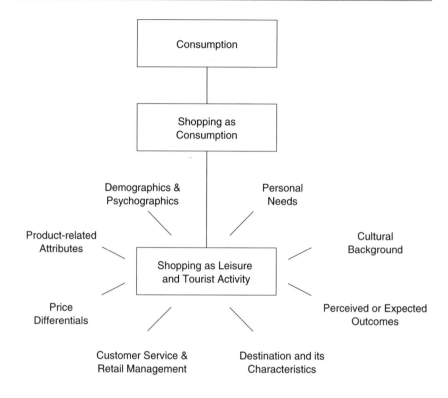

Figure 1.1 The elements of leisure and tourist shopping

shopping experience a leisure endeavor and an activity that millions of tourists pursue every time they travel.

The primary intrinsic variables include shoppers' demographic and psychographic characteristics (e.g. age, gender, level of affluence, behavior), personal needs (e.g. ego enhancement, socialization, functional need, a sense of escape), cultural background (e.g. nationality, race, ethnicity, traditions), and perceived or expected outcomes (e.g. acquiring authentic products, finding novel experiences and merchandise, buying gifts for people at home). The extrinsic influences are primarily comprised of retail venue features (e.g. store environment, size, type), the destination and its characteristics (e.g. heritage cities, beachfront communities, rural areas), customer service and retail management (e.g. catering to the needs of foreign visitors, providing customer comforts, thoughtful salespeople), price (e.g. relative prices, special prices, cost differentials in different countries), and product-related attributes (e.g. quality, authenticity, variety).

Although this is not an exhaustive list, it does incorporate the most influential factors that cause leisure and tourist shopping to vary from other forms of consumption and utilitarian purchasing. Although some of these issues will receive more attention and coverage than others based on the information, data, and observations available, all of them will be addressed in one fashion or another throughout the chapters of the book.

The next chapter examines shopping in the context of leisure, i.e. shopping as a leisure experience in general and its various manifestations as a recreational activity. The third chapter specifically highlights the situation where people travel with shopping as their primary motive. It proposes merchandise, destination image, and price differentials as the most prominent reasons for the growth of shopping tourism. The role of shopping as an activity that people undertake while on vacation, other than shopping as the primary motive for travel, is the focus of Chapter 4. The importance of shopping as an ancillary activity in tourist destinations is discussed, followed by the most important factors that influence people to shop and the consumer activities they pursue. Chapter 5 addresses the question of what tourists buy. While the general range of goods bought by tourists is examined briefly, the majority of the chapter focuses on the role of souvenirs as the foremost object of tourists' desires and the changes to handicrafts and other souvenirs wrought by tourist consumption. The next chapter provides a description and conceptual overview of the various types of venues in which leisure and tourist shopping occurs. This ranges from establishments that cater primarily to local residents (e.g. grocery stores and farmers' markets) to retailers that cater primarily to tourists (e.g. souvenir shops, museum shops, and airports). The main issues related to each type of shop or venue are considered as they relate to the interest of leisure and tourism.

From a retail management perspective, Chapter 7 provides a basic overview of several management principles associated with leisure and tourist shopping. Managing places, venues, shoppers, employees, and destination community members is an important element of successful business – particularly so in the tourism context. The concluding chapter briefly summarizes several of the main concepts and theoretical issues that are brought out in the book and directs readers to issues that have not been well addressed in any body of literature on tourism and leisure shopping and which would benefit from additional research attention.

Chapter 2

Recreational Shopping, Leisure, and Labour

Introduction

Shopping has become one of the most common leisure activities in the world today. According to a British research report noted in Jansen's (1989) study, by the end of the 1980s shopping had become the leading leisure activity in the United Kingdom on a par with spending a day at the beach.

Throughout most of recent history, shopping has been viewed as a laborious activity, one that must be undertaken as a means of survival. The activity rarely, if ever, possessed qualities that could be considered enjoyable. However, times have changed and shopping during the past century has become much less of a utilitarian chore and more of a free-time activity to be undertaken as a pleasant pursuit or, at least, as containing some elements of leisure (Bacon, 1991). While Bellenger and Korgaonkar (1980) and other observers have noted that shoppers can be viewed as either recreational or economic consumers, Jarboe and McDaniel (1987) suggest that this distinction may not be as clear-cut as what has tradition-ally been believed. Shopping, they argue, is a complex phenomenon that may involve several subsets of both recreation and utilitarian activity and a combination of both. Littrell (1996) provides some examples where both conditions apply. Bargain shopping can serve both economic value and hedonic pleasure as paying a lower price saves money and can result in a surprisingly unexpected exchange. Also, meeting intended buying goals (utilitarian) can serve to enhance the 'self-concept' and provide a sense of satisfaction.

Carr (1990) designed a functional-leisure shopping continuum (Figure 2.1), which suggests that there may be different degrees of functionality and leisure in shopping behavior. On the functional end, quartermastering is seen as routine purchases of essential items. It is usually boring and laborious. Next toward the leisure end is technical shopping, which refers to buying mechanical items that have a job to do (e.g. refrigerators,

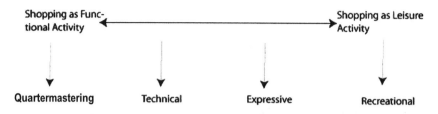

Figure 2.1 Functional-leisure shopping continuum (after Carr, 1990)

computers, cars, etc.). Technical shopping is fairly functional in that it usually demands considerable planning, decision-making, and information-seeking. Expressive shopping is more leisured than the previous two forms and entails people buying goods that will allow them to project an image of themselves that they wish to portray. Shopping for clothing, make-up, jewelry, and cars typically falls within this category, as these items allow consumers to create an identity by which they can be recognized and/or admired. Finally, on the right of the spectrum is recreation shopping, which is when shopping is felt to be a pure leisure activity.

Because this dichotomous relationship exists, there is a need to understand shopping as leisure and how it contrasts with shopping as laborious activity. In response to this need, this chapter aims to examine the role of shopping as a leisure pursuit in contrast to its utilitarian function and highlights the social, cultural, economic, psychological, environmental and temporal factors that affect the leisure shopping experience. It begins first by reviewing various shopping and shopper typologies that have been developed over the years, as they pertain to utilitarian and hedonic forms of shopping. The chapter then examines the traditional view of utilitarian shopping, followed by a longer assessment of changes in thinking about shopping as a leisure pursuit and its leisure components.

Shopping and Shopper Typologies

Since the Second World War, consumption and shopping have changed in ways that have had weighty impacts on corporate and retail planning (Lesser & Hughes, 1986). This transformation has been a key factor in the development of many different types of shopping typologies, which have been created by various authors in an effort to understand the changing demand for products and experiences. Since the mid-1900s, several retailing scholars have proposed shopper and shopping taxonomies related to motivations, products purchased, activities undertaken, and locations of retail. While the notion of leisure shopping was not explicitly explored by consumer scientists until the late 1970s and early 1980s, the collection of typologies developed since the 1950s shed some light on early notions of the role of leisure in shopping.

Stone (1954) was among the earliest scholars to categorize shoppers by their motivations and actions. His typology, which focused on housewives of the 1950s, was comprised of four consumer types: economic, personalizing, ethical, and apathetic. *Economic shoppers* are those for whom the act of shopping was unmistakably intended for the acquisition of products, paying special attention to price, quality, and variety. *Personalizing shoppers* define shopping as an interpersonal experience where customers individualize their role in the store by forming personal relationships between themselves and store employees. This type of consumer was seen as being less concerned about product selection and price and more interested in being recognized and friendly with shopkeepers and clerks. This is perhaps one of the earliest allusions to the leisure side of the shopping experience. Stone's *ethical* category has a tendency to feel obligated to support specific types of stores, such as local mom-and-pop shops, as opposed to large department stores where everything is streamlined. Often, this was done at the expense of lower prices and wider selection. Finally, the *apathetic shopper* is one who did not like shopping at all. The retail location was of no importance, as shopping was considered an arduous task that had to be done regardless of venue. Stephenson and Willett (1969) later presented a similar four-part typology comprised of store loyal, convenience, compulsive, and price/bargain conscious shoppers (cited in Jarboe & McDaniel, 1987: 47).

Based on their survey of shopping activity and lifestyle in 17 communities, Lesser and Hughes (1986) identified seven types of shoppers. *Inactive shoppers* are those who have very restricted lifestyles and shopping interests. They rarely engage in outdoor pursuits, and they do not express enjoyment of, or interest in, shopping. For inactive shoppers, price, service, and product selection are less important than for other consumer groups. *Active shoppers* live more demanding lifestyles, engage more in outdoor activities, and are generally more inclined to be do-it-yourselfers. This middle-class group enjoys shopping around for bargain prices and seeks products that reflect a higher social class. *Service shoppers* are very concerned with in-store service quality. They seek shops with friendly and helpful staff and are quick to become impatient, demanding high levels of attention from employees. They are generally willing to pay higher prices and become loyal consumers in exchange for better service. *Traditional shoppers* are also interested in outdoor activities and are typically 'do-it-yourselfers'. However, in contrast to active shoppers, they are not enthusiastic about shopping and are less comfortable in spending money.

Dedicated fringe shoppers desire to be different. These are among the first to try new products, are almost always do-it-yourselfers, and are generally active information seekers. They tend to be less interested in socializing as part of the shopping experience, which leads them to be avid catalogue and Internet shoppers. *Price shoppers* can be identified by their excessive price consciousness. They are willing to search far and wide to find special deals. Price shoppers are even willing to give up service quality, product quality, and selection to save money. *Transitional shoppers* are generally found in their early stages of the family life cycle. They are still formulating lifestyle patterns and consumption habits. Transitional consumers are generally younger and are able and willing to try new products. *Convenience shoppers* want ease of buying and are not concerned about price and service. *Coupon-saver shoppers* rely heavily on coupons and advertising to guide their purchasing decisions. They tend to be more sedentary, having little interest in the outdoors or do-it-yourself projects. *Innovator shoppers* are a more upscale market segment and are inclined to buy new products and make more impulse buys. Finally, *unclassified shoppers* do not fit into any of the other types that Lesser and Hughes could identify.

From their research at West Edmonton Mall, Finn *et al.* (1994: 136) identified five types of mall-specific shoppers. First, *light consumers* are those who had a specific shopping purpose in mind, such as a particular item or picking something up at a certain store. The second type they identified is the *multiple shopper*: these are the consumers who planned to buy more than one item or shop at more than one individual store. *Leisure users* are the third type. This group has more of a recreational or entertainment goal in mind when heading for the mall, including browsing or participating in other forms of entertainment. Fourth, *social users* go to the mall to show someone around or to meet someone there for a meal or drink. Finally, they identified *combined purpose consumers*, i.e. those who have several purposes, including shopping for a specific item, browsing, entertainment, to show someone around, and/or to eat a meal.

In common with Finn *et al.* (1994), other classifications of mall shoppers have been developed, including that by Bloch *et al.* (1994: 33), whose first category is *mall enthusiasts* – individuals who engage in many behaviors at the mall including significant levels of purchasing, usage of other services and activities at the mall, and highly experiential consumption. Mall enthusiasts view the mall as an important attraction and play many roles in the shopping center habitat. The second group is what Bloch *et al.* label *traditionalists*. Like enthusiasts, members of this consumer group also have a strong inclination to participate in mall-centered activities. As its name indicates, though, this group includes people who primarily visit the mall to take advantage of typical services and to buy store merchandise. The third category of mall users is most distinguishable by its higher-than-average propensity to pass time in the center eating and perusing. These shoppers, the *grazers*, also scored a bit above average in product purchasing, likely owing to impulse buying during browsing. The name of the final grouping in the taxonomy is *minimalists*, owing to their relatively low average participation in all mall-related activities, including purchasing. Minimalists tended to be reluctant mall-goers, those who are uninterested in socializing and who are uninvolved with browsing, eating, or other mall services and activities. Most of these people would consider malls to be a hassle because of time constraints, overcrowding, and other factors: they desire to get in and out of the mall as quickly as possible.

Finally, Marjanen (1995) examined several additional typologies that are based on retail location and product purchase types (e.g. in town, out of town, rural, urban, convenience goods, specialty items, etc.). Although the classifications reviewed in this section were developed from economic and marketing perspectives, all of them allude, either implicitly or explicitly, and in part to the dichotomous notion of shopping as a leisure or labored experience.

Utilitarian Shopping

Utilitarian shopping (also known as functional, economic or convenience shopping) has been differentiated for many years in the retailing literature from the less obligatory form of shopping most commonly referred to as hedonic purchasing. Usually, when observers discuss shopping in laborious terms, they do so in reference to economic or utilitarian consumer behavior. In most cases, shopping is laborious for consumers when it is viewed as an unavoidable need, done in a highly efficient and directed manner, a negative experience, when consumers face difficult, frustrating, and monotonous decisions and when it is not done of one's own free will and choice (Babin *et al.*, 1994; Bellenger & Korgaonkar, 1980; Jansen-Verbeke, 1987; Jarboe & McDaniel, 1987; Jones, 1999; Littrell, 1996; Prus & Dawson, 1991). The utilitarian factor may also be a result of product characteristics. Utility is typically measured as a function of a product's tangible attributes and its ability to satisfy some perceived need (Hirschman & Holbrook, 1982: 94). In most cases, functional consumers' choice of store will be based primarily on price and product availability (Bellenger & Korgaonkar, 1980). Functional shoppers also generally know what they are looking for ahead of time, and their efforts are geared toward problem-solving and goal realization through shopping (Littrell, 1996).

The primary underlying theme of Underhill's (1999) book is the difference between the male and female shopping encounter. He claims that there are clear differences in the shopping preferences of women and men.

'Men and women differ in just about every other way, so why shouldn't they shop differently too?' (Underhill, 1999: 98). For many men, he claims, shopping is a treacherous and arduous occurrence, which is something typically avoided. When men do shop, however, according to Underhill, they move faster through the aisles, spend less time looking, and hesitate to ask where things are. If a man is unable to find the section for which he is searching, 'he'll wheel about once or twice, then give up and leave the store without ever asking for help. You can watch men just shut down' (p. 99). This illustrates that, for some people, shopping is a painstaking chore that must be done, while for others, it provides a social outlet and a sense of belonging. As the social context varies, the same experience of shopping in the same place will have radically different meanings for different individuals (Jackson & Holbrook, 1995). In this sense, 'we all move through the same environments, but no two of us respond to them exactly alike' (Underhill, 1999: 95). For many women, shopping with small children is a source of anxiety, resulting in a stressful and unenjoyable retail experience, while, for others, it adds the the experience in a positive way (Jackson & Holbrook, 1995).

Prus and Dawson (1991: 154–9) noted three main themes as being endemic to the utilitarian purchasing experience (Table 2.1). The first is when consumers face undesired ambiguity, which is perceived as discom-

Table 2.1 Themes associated with utilitarian shopping

Undesired ambiguity	*Closure*
Vague information	Pressing obligations
Imprecise comparisons	Limited options
Contradictory definitions	Necessary actions
Accountability to others	Time pressures
Fitting problems	Financial constraints
Neglect by salespeople	Encouragement from others
Distractions	Unavailability of merchandise
	Embarrassing events
	Unlikeable purchases
Boredom	
Uninspiring purchases	
Being slowed down	
Routine purchases	
Thinking of doing something else more enjoyable	
Fatigue	

forting, perplexing, or distressful. Ambiguity takes on many forms in the shopping context, including vague information, imprecise comparisons, contradictory definitions, accountability to others, fitting problems, neglect by sales clerks, and being distracted. Vague information concerns buyer knowledge of products. Often, people must purchase something they know little about, which causes stress and this is often compounded by vendors' tendencies to assume that buyers know more about what is being purchased than they actually do. Imprecise comparisons tend to be frustrating to customers when they are uncertain about the relative worth of objects being compared and when people are unclear about the standards they wish to apply in making assessments. Fitting problems occur when people are unable to find items in their desired sizes, are concerned about how something will look on them, or whether certain objects are fitting for other people or settings. The shopping experience also becomes laborious when people encounter contradictory definitions. This is especially the case in relation to prices, quality, fit, and style. The problem is compounded when their initial reactions to products are not shared by others. Experiencing accountability to others reflects the discomfort associated with having one's purchases critically assessed by other people in a group setting. Feelings of neglect by sales clerks relate not so much to being bothered by sales staff but being unable to obtain information when it is desired. Finally, being distracted tends to make purchasing decisions more difficult and perplexing when shoppers are unable to concentrate on the decision before them. These distractions include children, other shopping companions, things on a person's mind, loud noises, and large crowds.

Second, experiencing closure refers to circumstances wherein people participate in actions as a result of pressing obligations and limited options. This does not indicate desired actions but instead reflects ways of fulfilling urgent needs, such as paying bills. Many people approach shopping from this perspective, which makes the activity one of limited choice and simple necessity. Various forms of closure have been identified, resulting from time pressures, financial limitations, encouragement from others, unavailability of certain products, and embarrassing or unlikeable purchases and contexts. In these instances, consumers feel forced to make purchases under conditions they would rather avoid (Prus & Dawson, 1991).

The third theme is experiencing boredom, which is reflective of uninspiring purchases and perceptions of being slowed down. Purchases that people see as routine, uninteresting, and required contribute to the sense of shopping as labor. This feeling is compounded when people imagine themselves doing something more enjoyable. Shopping with companions who move at a slower pace is also a factor in shopping fatigue and creating laborious conditions (Lichfield, 1990; Prus & Dawson, 1991).

In addition to Prus and Dawson's three issues, concern about personal safety makes shopping less than desirable. While the majority of shopping centers are safe and well protected and statistically people generally believe shopping malls are safe places, some people choose not to shop in malls and other large venues because of safety concerns (Bloch *et al.*, 1991). Witnessing a shoplifter being apprehended by security, getting stuck in traffic, seeing a car accident, being in a car accident, or otherwise being hurt are events that can make a shopping experience negative, which might otherwise have been positive and enjoyable (Bacon, 1993; Jones, 1999).

One of the most traditional and pervasive assumptions in consumer behavior research is that purchases and buying patterns are preceded by a rational decision-making process. Various models have been developed over time to examine and understand this process but all of them appear to have at their foundations the following justifications:

- More than one alternative action exists and, thus, some level of choice must take place.
- Various criteria are evaluated by consumers, which help them forecast the consequences of each alternative.
- The selected option is decided by a decision rule or evaluative procedure.
- Information acquired from external sources or retrieved from memory is processed in carrying out the decision rule or evaluation procedure (Olshavsky & Granbois, 1979: 93).

Thus, utilitarian shoppers are generally characterized as information-seekers, who search for knowledge that will inform their decision-making. The fundamental notion of the traditional explanations of the process of consumption is that people are goal-oriented, inclined to seek information regarding which products to buy, and that information searches will result in a purchase. Since the early 1980s, however, other observers have begun to suggest that not all information-seeking results in actual purchases. Instead, information-seeking (e.g. via the Internet, magazines, television, etc.) may be carried out as a form of entertainment, as a way of gaining general knowledge about a product or place, or as a way of fulfilling people's curiosities (Hirschman, 1980, 1984; Hirschman & Holbrook, 1982; Hirschman & Solomon, 1984; Holbrook & Hirschman, 1982). In the words of Vogt and Fesenmaier (1998: 553), 'they are always searching and not necessarily because they are planning to buy'. Thus, information search activities occur very often for more subjective needs, such as emotional stimuli and enjoyment, more than for simply functional and immediate purchasing needs. This hedonic perspective on information search views consumers as pleasure-seekers who are engaged in amusing, fun, and stimulating activities (Vogt & Fesenmaier, 1998).

Despite the traditional view of consumer behavior, Olshavsky and Granbois (1979) boldly noted early on that, in some cases, no pre-purchase decision process exists. Their controversial conclusion had important repercussions for shopping theory, as they introduced the argument that the traditional understanding of consumer behavior can provide an explanation for only some types of purchasing. This conclusion led to broader thinking in the realm of shopping research and wider ideas were developed relating to consumer performance, especially leisure consumption.

Leisure Shopping

It is necessary at this point to reiterate the difference between buying and shopping. In precise terms, buying refers to obtaining a specific item from a seller, while shopping more broadly entails sorting, comparing, checking prices, selecting styles, browsing, walking, and meeting with other people (Angle, 1974; Bloch *et al.*, 1989; Bromley & Thomas, 1993; Bussey, 1987; Roberts, 1987). Shopping, is therefore, not always about acquiring new merchandise. Instead, its purposes also include servicing needs that are unrelated to product acquisition, including a desire to meet people, feel wanted, exercise, or spend leisure time with friends and relatives (Tauber, 1972). According to Hirschman (1984), a significant part of the shopping experience is novelty-seeking and innovativeness. Individuals seek out novel stimuli through the total shopping experience, which may be particularly enhanced when new venues are visited, new environments are introduced, new friends made, and new merchandise examined. Thus, shopping is a multidimentional activity that involves social interaction, economic exchange, and, very often, the participation in non-purchasing activities. Indeed, it is argued that shoppers' quest for a leisure experience is more substantial than the acquisition of objects (Babin *et al.*, 1994; Christiansen & Snepenger, 2002; Jones, 1999; Kamphorst, 1991; Sherry, 1990; Westbrook & Black, 1985).

The most critical new development for the present discussion is that related to hedonic or recreational shopping. Recreational shoppers are consumers who enjoy shopping as a leisure-time activity – a significant issue in most societies in the developed world. According to a study cited by Jackson (1991), a nationwide survey of American adults indicated that some 31% of the population saw shopping as a recreational pastime. An earlier study by Bellenger and Korgaonkar (1980) found that 69% of their 224 survey respondents claimed to enjoy shopping as a use of their leisure time. Yet another study concluded that in the mid 1990s, some 75% of

Americans went to a mall at least once a month, and time budget analyses showed that Americans spent more time in shopping centers and malls than any other place outside of home and work (Bloch *et al.*, 1994: 24).

For many leisure shoppers, shopping represents an important outlet for social interaction (discussed later) and provides temporary relief from routines and monotonous environments. It may also confirm one's status and provide opportunities for self-evaluation (Terry, 1977).

In general, recreational shoppers are less likely to have an idea of what they will purchase and less concerned about distance to travel. They will also tend to make more spontaneous buys, shop more often, spend more time shopping per trip, shop with others, and continue shopping after making a purchase (Bellenger & Korgaonkar, 1980; Bellenger *et al.*, 1977; Downs, 1970; Jarboe & McDaniel, 1987; Roy, 1994; Swanson, 1994). In simple terms, this is because people who are interested in shopping are prone to spend more time doing what they enjoy (Wakefield & Baker, 1998: 22). In addition to these specific behaviors, recreational shoppers are more affected by store environment, and extra amenities play an important role in their decision to return (Hirschman, 1986; Johnson & Mannell, 1983). Recreational shoppers are less task-oriented, have more fun, and enjoy the ludic and playful aspects of shopping (Holbrook & Hirschman, 1982). They are more inclined to enjoy the complete process of retail consumption – 'looking, trying, and buying' (Graham *et al.*, 1991: 346).

Additionally, while convenience shoppers tend to be more inclined to conduct information searches for economic and utilitarian purposes, recreational shoppers are believed to perceive a higher, subjective value in gathering information. As noted previously, this translates into their being more involved in information-seeking for pleasure, fun, and self-fulfillment (Bellenger & Korgaonkar, 1980). It is this second type of shopper, the leisure consumer, which is of primary interest in this chapter and indeed in the entire book. Leisure shopping is a form of experiential or playful consumption that produces experiences enjoyed for their own sake (Bloch *et al.*, 1991: 445). Jackson (1991: 283–84) carries this notion further by presenting a three-part typology of the relationships between shopping and leisure (Figure 2.2).

His first linkage is shopping *for* leisure. This relationship refers to individuals purchasing goods that can be used later during leisure time. Examples include books, music, games, and sporting equipment. Bussey (1987) includes vacation holidays as well in this type of category. Second is shopping *and* leisure, which denotes shopping which is done in conjunction with recreational activities along the way or at the retail establishment. Shopping malls are a good example of this as they provide many opportunities for other forms of leisure, such as movie theaters, video arcades, and

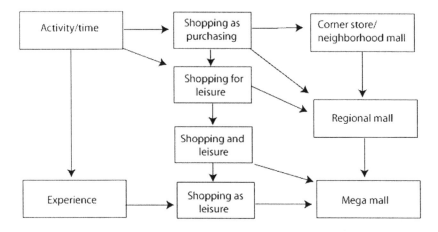

Figure 2.2 Linkages between shopping, leisure, and venue (after Jackson, 1991)

dining out (Bussey, 1987; Morgan, 1990). Finally, shopping *as* leisure refers to the act of shopping itself as a recreational pastime. Filling time, browsing, and watching other people are just a few of the ways in which shopping is seen as a leisure-time activity.

In conjunction with leisure time, Johnson and Howard (1990) proposed a three-part typology of leisure-shopping environments. The first form is *ambient leisure*, which entails the creation of a pleasant shopping environment, in an effort to extend the shopping stay and to attract customers from competing centers. Ambient shopping at a mall, for instance, would include visits to a food court, seeing a performance, or sitting to watch people pass by. In this case, design and décor are important influences for leisure shopping. The second form is what Johnson calls *magnet leisure in a new generation shopping mall*. This model denotes that leisure facilities are designed in their own right to attract leisure and dual purpose traffic (shopping and other recreational activities). West Edmonton Mall is a nice example of this, where people may go to enjoy various activities without even spending time in the shops themselves. The synergy between shopping and other recreational activities is considered a major strength as the potential for impulse purchases is strong. The third form is *heritage-destination leisure*, which emphasizes historic areas as the main attraction for leisure visitors with nearby shops and eating establishments feasting off the traffic. This is especially important in the historic cities of Europe and North America (Jansen-Verbeke, 1989; Pearce, 1998, 1999), where specialty shops and festival shopping have developed near cathedral areas, harborfronts, and major museums.

Along the lines of Johnson's (1990) second form of shopping environment, there are notable commercial benefits from satisfying human and social leisure needs in retailing contexts aside from merchandising itself. By expanding the retail environment into a broader leisure setting, commercial establishments are able to draw in more people and keep them for longer periods of time, which research shows will result in higher expenditures (Howard, 1990b; Jansen-Verbeke, 1990b; Jones, 1999; Lichfield, 1990).

Impulse purchases are one result of leisure situations and an important source of income for retailers. Simply noted, impulse purchases occur when a decision is made to buy something after the shopper has entered the store (Bellenger *et al.*, 1978: 17), which reflects the tendency of impulse purchases to result more from a need to purchase than a need for any particular item (Babin *et al.*, 1994). These unplanned sales are crucial for merchants and efforts should be made to create conditions that will induce this behavior, although unplanned purchases are also dependent on product and consumer characteristics (Iyer, 1989), which are much more difficult to control. Leisure shoppers are much more inclined to make impulse purchases than economic shoppers, as the former spend more time in shops and are influenced more by various internal and external sensory stimuli (Iyer, 1989; Sherman *et al.*, 1997; Stoltman *et al.*, 1990; Sun, 1998; Tauber, 1995). Stern (1962: 61–2) highlighted nine factors that promote impulse buying:

- Low price exerts considerable control over spontaneous purchasing decisions.
- The degree of consumer need for an item also influences consumption. While most impulse items are unnecessary, there may be a marginal need for them.
- Mass distribution creates conditions where consumers receive a lot of exposure to a product in many different retail outlets.
- Self-service operations allow people to buy more quickly and with greater freedom than clerk-service operations.
- Widespread advertising creates knowledge and / or hidden images of products in people's minds, so that when they see them, their previous experience or interest is stimulated.
- Prominent shop displays create opportunities for shoppers to see items they might like to have.
- Items that have short product lives are clearly more subject to more frequent purchase than longer-lived goods.

- Small size and light weight may be a factor too, as these entice shoppers to buy things that might be easy to carry.
- Products that are easy to store are also appealing. The issue of where to keep the item once the shopper gets it home may also affect impulse-buying.

Early research from the 1960s (e.g. Kollat & Willett, 1967: 21; Stern, 1962: 59–60) outlined several forms of impulse-buying. These include the following:

- Pure impulse buying is the most obvious kind of unplanned buying. It is the purest impulsive buying action which breaks the normal buying pattern. In this case, before entering the store the shopper does not recognize a specific need for a product, or the need may be suppressed until the shopper has been exposed to in-store stimuli.
- Reminder impulse purchases are those created when a shopper sees a product and remembers that the stock at home is low or s/he recalls a television advertisement or other information about the item and a previous decision to buy.
- Suggestion impulse-buying occurs when a consumer notices an item for the first time and imagines a need for it, even if s/he has no prior knowledge of it.
- Planned impulse-buying happens when shoppers enter a store with some specific purchases in mind but with the expectation and goal of making other purchases that depend on coupon offers, sales, and availability. Sometimes, the consumer may know the type of product s/he wants to buy but not necessarily the brand.

Nonetheless, despite its potential to increase the competitive advantage and consumer expenditures, the leisure approach has generally been treated with suspicion by the retail industry (Howard, 1990a). Even as early as 1978, as a result of its study findings on the leisure role of shopping malls in the lives of women, the Department of Environment, Housing, and Community Development of Australia recommended an increase in these various new fusions of leisure and shopping, owing to the important role that malls play in the leisure pursuits of women, teenagers, and families. Despite their initial misgivings, many shopping centers and malls have begun to meet the changing needs of consumers and have become, in essence, community centers, offering a wide range of recreational attractions in addition to shopping (Bloch *et al.*, 1991; Brennan, 1984; Feinberg *et al.*, 1989; Finn & Rigby, 1987; Gratton & Taylor, 1987; Johnson & Mannell, 1983; Kowinski, 1985; Martin & Mason, 1987; Rosa, 2001). This new mall form, which has really only developed since the mid-1980s, was dubbed by Sargent (1988: 20) as 'leisure shopping and entertainment interbreeds' and provides what some observers call 'shoppertainment' (Beddingfield, 1999; Rosa, 2001). From their study of mall users, Bloch *et al.* (1994) identified the top ten mall activities as:

(1) shopping in a mall store to buy something;
(2) browsing in mall stores without intending to buy;
(3) making an unplanned purchase;
(4) buying a snack;
(5) socializing with friends or family;
(6) looking at mall exhibits or shows;
(7) eating lunch or dinner;
(8) walking for exercise;
(9) talking with other shoppers met in the mall; and
(10) getting a haircut.

West Edmonton Mall and the Mall of America are among the most widely cited forms of the shoppertainment phenomenon, which people visit less often to purchase something than to participate in one or more of the multitudinous other recreational activities (Finn & Rigby 1987; Wong, 1980). As will be noted in more detail in Chapter 6, these mega-malls provide 'new kinds of "lifestyle" shopping, blurring the boundaries between recreational and laborious activity' (Holbrook & Jackson, 1996: 193).

In an effort to increase the commercial value of traditional shopping spaces, malls are being designed and remodeled to enlarge their recreational content in several ways:

- The environmental and architectural aspects of mall design are now being emphasized. Lavish designs are showing that even everyday folks can shop in elegant settings, and interior landscaping and natural lighting are replicating open space and outdoor settings.
- Social functions are being programmed for shopping centers and malls, including special events and concerts, walking clubs for seniors, and the expansion of food services and entertainment to bring people together.
- Designers and managers are augmenting the traditional shopping experiences with recreational attractions and activities, such as food courts, movies, and arcades, and they are beginning to add supporting services such as day-care centers and banks, which will assist in allowing parents to browse and shop (Bloch *et al.*, 1991: 446–7).

The realization that shopping and leisure have a symbiotic relationship has caused retailers to recognize the need to compete for the attention of consumers, especially since modern-day shoppers have more sophisticated tastes, more discretionary income and time, and their boredome threshold is very low (Howard, 1990b: 8). Among other things, the benefits of leisure shopping for merchants include the following ones.

- The leisure–retail combination expands the shopping catchment area. If the shopping and leisure attraction is large (e.g. West Edmonton Mall or Mall of America), there may be national and international appeal for merchandise.
- The added leisure component generally means that visitors will stay longer in a combined shopping and recreational center.
- Visitors will tend to spend more in recreation and shopping center combinations. While there is a possibility that other recreational activities might redirect income from the retail stores, the recreation component encourages more people to make visits than they might have done otherwise, resulting in higher overall retail expenditures.
- The recreation and shopping combination attracts more visitors.
- Combined recreational amenities and shopping helps attract target consumers, such as family groups and middle-class clientele.
- The leisure–retail mix creates a highly marketable image for the region where it is located (Johnson, 1990).

Browsing, or window shopping, is an important form of the non-purchasing behavior mentioned earlier. It is a common element of shopping, as it allows people to employ many of their senses, spend time with others, get exercise, and conduct certain levels of first-hand information-searching. Jarboe and McDaniel (1987: 48) hypothesize that browsers will tend to demonstrate several unique characteristics:

- they are more inclined to shop in stores where they had not previously planned to shop;
- while they may not plan to make any actual purchases, they enjoy looking around;
- browsers are more likely to buy merchandise they had not previously planned to purchase;
- when going from store to store, they are more liable to look at window displays; and
- finally, they generally spend longer in malls and shopping centers than non-browsers.

In his 1977 study, Terry found that nearly all of the women he surveyed enjoyed shopping and approximately one-quarter of them went to the mall solely for the purpose of pleasure rather than for any utilitarian purpose. In another study, over half of the women surveyed identified window shopping, or browsing, as their favorite activity at a shopping center. For them, the shopping experience had little to do with actually purchasing products. Instead the main appeal was entertainment, socializing, and diversion from their daily routines (Department of Environment, Housing, and Community Development, 1978: 55). According to Jarboe and McDaniel (1987: 46), browsing serves many functions for different shoppers. It may simply be a recreational activity motivated only slightly by the desire to purchase something or a way of gathering information for future purchases. Either way, browsing/window shopping is essential to the success of retail operations and is seen as a low-cost, or free, leisure pastime or an easy way to spend a stormy day (Bloch *et al.*, 1991). For retailers, it amounts to free advertising.

Motivations and factors affecting the leisure shopping experience

There is little doubt that the leisure component of shopping is affected by a state of mind and takes place during a time that is not obligated to fulfilling work responsibilities (Fiske, 1989; Jansen-Verbeke, 1990b; Martin & Mason, 1987). Even grocery shopping, which many people treat as laborious and purely utilitarian, for many people becomes a recreational event where pleasure mingles with work (Bowlby, 2001; Wade, 1985). Researchers have identified several internal (customer) and external (retail environment) influences that contribute to making shopping and its associated activities a leisure pursuit. The internal factors generally refer to issues such as social involvement, allotted time, task completion, product involvement, and financial resources. The external or retailer factors are the ways in which retailers influence shoppers' experiences. These typically include product selection, special prices, retail environment, and salespeople (Jones, 1999; Wakefield & Baker, 1998). While both consumer and retailer factors are important in influencing the experience, according to Jones' (1999) study, it is the consumer, or internal, factors that are most influential. However, when experiences are non-entertaining or negative, the retailer, or external, factors are the most dominant.

According to Wakefield and Baker (1998: 518), certain variables affect the excitement levels of shop customers, which, in turn, result in certain behaviors. Their model (Figure 2.3) suggests that tenant variety, physical environment, and involvement with shopping directly influence excitement – a positive emotional state that involves high levels of pleasure and arousal. Excitement, they argue, leads to a stronger desire to remain at the shopping center, to return again, and results in less outshopping behavior. Donovan *et al.* (1994) confirmed this hypothesis in their research. The following sections examine the consumer and retailer factors that affect the leisure shopping experience most.

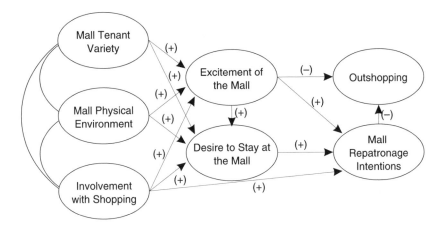

Figure 2.3 Model of mall excitement (after Wakefield & Baker, 1998)

Socializing

As noted previously, the ability to socialize with relatives and friends and to meet new people is one of the most important factors in making shopping an enjoyable, or leisure, experience (Anthony, 1985; Bergadaa *et al.*, 1995; Bloch *et al.*, 1991; Christiansen & Snepenger, 2002; Feinberg *et al.*, 1989; Graham *et al.*, 1991; Lehtonen, 1994; Lewis, 1990; Tauber, 1972). In Uzzell's (1995: 308) words, 'the reward of shopping lies in being able to do it with others', which reflects consumers' needs for approval, affiliation, and recognition (Kaplan, 1987: 15).

While the activity of shopping itself may be seen as a social pursuit that provides entertainment, excitement, and joy, retail venues themselves also create an atmosphere for social exchange. Browsing, socializing, and filling time are important activities undertaken at shopping venues (Jackson, 1991; Jacobs, 1985). Terry (1977) argued that the social meaning ascribed to a particular place is what gives people the satisfaction they are looking for in their individual experiences. This notion may have had its beginnings during the 18th and 19th century at the general store. The community general store was a place of male retreat, where a man could be idle in the company of other men, spitting, drinking, reading newspapers, and making up stories (Nelson, 1998). As the forms and functions of retail outlets changed, the locational focus and audience also began to change. In the early 1900s, corner drugstores became popular hangouts among teenagers for their sweets, sodas, ice cream, and peer companionship (Terry, 1977).

Later in the 20th century, in conjunction with the process of suburban-ization, shopping malls were developed to serve the consumer needs of an increasingly affluent and mobile society. With the development of suburbs, people began moving into single-family homes that were not physically or socially connected. This process and location did not allow large crowd interaction, so the malls, department stores, and corner conve-nience stores became surrogates for town squares and plazas that were absent in most suburban communities (Angle, 1974; Chubb & Chubb, 1981; Riehle, 1987). In the words of Westover (1976: 19), malls began 'seizing the role once held by the central business district, not only in retailing but as the social, cultural and recreational focal point of the entire community'. For suburbanites, the shopping center became 'the convenient all-purpose place to go for everything from a Sunday stroll to a symphony concert'. As a result, malls became the haunt of people of every age, leading Terry (1977: 197) to call them 'browsing centers', 'relaxing centers', or 'entertainment centers'. Kowinski (1985) describes shopping malls as central elements in modern society, playing such a critical role that they have recently been referred to as a consumer habitat (Bloch *et al.*, 1994). According to Bloch *et al.* (1991: 445), there were more malls than movie theatres in the early 1990s, and their research demonstrated that people spent more time in malls than anywhere else outside of work and home.

In Jones' (1999) study, some 36% of the respondents noted socializing aspects as being very important in their recreational shopping. This has tra-ditionally been one of the most important reasons for housewives and young mothers spending time at shopping centers with or without their children. Most research shows that going to the mall gives them a chance to get away from their mundane environment of homemaking and gives them an opportunity to relax, interact with other adults, and engage in self-reflection (Glennie & Thrift, 1996; Tauber, 1972). Approximately 37% of the participants of one early study listed 'getting away from home' as a positive feature of a shopping trip. They also observed that it provided variety, entertainment, and excitement to their routines, while at the same time confirmed their status as responsible homemakers. For 60% of the housewives, the shopping mall was used repeatedly on a weekly basis to meet their needs for social interaction (Department of Environment, Housing and Community Development, 1978).

The most popular group of shopping companions is friends. According to one recent study, about 70% of shoppers at a mall preferred to shop on their own, with a friend or a group of friends rather than with family members. Less than 2% claimed to enjoy shopping with a spouse or children (Holbrook & Jackson, 1996). In Australia, the Department of Envi-ronment, Housing, and Community Development (1978: 56) found that shopping with another adult helped distinguish between those who did and did not like shopping. Of the women in that study who claimed to enjoy shopping, 42% usually visited the mall with an adult companion. In most cases, it was a female relative but many were often accompanied by a friend or neighbor and 25% of the time they went with their husbands.

Graham *et al.* (1991: 347) regard shopping sociability as having two meanings: passive and active. People-watching is a good example of passive sociability, which allows individuals to watch and mingle with others but remain anonymous. People who want to be more actively involved use shopping centers as a venue for meeting people and interacting with them in various ways. Graham *et al.* (1991) use Kowinski's (1985) term 'mallingering' to identify the action of visiting malls when one desires to be actively or passively sociable.

Most notable among mall socialites and perhaps the most active in 'mallingering' are teenagers and the elderly. Kowinski (1986) explained that teenagers are so loyal to mall browsing that they refer to themselves as 'mall rats' (males) and 'mall bunnies' (females). According to some of the teenagers he interviewed at American shopping malls, 'a Mall Rat is someone who is here every day . . . We put on our cool faces and walk around and try to meet girls, and scare all the other guys' (Kowinski, 1986: 37). The primary motive, Kowinski notes, is the opportunity for teenagers to 'strut their stuff', to find acceptance in large groups of other people in the same age bracket.

Most adolescents spend the majority of their mall time assembling near video arcades and food courts (their territory) or 'cruising' the corridors. They generally congregate in the late afternoon and evenings after school to show off their new haircuts, makeup and clothes, talking, smoking, and waiting for something to happen (Lewis, 1989: 884). Most of them stay late, spending little or no money, until the stores close and the mall shuts its doors. Unfortunately, the mall has also been a place where young people can buy and experiment with drugs and shoplifting (Anthony, 1985). For many teenagers, the mall is an escape from home and school. One young woman in Lewis' (1989: 885) study, went to the mall 'to get away from home, get away from problems because I can't stay at home. Because my mom's always on my case when she's not off partying with her boyfriend . . . They bother me. So, I come to the mall'.

According to research by Anthony (1985), teenagers nearly always visit the mall with others. Of the youth in his study, 90% visited the mall in the company of one or two other people and only 9% visited alone. Most (83%) went to the mall with their friends, only 15% went with their parents, and only 2% claimed to have visited the mall with a sibling. The same study demonstrated that, in addition to shopping, the most important activities undertaken by teenagers at a mall were looking for members of the opposite sex, playing video games, having fun, seeing friends, people-watching, eating, and just filling time. Although marketing researchers have traditionally argued that the length of time spent at a mall affects the chances of a person's making a purchase, this does not appear to be the pattern for adolescents. For teenagers, hanging around at the mall usually does not involve spending much money (Anthony, 1985: 311).

The elderly are also important users of the mall, although their primary aim is not usually to make purchases. According to Maynard (1990: 35), this is because 'aging makes people slightly more likely to do two things – save money and enjoy life more, often at the expense of fewer retail purchases: people become less interested in having things and more interested in doing things'. The activities of the elderly and retired at malls are typically twofold. First, they sit, socialize, and watch the action around them (Graham et al., 1991). For these people, the mall atmosphere is important, especially when there are small children around. They also find comfort in being with other people of their own age group and in escaping from loneliness and fear (Kowinski, 1986: 37). The second main non-purchasing activity is called mall-walking (Duncan et al., 1994). With the knowledge that walking is good for their health, many older people select shopping malls as settings for walking, because they are one of the few places that long distances can be covered with six important comforts: air-conditioning in summer and heating in winter, the companionship of other people, interesting scenes to observe, toilets, relative safety, and refreshment stands (Cockerham, 1994; Fletcher & Macauley, 1983).

Escapism, sensory stimulation and arousal

An important element of the social motives, and as alluded to earlier in the context of housewives, shopping for recreationists involves elements of freedom, fantasy, and escapism (Babin et al., 1994). A shopping trip provides pleasure from bargaining and window-shopping, physical exercise, self-gratification, and increased social status. Elements of spontaneity, captivation, arousal, and excitement are fundamental motivations for hedonic forms of shopping (Tauber, 1995).

As noted elsewhere in this chapter, sensory stimulation is an important element of consumptive activities. Hirschman and Holbrook (1982: 92) discuss multisensory stimulation at considerable length and note that shopping, purchasing, and consumers' interaction with products enhances sensory modalities including sounds, visual images, scents, and tastes. Emotional arousal refers to motivational phenomena that include expressive, experiential, and neurophysiological components, which elicit reactions of jealousy, fear, rage, rapture, and joy. 'Emotive response is both psychological and physiological in nature, generating altered states in both the mind and body' (Hirschman & Holbrook, 1982: 93).

Time

Severe time limitations make shopping more arduous and appear to take away from the unhurried style of leisure shopping. Consumers seem to enjoy having a sense of unlimited time and temporal freedom to browse and stroll about. Jones' (1999) study noted that shoppers who felt rushed for time or had some kind of limits on their time in retail pursuits did not consider their experience a leisured one. Conversely, some participants felt that too much time spent shopping also influenced their experience in a negative manner. It appears, then, that having a choice in time terms can make or break the leisure shopping experience. Too much time to shop, usually the plight of accompanying companions, can cause mental tiring from the incessant display of goods and physical fatigue from hours of walking, inspecting merchandise, and carrying shopping bags (Lichfield, 1990).

Limited time is a sign of a harried society and, in the developed world, many people are living time-compressed lifestyles, which has, in recent years, turned what used to be a pleasurable activity into a chore that many people dread (Fram & Ajami, 1994; Lengfelder & Timothy, 2000). This is especially so on weekdays. Weekends are more commonly seen as favorable times for leisure shopping (Westover, 1976).

Another time element that is less commonly considered is seasonality of shopping. There are notable seasonal variations in leisure and tourism shopping, just as there are in demand for other forms of tourism and recreational activities (Johnson, 1990; Mintel International, 1996a; Patton, 1986; Timothy & Butler, 1995). The autumn and winter holidays in North America (e.g. Halloween, Thanksgiving, Christmas) are the busiest shopping season of the year. In the United States, the day after Thanksgiving is typically the busiest shopping day of the year, because it marks the beginning of the Christmas season. In fact, according to Fisher (1996), the month between Thanksgiving and Christmas involves fully 25% or more of the year's annual retail sales and determines the year's profits and losses for many merchants.

Task completion

As mentioned earlier, leisure shopping is generally not associated with task fulfillment. In fact, for many people, the presense of a specific purchasing task may reduce the leisure nature of a shopping trip. However, many of the respondents in Jones' (1999) study (34%) noted that when they did have a specific task in mind or a particular purchase to make (e.g. a new pair of shoes), making the targeted purchase led to a more enjoyable experience. Holbrook and Hirschman (1982) noted this in their discussion of how task definition and completion can influence consumption. Jones' participants stated that even when they did not have a specific purchase to make, they enjoyed the act of purchasing and leaving the store with something new. Prus and Dawson (1991) noted a similar finding in their study.

Product involvement

Product involvement can be seen from two perspectives. The first is when customers are able to handle and interact with products. Trying on new clothes, reading books, and testing computers are all ways of enhancing the shopping encounter. First-hand exposure to products, according to Simms and Narine (1994), is the most important source of information leading consumers to buy. The second perspective is when people have a personal interest in the merchandise being considered (Holbrook & Hirschman, 1982; Jones, 1999). Wakefield and Baker (1998) used car shows, stamp shows, fashion shows, toy exhibitions, and other related activities as examples of how shopping appeals to people who are involved in these types of pastimes. In this sense, people who are heavily involved in fishing and camping would find more pleasure in shopping for fishing rods, sleeping bags, and tents.

Involvement may be either enduring or situational. People who have an enduring (long-lasting) involvement with shopping may receive enjoyment directly from time spent exploring the shopping environment. Situational (temporary) involvement may be important at certain times owing to specific situations, such as when someone needs to purchase a new computer or automobile. Recent research reveals that higher involvement results in increased arousal with the experience of consumption (Wakefield & Baker, 1998).

Financial resources

The more financial resources individuals have, the more they tend to enjoy their purchasing activities (Holbrook & Hirschman, 1982). Some of the respondents in Jones' (1999) study conveyed that having a sense of unlimited financial resources while shopping contributed significantly to their level of enjoyment. A sense of freedom and excitement is the most commonly cited reason for this influence. Study participants noted that the boundaries set by having limited funds usually reduced the level of enjoyment.

Product selection

It is a well-known fact in retailing studies that consumers seek variety in their purchasing activities (Holbrook & Hirschman, 1982; Hoyer &

Ridgway, 1984). Consumers have a tendency to enjoy shopping more when stores carry a broad selection of products and unique merchandise not readily available in every shop. Similarly, consumers enjoy shopping better in malls and shopping centers that have a wide variety of stores selling a broad range of items (Jones, 1999). Product quality also contributes to people's perceptions of leisure shopping. In research done by the Bureau of Tourism Research (1990) of Australia, beauty, lack of availability at home, high-quality workmanship, nice design/style, and authenticity were viewed by consumers as product characteristics that helped create a satisfying leisure shopping experience.

Prices

Shopping for good values can have the effect of making consumers feel like smart shoppers and is an important part of entertainment-based shopping. The feelings are compounded when people discover a good bargain or participate in a major sales event. Negotiating a good price can also have a positive effect as consumers obtain price concessions from merchants or gain an economic advantage (Tauber, 1995; Westbrook & Black, 1985). Nearly 20% of Jones' (1999: 134) study participants recalled the importance of finding bargains in generating feelings of excitement and pleasure. By the same token, 8% of respondents noted that high prices were an issue in their non-entertaining shopping experience. The latter respondents appeared to be disappointed at high prices because they spent more money than anticipated.

Retail environment

The retail setting, according to Prus and Dawson (1991: 149), includes all aspects of a shopping context that people encounter in their shopping pursuits. This relates not only to products and salespeople but also to store layout and design, tenant variety in shopping centers, and the physical locations of the shops themselves.

Visual content and architectural design in shopping centers and stores have been shown to affect the leisure nature of shopping, frequency of visit, and length of stay (*Barron's*, 1998; Bellenger & Korgaonkar, 1980; Kent, 1989; Kowinski, 1985; Sherman *et al.*, 1997; Wakefield & Baker, 1998). Store environments act both as an attraction and as a deterrent to leisure shopping (Christiansen & Snepenger, 2002; Jones, 1999; Kinley *et al.*, 2003). A pleasant atmosphere, including décor, spatial organization, cleanliness, and merchandise layout, contributed to shopping being leisured and desirable. By the same token, non-entertaining shopping experiences were created by disorganized store designs, bad décor, crowded conditions, and overall bad surroundings. Sensory stimulation through store design and various intangible characteristics (e.g. sounds, smells, etc.) provide relief from boredom, escape from mundane tasks, and create moods and emotions that are conducive to enjoyable shopping beyond simple product acquisition (Bloch *et al.*, 1994; Chubb & Chubb, 1981; Hirschman, 1984; Lehtonen, 1994; Sherman *et al.*, 1997; Wakefield & Baker, 1998; Westbrook & Black, 1985).

Tenant variety also appeals to consumers. In the 1978 study by Australia's Department of Environment, Housing, and Community Development, some 82% of the shoppers surveyed replied that variety of shopping available was their primary reason for visiting a major shopping center. There is evidence to suggest that variety in tenant mix at malls will influence consumers' shopping center choice, frequency of visit, and shopping center image and will avert the leakage of valuable expenditures from the local economy through outshopping (Wakefield & Baker, 1998: 522). Wakefield and Baker's findings suggest that a variety of shops influences excitement levels as well. Tenant diversity includes shops, eating establishments, and entertainment opportunities (Chubb & Chubb, 1981).

The idea of clustering becomes a benefit in multistore shopping centers. By locating close to direct competitors, consumers can compare prices, products, and services better, which is an important motive for visiting shopping malls (Jarboe & McDaniel, 1987). 'A mall that offers store balance and tenant variety is likely to attract more shoppers because of the excitement it generates, and because one-stop shopping allows consumers to conveniently compare product offerings' (Wakefield & Baker, 1998: 521). For this very reason, retail developers use clustering as a planning principle so that merchants can take advantage of consumers' multipurpose shopping tendencies.

A third perspective on the retail setting includes the venue in which a shop or cluster of shops is located. The geographical setting is important but has not been well addressed in the literature, although a few authors have examined leisure shopping in rural regions and historic urban quarters (Getz, 1993a; Jansen-Verbeke, 1987; Orbaşli, 2000). Jansen-Verbeke (1987, 1989) and Timothy and Wall (1995) noted that shopping areas, most remarkably central urban retail districts with their physical characteristics (e.g. historic buildings, sidewalk cafés, and pubs), facility diversity, and morphological structure, are considered by many shoppers to be highly attractive places that lead to a leisure mindset. The distinctive Bavarian theme of Frankenmuth, Michigan, has created a successful shopping-based tourism industry in that community. The community's Christmas theme has also enhanced its shopping appeal, as people travel sizeable distances to enjoy the distinct, albeit blatantly contrived, environment as they shop for wood carvings, Christmas decorations, glassware and candles, and dine in one of the many German restaurants (Chubb & Chubb, 1981).

Salespeople

Of Jones' (1999) study respondents, 10% pointed to the role of salespeople in helping to create their leisure shopping experiences. This is usually a result of helpful and courteous staff, who are able to build a relationship with the customers. The opposite may also occur. One-quarter of the study's respondents mentioned employees as a part of the reason for having negative experiences. It is particularly the over-aggressive nature of store clerks that diminishes the entertainment or recreational factor in shopping.

Satisfaction with shopping

All of these elements work in concert to create a satisfying shopping experience, influenced by internal and external stimuli. Satisfaction with shopping, according to Wong and Law (2003), is a factor of people's expectations and perceptions of the activity and the subsequent outcomes. The very characteristics described earlier in this chapter that make shopping a leisure pastime also render the experience a satisfactory one. According to the research literature, shopper satisfaction is determined by four primary elements: product characteristics, service and performance, customer characteristics and behavior, and environmental influences (Wong & Law, 2003). The most important product characteristics are value for money, merchandise selection, and product quality (Heung & Cheng, 2000; Jansen-Verbeke, 1990a, 1990b; Mak *et al.*, 1999; Wong & Law, 2003). The study by Turner and Reisinger (2001: 24) concluded that satisfaction among tourists is directly related to obtaining the product attributes they consider important. Under the service and performance category, the most notable elements are fast and efficient service, high-quality and conscientious service by merchants, and attitudes and knowledge of staff (Heung & Cheng, 2000; Jansen-Verbeke, 1990a, 1990b; Wong & Law, 2003). Characteristics of the shoppers themselves, which determine satisfaction level, include gender, age, socioeconomic status, family status, and nationality (Kozak, 2001; Turner & Reisinger, 2001). Wong and Law (2003: 409) found that there are considerable differences between Asian and Western travelers' perceptions and expectations toward the attributes of shopping, which may result in different levels of satisfaction even within the same undertakings. Among the most important environmental influences are store reputation, retail location, opening hours, and the environments inside and outside the shops (Jansen-Verbeke, 1990a, 1990b; Mak *et al.*, 1999).

Shopping satisfaction is usually measured using various pre- and post-activity analyses of expectations and outcomes. The expectancy disconfirmation is a useful and common tool for understanding consumer satisfaction in retailing. It refers to the purchase of goods and services with pre-purchase expectations about anticipated outcomes: once purchases have been made, the results are then compared with the initial expectations (Oliver, 1980, cited in Wong & Law, 2003: 403). Obviously, understanding customer satisfaction provides valuable information about how well a destination or retail establishment is meeting shoppers' needs. Customer satisfaction can result in repeat business, so understanding it in the context of leisure and tourist retailing is an important undertaking by retail establishments.

Leisure Shopping at Home

Most of the information examined so far in this chapter is based on consumer experiences at shopping venues. However, there is another form of leisure shopping that has not been well examined in the retail or leisure literature but which deserves mention in this context: mail order and Internet shopping. Catalog retailing has a long history in North America and Europe and has been an important component of consumer behavior in developed societies for decades. This form of shopping, which is typically done in the comfort of home, is commonly seen as a pleasurable activity and a form of leisure. Chubb and Chubb (1981) noted that mail-order systems are a source of pleasure in a variety of ways. Catalogs are typically well illustrated and provide some home-shoppers with an escapist form of entertainment, where fantasies can be fabricated. Catalogs also make it possible for the elderly, the bed-ridden, children, people who live in remote and isolated areas, and people with severe disabilities to participate in a form of 'window-shopping' without having to visit a retail establishment in person.

Many reasons exist for the increasing popularity of Internet shopping but there are a few that stand out as being the most influetial. First, it generally takes less time than physically shopping in retail stores. Second is the ease of searching for bargains from a variety of suppliers without having to travel from shop to shop (Balabanis & Vassileiou, 1999; Charin, 1999). Third, many people feel that Internet and catalog shopping from home is safer than spending time in places where large numbers of people congregate (Underwood, 1994). Finally, there is the ability to avoid large crowds, particularly during holiday seasons (*Consumers Digest*, 1997). The following quote demonstrates many shoppers' feelings and clarifies why so many are opting to shop online from home.

I despise the malls, the stagnant traffic, the noise, the impatient crowds, the pushy sales people, the long lines, and the inconvenience of it all. Call me a shopping Scrooge, but physical stores for me are out! . . . Last year, I purchased only two Christmas gifts via the Internet, but this year I . . . orderd all my Christmas presents from the Net. (Blake, 1996: 70)

Despite its present popularity, home-shopping is not enough for most consumers, because, as O'Connor (1999: 145) notes, people like to go out to shop because of the social dynamics and because they like to compare products, quality, prices, and colors. Similarly, many people are leary to make purchases online because they have negative perceptions of Internet shopping security. Giving credit card numbers over the Internet is still a concern for many people (Jones & Vijayasarathy, 1998). O'Connor (1999) predicts, however, that home-based shopping will increase in popularity as people become more familiar and comfortable with technology.

Summary

This chapter examined the leisure and utilitarian characteristics of shopping and the various sociocultural, economic, and environmental factors that determine whether or not it is viewed as leisure or labor. The utilitarian side of shopping is described as being efficient, frustrating, difficult, monotonous, arduous, goal-driven, and boring. Leisure shopping, however, is a product of more than the simple acquisition of objects, although this may be an important element in the experience. For leisure shoppers, the social implications are of upmost importance, including spending time with friends and family members, making new friends, and watching people. Shopping also provides an outlet or escape from daily routines and mundane environments. Shop design, merchandise mix, décor, and helpful salespeople play a major role in sensory stimulation and the creation of relaxing and enjoyable consumptive experiences. Having adequate time and financial resources also contributes to the leisure element of shopping. Product selection and value and individual involvement with the product are important leisure variables as well. In addition, electronic shopping via the Internet and telephone are now well-established forms of leisure shopping.

Chapter 3

Shopping Tourism

Introduction

Shopping is among the most common and enjoyable activities undertaken by people on holiday and, in many cases, it provides a major attraction and basic motivation for travel. With the recent growth of more efficient transportation systems, increased technology, and widespread use of credit cards, people have been able to travel further a field to shop. In many instances, new-found levels of mobility have resulted in increased shopping in places far away from people's home communities. On a relatively small scale, this form of outshopping has existed for centuries but with new innovations and, as societies have become more mobile and affluent, many more opportunities have opened up for people to travel considerable distances, often even overseas, to shop.

Butler (1991) noted that the relationships between shopping and tourism could be divided into two categories. The first is where the primary purpose of the tourist trip is to shop. The second is where shopping is done as a secondary activity during a trip which might be motivated primarily by something other than shopping (e.g. sunbathing, ecotourism, etc.). This division between the two types of tourist shopping is clear and basic and, for heuristic purposes, has been adopted here. The focus of this chapter is the role of shopping as the main purpose for traveling, including the primary reasons for its popularity and growth. Shopping's role as a form of tourism is first examined within the framework of products purchased, the selected destination, and price advantages/value. The chapter concludes by looking at cross-border shopping, or shopping in border regions, as an importance example of shopping as a form of tourism.

Shopping as a Form of Tourism

Of the two forms of tourist shopping noted by Butler (1991), shopping as an added attraction to the destination being visited probably accounts for the majority of tourist expenditures on retail items. Nonetheless, shopping as the primary reason for taking a trip is an important factor for millions of travelers each year (Beck, 1998; Jansen-Verbeke, 1991; Timothy & Butler, 1995). McCormick's (2001) study found that 51% of travelers surveyed said shopping was the primary or secondary purpose of one or more trips during the previous year. Similar results were found by the Travel Industry Association of America (2001), which estimated that 47% of all shopping person-trips were taken by travelers who claimed shopping as their primary or secondary reason for traveling.

A quick search on the Internet reveals many types of specialized international shopping tours that can be purchased online or through travel agencies. Shopping tours to Europe from North America and Asia have become quite popular in recent years. For example, one US-based tour company offers a five-night Christmas shopping tour to Paris. In 2000, for approximately US$500, shoppers could fly from New York City to Paris, spend five nights in a hotel, eat breakfast daily, attend a free fashion show, receive a 10% discount card at Le Printemps department store, and free admission and a 25% discount card for the Lorenzi Diamond Museum (*Travel Weekly*, 2000a). The city of Florence has also initiated escorted shopping tours. On a typical tour, visitors are taken to famous shops like Gucci, Prada, and others specializing in gold, cashmere, leather, and silk. Participants also get an opportunity to visit the homes of famous designers and dine with them. Before each tour begins, visitors are asked to indicate what type of products they are interested in buying so the guide can arrange visits to appropriate retailers and assist tourists in getting VAT tax reimbursements upon departure (*Travel Weekly*, 2000b). Handicraft tours throughout rural America and Christmas market tours through Austria, Germany, and the Czech Republic are also popular among traveling shoppers (Jansen-Verbeke, 1998).

Three primary factors stand out most clearly as the driving forces behind shopping as a primary reason for travel: the merchandise being sought, the destination selected, and price advantages (Figure 3.1), although as the diagram shows, these may overlap and work together as reasons for travel. These factors are not mutually exclusive. In fact, they feed off each other quite obviously. Price and merchandise variety/quality can, for instance, transform a place into a world-famous shopping haven. These three factors are examined in the sections that follow.

Merchandise being sought

It is not uncommon for people to travel in search of specific items they wish to purchase. In the context of textile crafts, Crippen (2000) argues that there is a distinct group of tourists who choose a destination because of a textile production technique, such as batik or ikat. Crippen (2000: 271) calls this form of tourism 'textourism' or specialized tourism featuring textiles

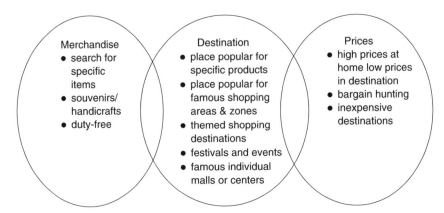

Figure 3.1 Factors influencing shopping as a motivation for travel

as a sole or key element. As well, collectors often travel in search of antiques to complement their collections at home (Michael, 2002). Places, such as Glendale, Arizona, the state's 'antique capital', rely heavily on this sort of specialized shopping tourism (Bartlett, 2000).

Mexico has become a famous shopping destination largely because of what it offers to retail consumers. Oaxaca is a sophisticated city that offers some of the best handicraft shopping in all of Mexico. Native and mixed European styles are popular there and the city is the source of many of the souvenirs and handicrafts sold throughout Mexico (Knickerbocker, 1995). Other items have become common commodities in Mexico, such as silver jewelry and clothing and, more recently, prescription pharmaceuticals have become one of the hottest products in Mexican border communities. This will be examined in more detail later in this chapter.

Some people travel to specialized destinations where duty-free goods can be purchased, ranging from expensive watches, jewelry, and clothing, to less expensive spirits and tobacco products. The Caribbean islands and Bermuda have become well-known shopping destinations owing largely to their status as international duty-free ports. The Bahamas and St Martin are popular examples of this (Weller, 1997). A unique duty-free destination that has long been popular among Europeans is Andorra, one of the world's smallest countries. The government's fiscal policy of duty-free shopping, in conjunction with the country's small size and fascinating history, has created a thriving tourism industry (Jenner & Smith, 1993; Taillefer, 1991). In the words of Reid (2000: 19), 'You take the biggest duty-free shopping area you've ever seen and multiply it a hundredfold', and that describes Andorra la Vella, the capital city. Reid also describes the situation as the main road through the country being 'one unbroken chain of shops', selling fashion clothing, jewelry, perfume, cosmetics, candy, cameras, computers, CD players, cell phones, skis, bicycles, tobacco, health food, liquor, and wine (Reid, 2000: 20).

The most valued items for sale in Hong Kong are electronic equipment, cameras, watches, furniture, Chinese antiquities, and jewelry; and every year thousands of people travel there to buy these specific items (Wakabayashi, 1995; Yogerst, 1993). The popularity of these items generally reflects their lower price tag in Hong Kong than in other places such as Europe and North America (Tanzer, 1996). According to one study of shoppers in Hong Kong, 68% of respondents purchased clothing and footwear, 50% bought jewellry, watches and gifts, and 22% purchased electronics. Although attractive prices were the primary reason these products dominate Hong Kong shopping, variety of goods, quality, fashion, and novelty are important factors in the decision to buy (Department of Hotel and Tourism Management, 2001).

The destination

Dozens of places around the world have developed into well-known tourist shopping destinations, either purposefully planned to be such or by default simply because they offered products that people found desirable (Begley, 1999; Birnbaum, 1996; Kreiner, 1996; Riegler, 1999). For the most part, famous shopping destinations are associated with one or a few primary products. For example, Venice is perhaps best known for its hand-blown glass and Hong Kong for its electronics (Lambert, 1996). This section describes several tourist locations that have developed largely because of their important role as shopping tourism destinations.

Themed shopping is an important part of tourism in many places. One of the best-known themed shopping destinations is Rovaniemi, located on the Arctic Circle in Finnish Lapland. For many years, Rovaniemi and the nearby Arctic Circle have been promoted as the land of Santa Claus – an image that has caught on throughout much of the world. This reputation has spread to the point that today, millions of letters come from children the world over to Santa's workshop and post office in Rovaniemi. This theme has led to the development of a successful shopping center and craft shop collection located directly on the Arctic Circle, complemented by visits from the jolly one himself and reindeers in the snowy fields nearby. Abundant shopping opportunities focused on themes of Christmas and life in wintery Lapland, coupled with a fair chance of seeing Father Christmas himself and his reindeer, Santa Village's reputation has grown beyond the boundaries of Europe (Nieminen, 2000; Pretes, 1996; Timothy, 2001).

In 2001, 45,000 'Christmas tourists' visited Finnish Lapland in December. In 2002, the number increased to 60,000. Owing to the popularity of the Christmas theme and its related shopping opportunities, charter flights from across Europe arrive directly in Rovaniemi throughout the holiday season. In 2002, 350 charter flights landed directly from abroad, primarily from the United Kingdom (*Helsingin Sanomat*, 2002). Groups from Greece and Russia also visit Rovaniemi to shop and celebrate Orthodox Christmas, and in Ukraine there is interest in introducing similar holiday shopping trips to Lapland.

As will be highlighted in more depth in Chapter 6, festivals and events are important venues for tourist shopping. Most festival themes derive from ethnicity, culture, religion, and food. Regardless of the type of festival, purchasing food, snacks, and handicrafts is nearly always involved in festivals and other events. In some places, the theme of shopping itself has been the center of attention for festival organizers. One of the newest forms of shopping attraction is the shopping festival of Dubai. Each January and February, the Dubai Shopping Festival (DSF) is held in Dubai, United Arab Emirates. Just Travel's (2003: para. 2) Website notes the following about the DSF: 'Forget Bangkok, Singapore or Hong Kong – Dubai is the latest and best shopping destination in the world.' The DSF was started in February 1996 and has run every year in January and February since then. In 2003, the festival attracted some 2.9 million visitors in only one month. Dubai has found success in promoting its shopping opportunities, which range from a wide assortment of modern and sophis-ticated malls to traditional Arab souks and street-sellers (Dubai Tourism, 2003).

Dubai is by far the most popular shopping destination in the Middle East and one of the most famous in the world. This is largely owing to the city's role as a major air transportation hub for flights between Europe and Asia. In common with several airports in Europe and Asia, the Dubai airport itself has become somewhat of a major shopping center offering luxury goods with low duty fees and no sales tax (Hunt, 2001).

Hong Kong is one of the most fascinating, product-diverse, and accom-modating shopping destinations in the world. As a result, the city has been dubbed a shopper's paradise (Cheng, 1999; Heung & Qu, 1998; Ko, 1999; Mak *et al.*, 1999). In recent years, tourism has provided nearly 10% of Hong Kong's gross domestic product, with shopping expenditures constituting more than half of the total tourism revenue throughout the 1980s and 1990s (Heung & Cheng, 2000; Law & Au, 2000). In 1996, Taiwanese visitors alone spent over HK$8.5 billion on shopping (Mak *et al.*, 1999).

While Hong Kong is well known for certain products, the ambience of the city with its glamorous malls, Chinese markets, and historic atmosphere has created an image that determined shoppers can hardly avoid. For more affluent North Americans and Asians, quick trips to Hong Kong are becoming more fashionable. For many years, long weekend trips have been offered from the United States to Hong Kong for the primary purpose of shopping. Today, four-day shopping tours are abundant, usually leaving the United States on the first day, arriving late on the second day, spending day three shopping with some sightseeing interlaced between shop stops, and then returing to the United States on the fourth day. Such a trip will typically cost approximately US$1000–1500 from the west coast. In spite of the cost, many visitors justify these short jaunts as saving considerable amounts of money overall as they buy enough merchandise at lower prices to justify the expense (Pesmen, 1994).

For many people, shopping is the sole or primary reason for their visit, so their ratio of expenditures on shopping is generally higher than that of others (Heung & Qu, 1998). In light of this, Tanzer and Tucker (1996: 176) state that in Hong Kong

shopping isn't something you do on your way to an activity. It is the activity itself, and its venues constitute the city's principal sights and monuments. Bargaining is an expression of the city's relentless drive and the highest tribute you can pay local citizenry'. Shopping tourism has contributed to alterations of the urban landscape of Hong Kong. Huge shopping centers, street vendors, and souvenir shops abound. The city's Chinese character and built heritage, according to Tanzer (1996), is ever more difficult to find owing to the modernized skyline, comprised of office towers and shopping centers. Even the picturesque harbor has been changed to accommodate higher levels of consumption.

Singapore comes in a close second in Asian shopping destinations. The country's tourism industry depends considerably on shopping and, in common with Hong Kong, it has consciously positioned itself as a major shopping hub (Hall, 1994; Lee, 1993a, 1993b; Lee & Boon, 1993). Shoppers from Southeast Asia are Singapore's most significant market, particularly affluent travelers from Indonesia, Thailand, and Malaysia, who are among the island's biggest spenders (Dhaliwal, 1998).

Among the most widely recognized shopping destinations in North America are New York City, Los Angeles, Honolulu, Toronto, and Montreal (Garnsey, 1999; Hein, 1996; Houston-Montgomery, 1994; Painton, 1994), although there are dozens of emerging shopping destinations, such as Las Vegas, Scottsdale/Phoenix, and Vancouver. According to a recent US Department of Commerce (1999) survey, the top five state destinations for shopping tourists were California (27%), Florida (25%), New York (21%), Hawaii (14%), and Nevada (10%), based on multiple responses.

In 1988 in Hawaii, 38 million people visited the Ala Moana Shopping Center alone. Of the total number of tourists who shopped at the center, 12% were Japanese, who spent US$80 million at the mall that year (*Chain Store Age Executive*, 1989). The popularity of shopping has been highlighted in Hawaii's marketing plans, especially in the state's recent campaign, 'Experience Aloha: Hawaii on Tour' (Fitzgerald, 2000).

As noted earlier, shopping malls, too, may become tourist destinations in their own right. The very nature of malls with their growing leisure infrastructures and services has elevated their role as resources for tourism and recreation. Many observers have noted the important role that malls play in the tourism system (e.g. Butler, 1991; Fairbairn, 1991; Gindin, 1984; Goss, 1993, 1999; Jackson, 1996; Jackson & Johnson, 1991; K. Jones, 1991; Kent *et al.*, 1983; McGoldrick & Thompson, 1991; Naylor, 1992; Rosa, 2001; Vester, 1996). The transformation of malls into tourist destinations in their own right and as major leisure centers has led to what Finn and Rigby (1992) have termed the 'mega-multi-mall', indicating a recent reorientation of purpose for large shopping centers to places of leisure and social interaction. Several mega-multi-malls have become the most popular tourist destinations in North America and the trend is developing in Western Europe as well (Balke & Rausch, 1990).

Mega-multi-malls have become the center of tourist attention for many countries and regions and, for millions of people, they are popular destinations. For example, Sawgrass Mills Mall in Sunrise, Florida, receives an average of ten million foreign tourists each year, of which approximately four million are from Latin America. This mall is particularly popular among visitors from Brazil, Argentina, Mexico, Venezuela, and Chile, many of whom fly directly to Florida from their home countries to shop (Elliot, 2001). Estimates suggest that each foreign visitor spends approximately US$200–300 per visit – a considerable economic impact for southern Florida (Painton, 1994). Similarly, it was estimated that, in 1986, non-local visitors to West Edmonton Mall spent approximately CA$227 million during their stay in Edmonton; and nearly half of these visitors claimed that their primary reason for traveling to Edmonton was to visit the Mall (Finn & Erdem, 1995).

Despite this widespread popularity, some observers note a decline in mall retail sales and in their general popularity since the early 1990s (*The Economist*, 1992; Sargent, 2002; Wakefield & Baker, 1998). Three primary reasons can be identified for the waning of mall popularity. First, too many malls look and feel too much alike, with many stores selling very similar merchandise. Second, people today are far too busy to spend time at the mall and they, therefore, make fewer trips as they seek to optimize their shopping time in other ways and in other locations. Finally, according to consumer research, people today tend not to enjoy the mall experience as they did when the first mega-multi-malls were established (Wakefield & Baker, 1998: 516). This decline notwithstanding, malls are still popular attractions for tourists and local recreationists.

It is difficult to determine precisely what it is about mega-malls that appeals to tourists. Some observers suggest that it is not the retail opportunities alone, nor is it the entertainment facilities alone. It is likely a combination of the two. Butler (1991) and Finn and Rigby (1992), in the context of West Edmonton Mall, argue that it is the uniqueness and novelty of the place that is the most wielding enticement.

The major attraction in the case of West Edmonton Mall surely lies in its image and scale. It is the largest shopping mall in the world, and as such, has been marketed as 'the eighth wonder of the world'. Since time immemorial, people have been fascinated with, and traveled to see, something unique, whether it be the largest, the fastest, the longest, or the most expensive item of its kind. (Butler, 1991: 291)

The West Edmonton Mall (WEM), located in Edmonton, Alberta, Canada, is the largest mall in the world. The four-phase construction of WEM began in 1981, when a 106,000 square-metre mall was built on 25 hectares of land. At that time, WEM had 220 retail stores and services and cost CA$200 million to build. In 1983, the mall was expanded to include an additional 105,000 square metres and 240 more retail stores and services. During this second phase, major recreation and entertainment facilities were introduced. Phase 3 of WEM's growth took place in 1985 with the addition of more entertainment features and attractions, more retail establishments, and themed streets (e.g. Bourbon Street and Europe Boulevard). The final phase of development ended in 1998 as the now 49-hectare site became home to even more leisure and tourism services (West Edmonton Mall, 2002).

Today, WEM comprises seven major attractions, themed streets, more than 800 stores and services, 26 movie theaters, 110 eating establishments, 58 entrances, hotels, dozens of activity centers (e.g. water park, amusement park, hockey rink, miniature golf course, indoor lake with submarines), and outdoor parking for at least 20,000 vehicles. The mall's inside area is 493,000 square metres (equivalent to the size of 115 American football fields). The total cost of building WEM is estimated to have been CA$1.2 billion. The mall is visited annually by some 35 million people, and employs 23,500 people directly (see Table 3.1) (Finn & Rigby, 1992; Finn *et*

Table 3.1 Characteristics of West Edmonton Mall and Mall of America

	West Edmonton Mall	Mall of America
Open	1981	1992
Size	5.3 million ft²	4.2 million ft²
Stores	> 800	> 520
Employees	23,500	11,000 (13,000 in high season)
Parking spaces	20,000	12,550
Cinemas	26	14

Sources: West Edmonton Mall (2002) and Mall of America (2002)

al., 1994; Kowinksi, 1986; West Edmonton Mall, 2002), earning the nickname 'the mother of all amusement malls' (Belsky, 1992: 213).

WEM is of paramount importance in the Canadian tourism system (Hallsworth, 1988; Henry, 1986; Howard, 1990b; Johnson, 1987; 1991; Kowinski, 1986). In terms of pure numbers, several studies have demonstrated its place is Canada's top tourist attraction (Bloch *et al.*, 1994), averaging more than 100,000 people a day, and having an economic impact of some CA$12 billion a year (Finn & Erdem, 1995; Hutchinson, 1994). WEM is an attraction not only for local recreationists, but also for nationwide and international visitors. Studies suggest that between 40% and 50% of all visitors to WEM are from outside the province of Alberta (Finn & Erdem, 1995; Hopkins, 1991). This amounts to being even a larger attraction than Banff National Park or Niagara Falls and, in fact, according to Ritzer and Liska (1997: 103), more Canadian package tours visit WEM than Niagara Falls.

The Mall of America (MOA), the second largest mall in the world, was completed in 1992 at a cost of US$650 million. Its area of 391,000 square metres houses 520 stores, 49 eating establishments, and dozens of entertainment facilities (e.g. an amusement park, indoor roller coaster, hotels, skating rinks, casinos, bungee jumping, a mini golf course, movie theaters, night clubs, and restaurants) (Belsky, 1992; Gershman, 1996). The mall's parking capacity is 13,000 automobiles and 11,000 people are employed on a regular basis (13,000 in summer and during holiday periods) (Mall of America, 2002; Nelson, 1998; Thorpe, 1994).

As mentioned earlier, the mall is divided into thematic regions, or retail destinations. The West Market section resembles a busy European marketplace with train-station-type architecture, street furniture, traditional stores, and vendors. The North Garden depicts a European landscaped garden with terraces, gazebos, and fine boutiques and shops. The focus of

South Avenue is luxury hotels with carpeted walks and sophisticated stores. East Broadway represents an American city with neon lights, chrome, and contemporary fashions (Goss, 1999: 52).

Commentators claim that MOA is the biggest attraction in the United States, being visited by more people than Disney World in Florida, Elvis' Graceland, and the Grand Canyon combined (Beck, 1998; Nelson, 1998). Within just a few months of its completion, MOA had attracted 1500 bus tours, including some 50 Japanese tour groups (*The Economist*, 1992). Today, more than 43 million people visit the mall every year (600,000–900,000 per week) and estimates suggest that between 10 and 15 million of these originate from outside a 200-km radius of the mall (Becker, 2000; Nelson, 1998). The majority of international visitors, which comprise some 6% of the total visitation, come from Canada, followed by Japan and the United Kingdom. The economic impact of 'that monument to consumption that put Minnesota on the international shopping map' (Dooher, 1997: 80) on the state's economy is estimated to be US$1.6 billion a year (Mall of America, 2002), of which 8% is contributed by foreign visitors (Goss, 1999).

MOA is a popular destination for shopping tour groups from Canada, Japan, Western Europe, Israel, and Australia (Becker, 2000; Nelson, 1998). In 1992, 1500 bus tours traveled to MOA and, in 1994, 3000 tours were booked. Northwest Airlines offers special package tours from around the world to the mall via Minneapolis-St Paul International Airport, which is located only ten minutes away by shuttle bus (Thorpe, 1994). In relation to local use, tourism is considered a major player in the economy of the MOA. Tourism accounts for 40–50% of all sales and is so important to the MOA economy that the mall has its own Tourism Department, which focuses on promoting mall tourism and helping people arrange trips (Goss, 1999; Pesmen, 1994; Wieffering, 1994).

In common with its Canadian counterpart, MOA is seen not just as a place to shop, but as an entire holiday destination, providing hotel rooms, transportation, activities, and business offices (Belsky, 1992). In the eyes of the popular travel media, the Mall of America is,

> not just a mall, and it's not really about shopping. It's an experience, it's a destination, it's a once-before-you-die kind of thing – a celebration of creativity and food and product of man over time, space, and weather. The Mall is magic, a Twilight Zone tucked out there in another dimension, with its own zip code and its own subculture. (Gershman, 1996: 84)

The appeal of shopping malls has been noted and capitalized on by major airlines and the tour sector. In the past, Northwest Airlines, for example, has offered a 'shop til you drop' tour that flew British and

Japanese consumers directly to the MOA. In the United Kingdom, consumers boarded a plane in London on Friday afternoon, arrived in Minneapolis on Saturday morning, shopped all day and arrived back in London early on Sunday morning. Northwest Airlines, the MOA's 'official airline', researched price differentials between Minneapolis and London and found that the differences were almost enough to pay for the whole trip (Painton, 1994: 58). Northwest Airlines has offered similar same-day trips from various parts of the United States and Canada to MOA for deep discounts on key shopping days of the year (Pesmen, 1994).

Price advantages

According to Keown (1989), relative prices are one of the most influential factors in generating shopping tourism. He hypothesized that the cheaper the prices in the destination, the more popular the destination would be for shopping. While it is obvious that many more variables come into play in shopping tourism demand, price is an important influence in the development of shopping tourism. People have long traveled outside their immediate home areas in search of retail bargains (this outshopping phenomenon will be discussed in more detail later in this chapter). 'Nearly everyone likes a bargain; nearly everyone likes to buy; nearly everyone likes to have a reason for going some place different to do so' (Lundberg, 1990: 46).

The growth in popularity of outlet malls and factory shops among tourists attests to the importance of good value and price. In 1997, some 40% of all travelers in the United States visited an outlet mall, 10% citing shopping as the primary purpose of their trip (Knight, 1999: 64). Painton (1994) remarked that low retail prices in the United States, ranging from 30–70% less than costs in Asia and Europe, brought nearly 50 million tourists a year into the country in the mid-1990s. The same can be observed in 2003, as the value of the US dollar to the Euro and Asian currencies fell drastically, thereby making shopping in the United States a desirable prospect, particularly for Europeans. In the USA, 'Every week thousands arrive with empty suitcases ready to be filled' (Painton, 1994: 58).

Thailand is an emerging shopping destination, which has grown in popularity in recent years in part as a result of its good value and low cost. Recently, Thailand has become popular both for its upper-class department stores and its inexpensive night bazaars where tourists can purchase handicrafts, clothing, ceramics, and cheap designer jewelry (Brown, 1995). The Tourism Authority of Thailand (TAT) is taking considerable strides in developing shopping tourism, in part as a way of counter-balancing the negative image that sex-related activities have brought to the international fore and also as a way of diversifying the tourism economy (Janssen, 1996;

Ngamsom, 1998; Parnwell, 1993). As part of these efforts, the TAT in cooperation with American Express, planned and executed Thailand's 'Grand Sale' in 1997. Dozens of shopping centers and department stores throughout the country participated in the event, which was aimed at boosting revenues from shopping tourism. Discounts of 20–70% were offered on Thai and imported designer products. This coupled with the advantageously low value of the Baht that year, was seen to be a considerable value for shoppers from abroad (*Far Eastern Economic Review*, 1997). Several other places in Asia are beginning to blossom as inexpensive shopping destinations as well, including Korea, Taiwan, and China (Lederman, 1995; Yogerst, 1993).

Cross-border shopping

A unique type of shopping tourism that has received considerable attention during the past decade is shopping in border areas – also known as cross-border shopping. This consumer activity takes place near international boundaries and contains elements of all three of the factors described earlier (e.g. merchandise, destination, and price). Cross-border shopping relates directly to the long-established notion of outshopping, which traditionally has been defined as people shopping outside their home environments or communities. The outshopping literature has heretofore focused primarily on domestic inter-urban and rural-to-urban shopping trips, where people travel from their own communities to shop, owing to a variety of perceived benefits (e.g. lower prices, better selection, product quality) in the destination (Humphreys, 1991; Jones, 1998; Papadopoulos, 1980; Prentice, 1992; Thompson, 1971). While domestic cross-border shopping (e.g. between states, provinces, cities) continues to be an important component of the outshopping phenomenon (Clark, 1994; Fox, 1986; Mikesell, 1971) and often has a leisure function (Timothy, 2001), this section focuses on the issues and dynamics of international-level cross-border consumption.

Economic, legal, and social differences on opposite sides of an international border create conditions that appeal to many types of tourists. As a result, activities such as gambling, prostitution, drinking, and shopping become important tourist activities in border regions. Cross-border shopping, wherein people travel beyond the boundaries of their own nation specifically to shop in a neighboring country, is common in all parts of the world. For people who live near a border, the trip may be short, lasting from minutes to hours, but for people who live farther from the border, the trip usually has a longer duration, sometimes lasting days and tends to be more leisure oriented (Timothy & Butler, 1995).

While border shoppers are, in most cases, day visitors or international excursionists, the activity itself should be considered a form of tourism because people travel abroad, spend money, use the tourism infrastructure, are often counted as international arrivals by official government agencies, and are commonly motivated by curiosity and pleasure (Jansen-Verbeke, 1990a, 1991; Matley, 1976; Murphy, 1985; Ryan, 1991; Timothy, 1995, 2001, 2002b). Some people also stay a night in the destination country (even if it is only a few kilometres away) for the simple reason that they can claim a higher duty-free allowance (Timothy & Butler, 1995). This specific form of international travel has become so popular that directories have been published in recent years to guide consumers to the best locations for border-land shopping (Cahill, 1987; Meldman, 1995; Szabo, 1996; Yenckel, 1995).

Four economic and sociopolitical conditions, which allow and facilitate the growth of cross-border shopping, exist (Leimgruber, 1988) (Table 3.2). First, as mentioned before, there must be enough contrast between the home location of the travelers and the potential destination across the boundary in terms of prices, quality of merchandise, and selection. Second, the potential consumers must be aware of what exists on the other side. They must have sufficient knowledge of what goods are for sale in the neighboring country either through previous personal visits or through various other media. Third, the border must be porous enough to allow a relatively easy flow of people between countries. Borders with fewer immigration and customs restrictions will be more inclined to be the focus of outshopping than those with extensive formalities and barriers. Finally, the traveling shoppers have to be able and willing to make the journey, particularly in light of issues such as personal mobility and currency exchange

Table 3.2 Conditions necessary for cross-border shopping to develop

• There needs to be enough contrast on opposite sides of the border to create a noticeable difference. This usually alludes to variations in product quality, price, and selection.
• Residents of the tourist generating country must be aware of what lies on the other side of the border. Potential shoppers must have enough information about the goods offered beyond the frontier through media sources or personal visits.
• Shoppers have to be able and willing to make the trip, particularly in light of exchange rates and personal mobility.
• The border, or entry requirements, must be permeable enough to allow people to visit with relative ease.

Source: Compiled from Leimgruber (1988)

Table 3.3 Factors that contribute to cross-border shopping

• Favorable exchange rates between currencies
• Higher taxes on one side of a border and lower on the other
• Economics of scale, small distribution channels, and a lack of competition in smaller economies, higher profit margins exist, raising the cost of consumer goods at home.
• A wider selection of products and services abroad than at home.
• Customer service in neighboring countries may be better than at home.
• Many people shop abroad owing to differences in the opening hours and days for shops, particularly on weekends and holidays.
• Shopping abroad is entertaining and enjoyable. For many people, the excitement of crossing a border is compounded by the assortment of products available.

rate differentials. When these conditions exist, the door to cross-frontier consumption opens up but several other motivations are the driving force behind the border-shopping phenomenon (Table 3.3):

- One of the most significant push-and-pull factors is a favorable exchange rate. Considerable research has demonstrated direct correlations between exchange rates and levels of cross-border shopping (Chadee & Mieczkowski, 1987; Di Matteo, 1993, 1999; Di Matteo & Di Matteo, 1993, 1996; Diehl, 1983; Patrick & Renforth, 1996; Prock, 1983; Timothy, 1999a). The economic rationale for shopping abroad is highly elastic, meaning that when even the slightest changes in the value of one currency occur, there will also be shifts in levels of cross-border shopping.
- Lower taxes have also long been considered a driving force behind this phenomenon. When sales and other taxes are lower in a neighboring jurisdiction, people who are taxed more heavily will travel there to shop (Bygvrå, 1990, 2000; Nielson, 2002; Timothy, 1999a).
- Distribution channels in smaller countries are usually not as cost-effective as those of larger states where there is a higher market demand. This means that profit margins in smaller countries are higher than those in larger states where competition is stronger (Canadian Chamber of Commerce, 1992; Timothy, 2001).

- Places that demonstrate a wider variety of merchandise in terms of brands, fashions, and product quality attract people across political boundaries to shop (Chatterjee, 1991; Government of Ontario, 1991).
- Quality customer service is a competitive advantage that some places possess and which contributes to the growth of cross-border shopping. Research has demonstrated that people enjoy the higher levels of service and personal attention they receive in neighboring countries (Canadian Chamber of Commerce, 1992; Government of New Brunswick, 1992).
- Hours of operation can also be an important motivation for some people to shop abroad. If stores are closed in the home country on Sundays, holidays or after a certain hour, they may very well remain open in an adjacent jurisdiction, especially on holidays that are only celebrated on one side of the border (Bygvrå, 2000; Goodman & Carr Consulting, 1992; Timothy & Butler, 1995).
- When a shopping trip is considered enjoyable and, in some cases, even functions as a family vacation or a weekend away, then the element of pleasure, or leisure, is an important motive (Goodman, 1992; Timothy & Butler, 1995). Ritchie's (1993) study confirms this claim, demonstrating that some 50% of the cross-border consumers in his study were motivated by pleasure. Another study by the Canadian Chamber of Commerce (1992) concluded that one of the main reasons Canadians shopped in the United States was because it gave them a chance to leave home and experience another environment. Additionally, many consumers include dining out, watching movies at a cinema, attending events, visiting historic sites, and participating in outdoor pursuits as part of their cross-frontier shopping excursions.

There are some notable spatial patterns with regard to cross-border shopping. Several observers have concluded that the further a consumer travels from home to shop, it is more probable that his/her motives will include a pleasure orientation (Jansen-Verbeke, 1990a; Ritchie, 1993; Timothy & Butler, 1995). Often the types of products and frequency of travel are also related to distance traveled to reach the border. According to a model by Timothy and Butler (1995) (Figure 3.2), the more distant shoppers live from the border the less frequently they will cross, but the value of the merchandise they buy will probably be higher. Thus, consumers who live within 50 km of the border (proximal zone) will have a higher tendency to cross more frequently and are more willing and able to go for commonplace items such as beer, groceries, petrol, cigarettes, and restaurant meals. Consumers who live further out (50–200 km – the medial zone) are less inclined to cross the border for everyday items. Instead, they

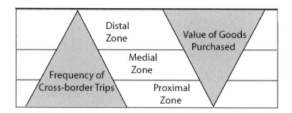

Figure 3.2 Spatial characteristics of cross-border shopping (taken from Timothy & Butler, 1995)

cross less often and purchase slightly higher-value goods (e.g. clothing, shoes, tools). Buyers who live more than 200 km from the boundary (distal zone) cross least often but, when they do, they travel with the goal of purchasing big-ticket items, such as dishwashers, furniture, and electronics. Clearly this is a mainstream pattern but variations will surely manifest. For instance, people who live far away will probably also fill up with gasoline and people who live closer may also buy new appliances on the other side of the border on one of their more frequent journeys (Timothy, 2001; Timothy & Butler, 1995).

It should also be noted that, in many border areas, some consumers live nearer to retail centers in the neighboring country than to shops in their own country. Assuming that people shop in locations closest to home and which offer the best and most cost-effective merchandise (Christaller, 1966), and barring major economic and political barriers, many shops have market areas that extend across political divides (Bygvrå, 2000).

Cross-border shopping is widespread and exists in many forms in nearly all locations throughout the world (Bygvrå, 2000; Jansen-Verbeke, 1998). In some places, the activity is the primary form of tourism. While shopping is common along nearly all borders in Europe, it has received the most attention in the following contexts:

- Denmark–Germany (Bygvrå, 1990, 1992, 1997, 1998, 1999; Weigand, 1990)
- Eire (Ireland)–Northern Ireland (Boyd, 1999; Fitzgerald *et al.*, 1988; Ryan, 1991)
- Central and Eastern Europe (Bachvarov, 1997; Hajdú, 1994; Hall, 1991; Kovács, 1989; Michalkó & Timothy, 2001; Minghi, 1994, 1999; Sándor, 1990; Williams & Baláž, 2000)
- Switzerland–Italy (Leimgruber, 1981, 1988, 1991; Ryan, 1991).

In the Americas, the international outshopping research literature focuses primarily on the Canada–US border (e.g. Ahmed, 1996; Di Matteo, 1993; Kreck, 1985; Timothy, 1999a; Timothy & Butler, 1995) and the Mexico–US border (e.g. Asgary *et al.*, 1997; Brown, 1997; Gibbons & Fish, 1987; Patrick & Renforth, 1996; Prock, 1983; Wasserman, 1996), although some attention has recently been directed toward boundaries in Central and South America (e.g. Caviedes, 1994; Mikus, 1994; Pearce, 1984). There is also a small but growing literature on this activity in Asia and Africa (e.g. Ngamsom, 1998; Peberdy, 2000; Piron, 2002; Toops, 1995; Zhao, 1994).

The following sections discuss case studies of cross-border shopping from Europe, North America and Asia that demonstrate the elements described earlier and which have featured prominently in the tourism and retail literature.

Mexico–USA

As mentioned previously, shopping along the USA–Mexico border is unique in that the motivations and products differ depending on the direction of consumption. The purchasing patterns of US residents in Mexico are based on three products – souvenirs, pharmaceuticals, and dental and medical services – and their activity is more leisure oriented than Mexican shopping activities in the United States.

The Mexican border towns have long been important international day-trip destinations for Americans and other tourists visiting the southwestern United States. The idea that people can park their cars in the US (or take a shuttle bus) and walk into a foreign country, a 'third world' country in fact, is an appealing prospect for many Americans and other international visitors. The Mexican border communities became especially popular destinations during the prohibition era, and even earlier in the late 19th and early 20th centuries, owing to their tolerance of alcohol consumption and prostitution (Arreola & Curtis, 1993; Arreola & Madsen, 1999). At the end of prohibition, border tourism wained until the 1950s, when it again revived on the basis of prostitution and shopping for goods that were difficult to acquire in the United States following the Second World War (e.g. tires, gasoline, some groceries, metal car parts). Since that time, the Mexican border towns have become well-known destinations for drinking, prostitution, bullfighting, authentic Mexican food, and shopping. In terms of total visitor numbers, the border towns are the most significant tourist destinations in Mexico, receiving millions of same-day and overnight visitors each year. The largest and most popular of these destinations are Tijuana, Mexicali, Nogales, Juarez, and Matamoros, with several popular but smaller communities in between.

As these Mexican towns and villages grew in importance as tourist destinations, demand for souvenirs also grew. Visitors to San Diego, California, and El Paso, Texas, commonly also visit their cross-boundary counterparts as part of their vacation experience. For many people, this is their first and only trip to Mexico (or even abroad), so their tendency is to desire souvenirs as tokens of their (usually) pedestrian journeys. This has created what Arreola (1999) terms a 'curio landscape' in most Mexican border towns, where streets and walkways are crowded with consumable symbols that stereo-typify the Mexico of tourism – sombreros (wide-brimmed hats), piñatas (papier-mâché figures), serapes (shawls/blankets), stone chess sets, carved mules and dolphins, seashell crafts, silver jewelry, clay pottery, leather products, and recently developed native handicrafts. The following narrative describes the 'curio landscape' of Nogales, Arizona's adjacent neighbor, Nogales, Sonora, Mexico:

> [It] is a pedestrian path marked by arrows that lead one across the border, through a rotating metal-barred gate, past a loiter space filled with standing customs officials, squatted begging street Marias, and assorted sidewalk vendors. Veering right along Calle Campillo, the first block in from the gate, one feels the first vocal blast of curio shop barkers in front of stores pressing you to come in and 'take a look'. Two blocks west you jog left and navigate along the sidewalk as well as in dense mini-malls and adjoining alleys, one discovers shops marked by signature cornucopic product displays of all things imaginable and some unimaginable. This, then, is the curio landscape, exotic yet familiar, raucous but safe ... This is the Mexico we have come to see, the Mexico-land of our imagination and the landscape that offers North Americans one of their most coveted and sacred rights – the freedom to shop. (Arreola, 1999: 33–4)

The other primary form of retailing for tourists in Mexican border towns is health care and pharmaceuticals. Medical care, dental care, and prescription drugs are costly in the United States and some insurance policies do not cover the necessary procedures and medicines. For some people, particularly the retired population, these items have become prohibitively expensive. People who live near Mexico and need these medications and services commonly seek them south of the border, where drugs are much less expensive because of market forces and demand (Borden, 2001; Valdez & Sifaneck, 1997; Vogel, 1995). For others, part of the appeal of spending the winters in California, Arizona, and Texas is those states' proximity to pharmacies in Mexico (Banks, 1998; de los Santos & Vincent, 1993; Vincent & de los Santos, 1990). The US government requires that all medications purchased in Mexico be declared at customs and all prescription drugs need to be accompanied by a prescription. However, many American drug consumers do not declare their purchases at the border, which, if discovered, may result in confiscation and fines (Koeppel, 1999). Dental and medical work is also considerably cheaper south of the border and many people get their annual physicals, dentures, and tooth fillings for a fraction of the price it would cost in the United States (Banks, 1998; Vogel, 1995). This form of consumption is evident immediately across the border. Second in number only to souvenir shops, pharmacies, dental offices, and medical practices line the streets near the main crossing points in nearly all Mexican border communities, creating a convenient conglomeration of services for people on fixed incomes and others who live nearby.

Mexican shopping in the United States has a somewhat different focus than the activities described above. The retail activities of Mexican day-trippers deal little with souvenirs and pharmaceutical drugs, and are notably less leisure oriented, although sightseeing, eating in restaurants, and visiting friends and relatives can also be important activities on the American side (Asgary et al., 1997). Instead, the focus is on household items, furniture, clothing, toys, and other day-to-day items that are perceived to be of a higher quality and less expensive than in Mexico (Pavlakovic & Kim, 1990). Many shops adjacent to the boundary on the US side accept Mexican currency and employees nearly always speak Spanish. Large US-based retail stores, such as Wal-Mart, are common in small, American towns adjacent to the border. In most parts of the United States, a large Wal-Mart store could not be supported in a community the size of Nogales, Arizona, or Douglas, Arizona, but these department stores are successful because of their usual location within 1 km or so of the international frontier. Thus, on the US side, the curio and pharmacy landscapes are replaced by a retail landscape of department stores, furniture and appliance centers, clothing and shoe outlets, and supermarkets.

According to Brown's (1997: 115) estimate, Mexicans spent US$20–22 billion in US border towns in 1995, which translated into more than one million American jobs. During the same time, in the border city of El Paso, Texas, alone, residents from Ciudad Juarez (Mexico) accounted for approximately 45% of all expenditures, totaling some US$1.4 billion in retail sales (Wasserman, 1996). Wasserman's study also noted that 70% of Ciudad Juarez's residents shopped in the USA at least once a year and 57% made more frequent trips. The small town of Douglas, Arizona (pop. 14,000), is heavily dependent on its cross-border neighbor, Agua Prieta, for much of its economic welfare. Research results from a 1998 study found that Mexican shoppers are responsible for over 30% of the Arizona town's retail earnings (US$38 million a year). It also found that 88% of the respondents claimed shopping as their primary or secondary reason for visiting

Table 3.4 Characteristics of Mexican visitors in Arizona border towns (n = 2612) by purpose of visit, 2001

Reason for visit	(%)	People arriving by car %	People arriving on foot %	People staying over night %	People on day trips %
Visit relatives	7.76	8.51	5.33	23.22	7.09
Vacation	2.51	2.45	2.18	7.82	2.30
Shopping	72.28	68.42	83.41	55.19	73.00
Medical	0.22	0.28	0.00	0.64	0.20
Business	1.52	1.66	0.63	6.30	1.33
Personal	0.72	0.93	0.01	2.58	0.64
Work	14.41	17.00	8.44	2.42	14.91
Other	0.58	0.75	0.01	1.83	0.53

Source: Compiled from Charney & Pavlakovich-Kochi (2002)

Douglas each month, spending on average US$74 each trip (Cochise College, 1998).

Asgary *et al.* (1997) found that 49% of the Mexican shoppers in Texas cities crossed the border primarily because of cheaper prices. The rest suggested that product quality, variety, availability, and customer service were the attraction. Table 3.4 highlights the characteristics and extent of Mexican shopping in Arizona border communities.

Several events have occurred in recent years, which have influenced the levels and types of Mexican shopping in the United States. The first is the devaluation of the peso. In 1976, the Mexican government devalued its currency by 50% as a strategy to decrease imports, increase exports, and curtail Mexican spending north of the border. The same thing occurred in 1982, when the peso was devalued by 200%, and again in 1994 (Patrick & Renforth, 1996; Prock, 1983; Timothy, 2001). This significantly curbed cross-border spending and resulted in the failure of many American businesses and the loss of many jobs (Diehl, 1983; Timothy, 2001). The second major event was the Mexican government's borderland mall-building program. Several malls were constructed during the 1990s in the largest of the Mexican border cities in an effort to keep middle- and upper-income Mexicans shopping at home (Wasserman, 1996). So far this program has seen only very limited success. The third occurrence was the Mexican government's recent decision to raise the monthly duty-free limit of goods entering Mexico from the United States from US$50 per person to US$400. This increase is only effective for people who live near the border and applies to basic daily merchandise (e.g. personal hygiene items, shoes, apparel, and food). Anything over that amount is subject to a 20.8% duty (Cochise College, 1998). This is a major breakthrough for both American retailers and Mexican shoppers, as many consumers from south of the border spend as much as 50% of their income in the United States (Wasserman, 1996). The final event is the tightening of border controls by the US government, which took place immediately following the terrorist attacks of 11 September 2001. Stricter border checks have created long queues backed up far into Mexico, economic disorder, and significant financial losses for US businesses as their foreign neighbors choose more often to stay home. Many merchants on the American side fear that a drawn-out war on terror might put them out of business (Flannery, 2001).

Canada–USA

While shopping by Canadians in the United States has a long history (Kreck, 1985), in the late 1980s the number of shopping trips and the level of spending by Canadians skyrocketed reaching its peak in 1991. The primary items purchased were household goods, including groceries, clothing, shoes, appliances, gasoline, cigarettes, and alcohol. The growth from an average of about 20–25 million Canadian shopping trips each year to some 60 million a year in the early 1990s was largely a result of a strong Canadian dollar. At its peak, this consumer movement was accused of victimizing the average Canadian, since thousands of jobs were said to be lost and thousands of retail bankruptcies were said to have taken place because of it. It was also blamed for huge losses in government tax revenues. Several studies estimated that some 55,000 Canadian jobs were lost and over CA$3.5 billion lost in sales in 1991 alone (Chamberlain, 1991; Government of New Brunswick, 1992; Government of Ontario, 1991). Canada's border communities felt the impact perhaps more than other areas, although the economic effects were noticable throughout the country (Kemp, 1992).

Whereas Canadian commerce suffered, business in the US borderlands prospered. In the state of North Dakota, Canadian sales reached an estimated US$2.5 billion in 1991, totaling over half of the state's retail sales (Goodman, 1992), and many border businesses on the American side reported 50–80% Canadian patronage (Scanian, 1991). Spurred by the popularity of cross-border shopping, many Canadian tour companies began to organize and sell one- and two-day shopping trips to the United States (Timothy, 2001).

Several Canadian studies were undertaken in the early 1990s in a frantic attempt to understand consumers' motivations for heading south (Chatterjee, 1991; Government of New Brunswick, 1992; Government of Ontario, 1991; Stevenson, 1991). Most found that the main reason was lower prices in the United States owing to the strong Canadian dollar, lower taxes, more retail competition, lower profit margins, and shops accepting Canadian currency on a par with the US dollar. Sunday shopping in the US, better service, enticing American promotional efforts, a different variety of merchandise, and free amenities were some of the non-economic reasons (Timothy, 2001).

After realizing the negative impacts of the southward shopping movement, the Canadian government and other organizations began to find ways to get residents to stay at home to shop (Ahmed, 1996). One approach was to tap into Canadians' sentimental side by running a promotional campaign that did everything from denouncing cross-border shoppers as unpatriotic citizens to running television and print advertisements that attempted to get Canadians to stay home and examine what their own country had to offer. However, much of this effort was futile as it became painfully clear that shoppers were more concerned about getting good deals and saving money than they were about patriotism (Timothy, 2001; Timothy & Butler, 1995). Another effort was to introduce Sunday shopping in some parts of the country where it had previously been banned. By illustration, in the province of Ontario, Sunday shopping was legalized in 1992 as a result of the cross-border shopping craze. A third effort involved the national government initiating changes at the border, including cracking down on the importation of certain goods by shoppers or levying heavier taxes on consumer items brought back into Canada. The government also insisted on removing tarrifs on some imports as a way of lowering consumer prices (Timothy, 1999a; 2001).

Beginning in 1992, the tides turned and Canadian expenditures in the United States decreased dramatically owing primarily to the weakening of the Canadian dollar and secondarily owing to the importation of American mega chains like Home Depot and Wal-Mart, which offered Canadians a wider variety and lower prices (Fox, 1995). This has incited many Americans to cross the border in the reverse direction to shop in Canada (Dunnan, 1998). The strength of the US dollar against the Canadian dollar in the late 1990s spurred millions of shopping day trips northward by Americans, particularly in search of expensive items such as electronics, appliances, furs, and, in some cases, real estate but also including everyday items such as diapers, food, and clothes. In contrast to several years earlier, recent years have brought about an increase in US-based tour companies offering shopping trips to Canadian malls and outlet centers (Timothy, 1999a; 2001). In response to this turn of events, Canadian border towns have begun improving their tourism infrastructures and building newer shopping facilities and expanding their old ones, just as their American counterparts did in the late 1980s and early 1990s. Since the change in direction of consumption, US border towns are feeling the same grim economic situation that faced their neighbors to the north just a decade ago. Many of the shops and shopping centers built during the 1980s to cater to the burgeoning shopping tourism from Canada are closed and the retail landscape of many US border communities is one of economic crisis and abandonement. Dozens of grocery stores, petrol stations, shoe shops, department stores, and restaurants in American border towns went bankrupt and closed their doors in the late 1990s. 'The derelict shopping landscapes of the earlier 1990s have become reminders of the short-lived zenith of Canadian consumerism, and communities that became too dependent on dollars from their northern neighbors have become virtual ghost towns' (Timothy, 1999a: 8).

The US response was slightly different from that of the Canadians. Instead of trying to get Americans to stop shopping across the boundary, shopkeepers and communities south of the border attempted to recapture the Canadian market. Ahmed and Corrigan (1995) and Ahmed (1996) high-lighted several actions that might be taken and, in fact, have been taken, by several US communities. First, an on-par currency program can be established, which aims to assess merchandise so that prices are marked in US dollars but could be paid in CA dollars, dollar for dollar. Thus, the Canadian dollar would be treated as equal to the higher-value US dollar (Ahmed, 1996).

Second, destinations can offer promotional gifts, such as coupons, gift certificates, and vouchers good for gasoline, meals, and food. Refunding the sales tax spent by Canadians is another alternative. Third, Ahmed (1996) recommended that the city of Minot, North Dakota, might want to consider offering a refund on sales taxes to Canadians if their collective expenditures totaled a specific amount during a single visit. Another option was to try to increase membership in the local convention and visitors bureaus and distribute a higher share of membership and marketing costs to the businesses that benefit most. Finally, there was the recommendation that communities should work together in a spirit of cooperation to promote the larger region as a shopping destination rather than each individual community acting on its own (Ahmed, 1996; Ahmed & Corrigan, 1995).

Central and Eastern Europe

Cross-border consumption in Central and Eastern Europe (CEE) has existed for some time but it became highly visible and more widespread during the 1990s. While patterns that resemble those in Western Europe and North America certainly exist in CEE, the activity in Eastern Europe is an entrepreneurial activity involving shopping for resale items rather than for personal-use items. Michalkó and Timothy (2001) examine this phenomenon in detail and the following section is based in part on their work.

The geopolitical changes that took place in Eastern Europe during the early 1990s have created considerable changes in tourism patterns in the region. One of the most obvious is cross-border shopping. During the decades preceding the fall of communism, cross-border shopping grew in social and economic importance throughout much of CEE. In state socialist systems where fixed prices, restricted access to products, and limited merchandise variety reduced buying opportunities, people had few possibilities to spend as much of their income as they desired. This resulted in shopping trips to more liberal nations in the communist bloc where nascent free markets functioned (Williams & Baláž, 2000), Hungary and Yugoslavia being the most open and accessible.

After the collapse of state socialism, a distinct border economy developed, which included informal trading – entrepreneurial shopping. This activity involved people traveling to neighboring countries with large amounts of meat, vegetables, clothes, shoes, and electronics in an effort to sell them and people who traveled abroad with empty sacks to purchase items to sell at home on their return (Michalkó & Timothy, 2001; Williams & Baláž, 2000).

During the same period, visitors from Western Europe, particularly those who lived in countries adjacent to CEE, began traveling eastward to buy merchandise at substantial savings. In the early 1990s, for instance, thousands of Germans crossed into Poland each week to buy inexpensive household products. In the early years, this was a one-way flow because most Poles, still economically disadvantaged after years of communist rule, could not afford to shop in Germany. Since then, however, the pattern has become one of bi-directional flow as the standard of living in Poland increased substantially during the 1990s (Bygvrå, 1999; Stryjakiewicz, 1998).

Apart from Hungarians and Yugoslavians, access to the West by residents of the East was forcefully controlled. Once capitalism was established, the West and more open eastern-bloc countries became the chosen destinations for consumers from the East. In the early 1990s, the economy of shortages and unbalanced development of the communist bloc encouraged eastern Europeans to shop in nearby nations for products and services that were scarce or expensive in the domestic market (Gołembski, 1990; Pál & Nagy, 1999; Michalkó & Timothy, 2001; Williams & Baláž, 2000). According to Minghi (1999: 34),

> With the end of the Cold War in the late 1980s and the inevitably long time-lag necessary for economic systems in the East to switch from

state control and ownership to a free market economy, it is hardly surprising that borderlands along the East-West interface underwent rapid change, including the instant development of the daily shopper phenomenon from the East to exploit the advantages offered by continuing price and availability in the West coupled with the new opportunity to move and transport goods much more freely. At the same time, changes in the political regimes meant that what would have been a serious crime of exploitation and profiteering against the state was now seen as a legitimate entrepreneurial demand-based activity.

These changes resulted in many border communities in Europe becoming major shopping destinations, where over half their populations were supported by cross-border trade (Stryjakiewicz, 1998). This shopping phenomenon began to be viewed during the 1990s as a unique form of tourism (Gołembski, 1990; Hajdú, 1994; Hall, 1995; Williams & Baláž, 2000). These cross-border trips were, for most traders, international excursions lasting less than one day but, for thousands of others, they became part of a multidimensional system of trade where hotels, eating establishments, and other services were used over a two- or three-day period (Michalkó & Timothy, 2001).

Because of its central location and broad economic policies, Hungary was an important part of the development of this Eastern shopping phenomenon. In the 1980s, markets began to develop throughout the country where goods brought in from Romania, Turkey, the USSR, and Poland were sold. Hungary's western border towns were particularly popular destinations for Austrians who rushed in to buy inexpensive consumer goods (Hajdú, 1994; Sándor, 1990). Once the Iron Curtain had fallen, citizens of other post-communist nations headed immediately for Hungary, which they did because of emerging free-market economies, rising living standards, and shortages at home. This marked the beginnings of Hungary's largest international tourism activity (Michalkó & Timothy, 2001).

China and its neighbors
A unique pattern of cross-border shopping has also emerged between China and its neighbors, particularly Russia and Kazakhstan. Along the Russia–China border, barter tourism – a form of cross-border shopping – developed during the late 1980s between the cities of Blagoveshchensk (Russia) and Heihe (China), which face each other on opposite sides of the Amur River. As relationships beween the two formerly hostile countries improved, their common boundary was opened up to trade and various

forms of tourism (Timothy, 2001). In 1988, the two cities started an exchange program, which allowed visitors from each side to visit the city across the border – cities that the people had seen for years but were inaccessible to them (Zhao, 1994). At that time, the possession of foreign currencies by individuals was still strictly regulated by both countries, so as a way of avoiding legal problems, arrangements were made to exchange equal numbers of visitors from both sides (approximately 200 people a day), provide them with food, accommodation, and sightseeing. This eliminated any need for currency exchange on opposite sides since each partner city charged visitors from its own country for the cost of hosting groups from across the river (Zhao, 1994; Zhenge, 1993). This arrangement worked well except that visitors were unable to purchase souvenirs and other merchandise while visiting the neighboring city. As a result, sightseeing was the only activity undertaken in the beginning but then a system was devised to eliminate the currency problem, which involved bartering for desired items with items from their own country as the medium of exchange (Nin, 1994; Zhenge, 1993).

This approach to cross-border shopping, which is similar to that in Central and Eastern Europe, caught on quickly far beyond the borderlands. Chinese traders from hundreds of kilometres inland traveled to the border for a chance to barter-shop in Russia. Cigarette lighters, jackets, cosmetics, and clothing from China where popular mediums of exchange on the Russian side and, in China, the Russians were greeted most warmly with bags of furs, watches, and leather products (Zhenge, 1993). Now that both countries have lifted their bans on the possession of foreign currency and while cross-border barter shopping still thrives in the area, it has given way to more traditional forms of shopping where rubles and yuan are the media of exchange (Timothy, 2001).

Summary

Shopping is a major motivator for travel overseas or closer to home. The primary reasons people travel specifically to shop are related to the products available away from home, the price differentials in the destination compared to those at home, and, finally, the image and environment of the destination, which may or may not have developed in conjunction with products and prices. Several places have become popular shopping destinations and the reasons for their development include these and several others. Shopping tours have developed as important forms of shopping tourism and have become popular in recent years to places such as Hong Kong, Singapore, and Italy.

To illustrate the issues and concepts introduced in this chapter, cross-border shopping was examined in considerable detail, looking primarily at the reasons for its development (e.g. price, product availability, lower taxes, better service, etc.) and the primary regions where it occurs. Border-land shopping is a significant form of tourism in many parts of North America, Europe, and Asia, and each region has different factors for its emergence and sustained growth.

Chapter 4

Tourist Shopping

Introduction

While shopping may not be the primary or sole allure of most vacation destinations, it is a universal tourist activity that adds to the overall attractiveness of almost every region of the world (Butler, 1991; Chen, 1997; Jansen-Verbeke, 1990b; Kent *et al.*, 1983; Kincade & Woodard, 2001; Law, 1993; McIntosh *et al.*, 1995; Page, 1992, 1995; Prus & Dawson, 1991; Reisinger & Turner, 2002; Turner & Reisinger, 2001). Oftentimes shopping provides an important competitive advantage for countries or regions in combination with other attractions (Jansen-Verbeke, 1998). The 'tax-free haven' status of many Caribbean islands, for example, adds a supplementary appeal to that region, which is best known for sun, sea, and sand. The availability of tax-free shopping in the islands gives them a competitive advantage over other beach destinations. The same is true of many areas where heritage and nature-based tourism are dominant.

The last chapter addressed shopping as a primary motivation for travel and described places that have developed into major tourist destinations as a result of shopping. This chapter examines the second relationship between shopping and tourism – i.e. shopping as one of perhaps many activities undertaken by people who travel primarily for other reasons. Heung and Qu (1998) and the Tourism Shopping Implementation Committee (1990) define tourist shopping as the expenditure of tangible goods by tourists either for consumption in the destination (excluding food and drink items) or for export to their home countries/regions. As noted in the previous chapter, this form of shopping in tourism is more widespread than the previous one and more is known empirically about the shopping behavior of tourists while on holiday. The position of shopping as a tourism development policy in some locations is examined, followed by a discussion on the appeal of shopping in tourist destinations or the reasons why so many (most) tourists shop while on holiday.

Shopping as a Vacation Activity

While the results of all studies conducted on the activities engaged in during vacation vary depending on time, location, and participant preferences, they almost inevitably include reference to shopping. In a generic sense, shopping tends to be either the most favored holiday-time activity or following at a close second (*The Business Times*, 1998; *Travel Weekly*, 2001). For Korean tourists, shopping is ranked second only to taking photographs (Ahn & Jeong, 1996, cited in Hobson, 1996). Industry research confirms that shopping is the number one vacation activity in the United States, which amounted to more than US$50 billion in tourist spending in 1995, with 40% being generated by foreign visitors (Arizona Shopping and Attraction Consortium, 2000). According to a US nationwide survey conducted by the Travel Industry Association of America, some 77% of all adults shop and purchase items while on holiday (Beck, 1998). Correspondingly, in a US Department of Commerce (1999) study, 89% of overseas travelers to the United States reported shopping during their visit. More recently, the Travel Industry Association of America (2001) found that shopping was the chief activity for 87% of foreign visitors to the United States and 33% for domestic travelers (Table 4.1). Shopping is not limited to pleasure travelers, for even business travelers find it hard to ignore opportunities to buy, and many schedule additional days on business trips so they can shop (Field,

Table 4.1 Activities undertaken by tourists in the USA, 2000 (in % of person-trips)[a]

Domestic tourists (%)		International Tourists (%)[b]	
Shopping	33	Shopping	87
Outdoor activities	17	Dining in restaurants	84
Historical/Museums	14	Sightseeing in cities	43
Beach	10	Amusement/Theme parks	31
Cultural Event/Festival	10	Visiting historic sites	31
National/State parks	10	Visiting small towns	28
Theme/Amusement park	9	Water Sports/sunbathing	23
Nightlife/Dancing	7	Touring the countryside	21
Gambling	8	Art gallery or museum	20
Sports Events	6	National Parks	20
Golf/Tennis/Skiing	4		

Source: Compiled from Travel Industry Association of America (2001)
[a] Multiple responses allowed
[b] Does not include Canadian and Mexican visitors.

1999; Sun, 1998). According to the Travel Industry Association of America (2001), 16% of all shopping done on trips in the United States is by business travelers.

Even in places where specific forms of tourism dominate, shopping is generally a favorite activity. In Las Vegas, for instance, gambling takes second place to shopping as a favored tourist activity (Beck, 1998; Curtis, 2001; Emerson, 1993). A study by Plog Research (cited in Beck, 1998) found that 67% of 8000 leisure travelers surveyed in Las Vegas listed shopping as a major activity, while only 18% listed gambling. A 2000 Las Vegas Convention and Visitor Association (LVCVA) study found that visitors spend US$116.14 per person on average on shopping, US$85.65 on shows, and US$62.46 on sightseeing (*Travel Weekly*, 2001). To enhance the city's shopping status, the LVCVA initiated the Shop Las Vegas program, which includes a shopping tour that highlights the city's malls, outlet shops, and resort shops. The program's Shop Las Vegas Passport provides gifts and discounts at participating retailers and a sweepstakes was created to award a deluxe trip for two to Las Vegas (*Travel Weekly*, 2001).

Likewise, shopping and ski resorts go hand in hand. Many ski resorts are becoming trendy shopping centers, particularly in the summer low season. In many traditionally snow-based destinations, such as Whistler, British Columbia, and Smuggler's Notch, Vermont, summer arrivals are beginning to outnumber winter visitors, reflecting in part at least the increased popularity of shopping. Domestic and international guests cite shopping as one of the top three activities at ski resorts in both summer and winter (Matheusik, 2001). In a recent survey of 50 North American ski resorts, managers identified the important role of shopping in the industry. They suggest that retailing is an integral part of the visitor experience; an important source of revenue with the potential to match or exceed ticket profits; a central meeting place for people; a tool for keeping visitors at a resort longer; and a unique selling proposition to differentiate one ski resort from another (Matheusik, 2001: 66).

Studies in the United States show that shopping expenditures typically account for 30–33% of tourists' total spending (Littrell *et al.*, 1994; Moreno & Littrell, 2001). Research findings generally suggest that tourists spend the largest amount of their on-site cash on accommodation, although shopping usually comes in a close second. Research in Australia in 1990 found that visitors spent on average AU$488 per person on shopping and AU$774 on everything else (i.e. accommodation, food, and drinks) (Bureau of Tourism Research, 1990). Tourist shopping in Australia is one of that country's most essential consumer segments, particularly among Korean and Japanese visitors. In Sydney, tourists spend more time shopping than in any other activity undertaken. Korean shopping alone contributed approximately

AU$74 million to the Australian economy in 1994 (Hobson, 1996: 29) and in New Zealand, Dudding and Ryan (2000) estimated that 60 cents of every dollar spent by tourists was in the retail sector.

Shopping studies in Hong Kong illustrate that there are cultural differences in spending patterns and that Asians spend the majority of their money on shopping, while visitors from North America and Europe spend more on accommodations. In Heung and Qu's (1998) analysis, mainland Chinese and Taiwanese visitors spent 61% of their money on shopping. US residents and Canadians spent in the order of 28% on shopping and European and Australian tourists spent between 32 and 37%.

Based on total expenditures by Taiwanese tourists to the island of Guam, Mok and Iverson (2000) proposed a three-part taxonomy of tourist-spenders: light spenders were those who spent less than US$879 on their trip to Guam; medium spenders were travelers who spent between US$880 and US$1206; and heavy spenders were the tourists who spent more than US$1206. The authors' findings suggest that Taiwanese tourists spend significantly more on shopping than any other local expenditure category. Light and medium spenders paid out 4% of their on-site expenses on shopping, while heavy spenders spent 46% of their local disbursement on shopping. The average local expenditures per person on shopping among the light spenders was $102.65, $158.66 by medium spenders, and $357.86 among heavy spenders (Mok & Iverson, 2000: 302).

Even people who do not normally like to shop (primarily men according to most studies) participate more in shopping activities while on vacation.

> Some women indicated that it was unusual for their husbands to go shopping with them at home, but their husbands would be shopping companions on trips. Several women smiled and recalled singular moments when their husbands purchased 'special' souvenirs for them when shopping together. (Anderson & Littrell, 1995: 339)

In fact, while many men do not like to shop at home, they often outspend women while in a tourist destination (McCormick, 2001; Mintel International, 1996b). Most people are too busy or cash-strapped to shop for fun at home very often, owing to work and family obligations; however, on holiday, they do not have the same home-bound pressures and are able to spend considerable leisure time and money shopping (Beck, 1998; Gordon, 1986; Stansfield, 1971, 1972).

Shopping as tourism policy and promotional strategy

Given this enormous demand for shopping by tourists, many destinations have begun initiating major shopping promotional campaigns and have adopted retailing and tourist shopping as official policies in their tourism development efforts (Jansen-Verbeke, 1991). Several small villages and towns in North America have adopted shopping as a tourism strategy (Getz *et al.*, 1994). The destinations highlighted in the last chapter (e.g. Dubai, Hong Kong, Thailand, and Andorra) are also good examples of countries and/or regions that have adopted shopping as an official promotional policy.

In some cases, shopping policies have been altered considerably as a result of tourism to the extent that retail-related laws have been changed to accommodate tourist demand. In Ontario (Canada), for example, Sunday shopping traditionally has not been allowed. However, with the growth in cross-border shopping, special concessions were made to try to keep Canadians from driving to the United States to shop and to draw American consumers north across the border (Timothy & Butler, 1995). One of these was to allow Sunday retailing, which had previously been restricted by the Retail Business Holidays Act to preserve a province-wide pause day. In 1992, however, this statute was modified by the Retail Business Establishment Statute Law Ammendment Act to grant special concessions to businesses that could demonstrate their direct association with tourism. Exemptions were awarded to retailers who could demonstrate a close connection and/or proximity (within 2 km) to a tourist attraction and a reliance on tourists visiting the attraction on a Sunday (Goodman & Carr Consulting, 1992).

In relation to promotional policies, two kinds of alliances have developed in the shopping arena in recent years. In some locations, major mall companies and other tourism-related retailers have begun forming cross-sectoral linkages. These include offering shopping day tours at popular destinations such as New York City and London. For these endeavors, alliances are formed between retailers and bus companies, tour operators, hotels, and even airlines (Andruss, 2000). The second form of shopping alliance adopts the chamber of commerce model that is widespread through much of the developed world. The primary purpose of these coalitions is to promote shopping as an important tourist activity and to increase sales through collaborative promotional efforts at a regional and/or national level. Founded in 1999 to aid in developing new opportunities and partnerships within the tourism industry, the Shop America Alliance (SAA) is a national-level partnership comprised of members including malls, specialty centers, festival marketplaces, outlet centers, and other leading retail and dining establishments (Shop America Alliance, 2001b). Its aim is to increase awareness of, and visitation to, retail destinations throughout the United States through cooperative marketing programs, strategic planning, and industry representation (Shop America Alliance, 2001a). The following objectives fall within the purview of the SAA:

- to boost the marketing of shopping centers, retailers, and restaurants in the tourism industry as a way of increasing sales and profits among partners;
- to facilitate marketing alliances and information exchange between retail and tourism partners;
- to create tourism marketing opportunities for its partners in a cost-effective way; and
- to represent the retail sector of tourism with local, regional, state, national, and international government organizations, trade associations, and political leaders to advance the tourist benefits and opportunities for retailers (Shop America Alliance, 2001a).

The International Council of Shopping Centers is an international body comprised of shopping malls and other retail centers that functions much in the same way that the SAA operates in the United States with similar mandates and procedures.

Shopping tourism associations also exist at the regional (subnational) level. At the end of the 20th century, the state of Arizona received nearly 20 million tourists a year, who spent more than US$12 billion, much of it on shopping. Some estimates suggest that between one-third and two-thirds of all shopping done at Arizona's main retail centers is done by tourists: 84% of the state's visitors make at least one purchase (Arizona Shopping and Attraction Consortium, 2000). Owing to Arizona's role as an important shopping destination, the Arizona Shopping and Attraction Consortium (AZSAC) was created in 1997 as a non-profit alliance in partnership with the Arizona Office of Tourism. Its goal is to enhance the promotion and synergy between retail, dining, attractions, and hotels to specific markets for Arizona, primarily Mexico, Canada, Japan, and Western Europe (Arizona Office of Tourism, 2001). The consortium works closely with the Office of Tourism, the state's convention and visitors bureaus, and chambers of commerce to promote the state's tourism industry. The focus is on increasing tourists' pre-arrival awareness of its members (e.g. malls, outlet centers, retail districts, specialty centers, individual retail stores, vendors, themed restaurants, attractions, gaming establishments, hotels, and museums) through international and domestic trade shows, advertising co-ops, information distribution, and media relations (Arizona Shopping and Attraction Consortium, 2000).

Tourists and the Need to Shop

There are, no doubt, endless reasons why tourists shop. Butler (1991) observed that self-esteem, prestige, nostalgia, vanity, and economic

Table 4.2 Possible motivations for tourist shopping

Motivation	Merchandise attributes	Type	Location	Example
Prestige	Unique	Crafts Local materials Local designs	Arctic Oceania	Soapstone Shells
Prestige	Exclusive	Clothes	Paris	Fashion
Economic	Cost-saving	Bargains Outlets Pirated goods Replicas	Asia USA Asia Asia	Electronics All Tapes/Videos Watches
Self-esteem	Trophies	Big game heads Named items	Africa Olympics	Pins
Nostalgia/ vanity		Souvenirs/mementos Gifts	Anywhere Anywhere	

Source: After Butler (1991)

Table 4.3 Reasons for shopping on most recent trip (in percentages)

Something to do	22
Wanted to buy something for other people	21
Had an event or holiday for which needed to buy something	15
Wanted a souvenir of the trip	13
Like to shop/always shop on trips	12
Friends/relatives took me shopping	6
Lower prices/save money	6
Wanted to buy items unique to the destination/authentic goods	4
Different selection of stores than those at home	3

Source:Travel Industry Association of America (2001)

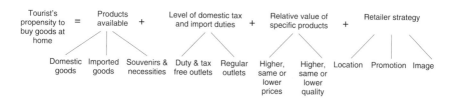

Figure 4.1 Model of Japanese tourists' propensity to buy (after Keown, 1989)

savings drive tourists to shop and can affect their choices of destination and merchandise (Table 4.2). Consumer research by the Travel Industry Association of America (2001) identified ten reasons people shop while on holiday (Table 4.3).

Likewise, Keown (1989) devised a model that may also help explain tourists' propensity to buy (Figure 4.1). He suggested that the types of products available, the level of import duties on foreign products and tax levels on domestic items, the prices/value and quality of goods in the destination compared to those at home, and merchants' retail strategies will influence the shopping behavior of foreign tourists. Others have recognized that demographic characteristics, attitude toward other cultures, currency exchange rates, lifestyles, purpose of travel, mode of transportation, where they are staying, and exposure to the destination culture may also affect shopping behavior and product purchases (Agarwal & Yochum, 2000; Bureau of Tourism Research 1990; Hobson & Christensen, 2001; Kim & Littrell, 2001; Kinley *et al.*, 2003; Mok & Lam, 1997; Paige & Littrell, 2003; Snepenger *et al.*, 2003; Turner & Reisinger, 2001). For heuristic purposes, Mok and Lam (1997) categorized these variables into four types of influences that affect tourist shopping behavior: tourist attributes, travel attributes, destination attributes, and situational attributes.

It is safe to assume that many of the same motives that drive people to shop locally in their home regions for recreational purposes (e.g. value, social belonging, escapism, sensory arousal, etc.) also influence tourists' propensity to shop while on vacation. However, there appear to be other reasons that are influential specifically in the tourism context. The elements Butler, Keown, Mok and Lam, and other authors have stressed are, in fact, more utilitarian in nature and are applicable to all forms of shopping, including that of a leisure and tourist nature. However, there are several factors that encourage shopping in the realm of tourism specifically. These are discussed in the sections that follow.

The desire for keepsakes and memories

Throughout history, people have purchased souvenirs or keepsakes in one form or another to remind them of their momentous journeys (Gordon, 1986; Levell, 2000; Mars & Mars, 2000; Scarce, 2000). For many travelers, purchasing a memento is an extremely important action and a trip would hardly be considered complete without having bought something to take home.

The primary reason people purchase keepsakes, or souvenirs, is to remind them of the place they have visited. Very often, mementos help people upon their return home to remember the special times they shared or the local culture or heritage they enjoyed (Littrell, 1990; Onderwater *et al.*, 2000). In research by Littrell (1990; Littrell *et al.*, 1994), international tourists were asked to describe the meanings connected to the textile crafts they had bought during their travels. Several categories of meanings were developed but, for this section, the most important were associations with place and culture and personal memories of travel. Thus, souvenirs provide travelers with a reminder of their experiences, as well as tangible evidence that they were there (Hitchcock, 2000; Littrell, 1990; Littrell *et al.*, 1994). In the words of Swanson (1994: 18), when someone sees or touches their souvenirs following a trip 'they are not only remembering that they were there but proving they were there'.

Likewise, in many instances, after returning home from a trip, souvenirs and other collectibles validate and can function to prolong the travel experience (MacCannell, 1976; Swanson, 1994). This is a crucial element of shopping, for in the post-trip period, usually referred to as the recollection phase of travel, memories may change and experiences are altered by time. Postcards and keepsakes help keep the memory of the experience alive. Gordon (1986: 135) argued that souvenirs are purchased as a way of locating, defining, and freezing in time a short-lived experience and allows people to bring remnants of an extraordinary experience back into the ordinary world. 'People . . . cannot stay in the extraordinary state indefinitely; they can, however, hold onto a tangible piece of the extraordinary time' (Swanson, 1994: 18).

For others, the primary motive for buying souvenirs is to demonstrate an appreciation of the workmanship of the items. As part of the destination encounter, some tourists find considerable pleasure in watching artisans demonstrate their skills. When tourists observe artisans painting batik, weaving baskets, throwing pottery or carving wood, a special meaning is established and they are more inclined to purchase craft items (Anderson & Littrell, 1995: 340). For many tourist shoppers, this is an attempt to connect with local craftspeople – 'an intimate human interchange which can transcend cultural differences between buyer and seller' (Littrell, 1996: 109). For craft purchasers, these exchanges and linkages are an important part of the trip. Possessing an item of superb artisanship allows tourists to 'continually search for and delight in details of an artisan's intricate weave, well-turned pot, or wood joining techniques. As one tourist described an Indonesian textile hanging in her home, "the more I look at it the more detail I appreciate in it"' (Littrell, 1996: 109).

Buying keepsakes on vacation also enhances people's personal collections at home. Cuneen (2000) highlights the popularity of collectibles and notes that they often carry with them a nostalgic meaning. According to Shackley (1997: 26), travelers also buy to collect either opportunistically when they see items that attract them or they are serious collectors who have a clear sense of what they want to buy and its particular value. In the case of Parks Canada merchandise, collectors see park-oriented products as being symbolic of parkland values and principles. For them, quality is not as important as the symbols portrayed in Parks Canada souvenirs (Mata & Stanley, 1995).

The quest for authenticity

A related and somewhat overlapping issue is that of authenticity. For many years, observers have argued that people often travel in search of authentic experiences and places (MacCannell, 1973, 1976; O'Meara, 2000; Ryan & Crotts, 1997), although the theoretical view of authenticity is often very different from the form of authenticity that tourists seek (Cohen, 1988a; Timothy & Boyd, 2003). Despite receiving a good share of criticism in recent years among scholars (e.g. Boniface & Fowler, 1993; Brown, 1996; Bruner, 1994; Butler, 1996; Schouten, 1995a), authenticity is an important aspect of the visitor experience in the realm of heritage tourism and level of satisfaction with a trip or specific site, and it often comprises much of the appeal for visiting historic places.

The question of the extent to which the tourist is really interested in authentic products or rather in the authentic setting of the places where souvenirs can be acquired has become a key issue in tourist consumer research. Tourists' propensity to shop varies according to their cultural background, the range and nature of shopping opportunities in the destination area, economic situations, and many additional variables. The production and marketing of craft souvenirs is the global answer to this new tourism market but it raises the question about authenticity and cultural convergence.

Generally authenticity is seen as a social construction of objects and the meanings that envelop them. In other words, authenticity is a subjective notion that may vary from place to place, culture to culture, and person to person. The subjective perceptions of souvenir authenticity can be negotiated by salespeople, consumers' own knowledge and experience, social tradition, and the producers' techniques and manipulations of materials and processes (Crozier, 2000; Onderwater *et al.*, 2000; Shenhav-Keller, 1995; Verlini, 2000). In the words of Hitchcock (2000: 9), 'shops selling souvenirs are a vital ingredient in the social creation of reality and may be organized in particular ways that enhance the authenticity of the goods being sold'.

Perhaps the most influential of these in determining authenticity is the meanings that the tourists themselves assign to their merchandise through a process of attribution of meaning. For most people, 'buying a souvenir is an act of acquisition of an object perceived as authentic' (Shenhav-Keller, 1995: 144). However, according to Jamison's (1999) study, the perception of the souvenir vendors was that tourists really do not care if the design is traditional or contrived. The study concludes it is obvious that tourists understand that fabricated and non-destination-specific items (e.g. stone chess sets, brass cigarette lighters, etc.) are not part of the craft tradition of indigenous cultures, but rather such items are made specifically for tourists. Nonetheless, the souvenirs tourists take home are still a sort of trophy, which must reflect their image of the country visited–it must look authentic, traditional, or primitive, because the authenticity of the artifact is a guarantee of the authenticity of one's experience abroad (Dougoud, 2000: 235).

In their study of handicraft purchasing, Littrell *et al.* (1993) identified eight criteria that tourists use to judge the authenticity of the craftworks they purchase. These include: originality and uniqueness, cultural and historical integrity, aesthetics, workmanship, craftspeople and materials, shopping experience, function and use, and genuineness or truth in advertising. Several other authors have proposed similar classifications, which are examined here in more detail together with those of Littrell and her colleagues.

- Product uniqueness is an important component of what makes something authentic in the eyes of many tourists and it is this perception that attracts tourists to 'specialty' retailing, where goods are not widely available and not mass produced (Anderson & Littrell, 1995; Law, 1993; Littrell, 1996; Pysarchik, 1989). When one-of-a-kind items can be purchased or when only a few of a certain product exist, a scarcity value is achieved, which many consumers equate to authenticity. For some tourist shoppers, the extent to which a particular product is unique to a specific destination is of considerable importance in determining its level of authenticity, and, thus its purchasability (Littrell *et al.*, 1993).

- Cultural and historical integrity is another value that many shoppers see as contributing to a product's authenticity assessment. This entails producers and marketers assuring accuracy in providing products themselves but also in the product information they disseminate (Borrus, 1988). For instance, many consumers might feel that 'real' Native American items must come from a Native American area and that design and motif should relate to the community's history, thereby adding meaning and heritage value (Littrell *et al.*, 1993). Thus, items that 'belong' to a particular place or culture are valued as important indicators of genuiness (Onderwater *et al.*, 2000) and cultural symbolism *versus* items of a more general type is an important element in cultural and historical-based authenticity (Asplet &

Cooper, 2000; Kim & Littrell, 2001; Shenhav-Keller, 1995). Thus, souvenirs sold in Israel should, according to Shenhav-Keller's (1993, 1995) work, be a material representation of historical 'Jewishness'. In the context of Israel, the theme of identifying with the nation's historic past and the rootedness of Jews in products purchased by tourists (Jewish and non-Jewish) create a stronger element of historical accuracy.

- The third element of authenticity is aesthetics. Alluring colors, artistic merit, and general visual appeal are important characteristics of desirable souvenirs (Littrell *et al.*, 1993; Shenav-Keller, 1995). The physical and aesthetic features of the product appear to be especially important qualities for textile buyers (Littrell *et al.*, 1994; Onderwater *et al.*, 2000). In many cases, tourist consumers determine authenticity based on their own judgements, such as what they themselves perceive to be beautiful (Littrell *et al.*, 1993).

- Workmanship is another crucial element of defining authenticity. Often authenticity is equated to, or at least partially determined by, product quality and attention to detail (Littrell *et al.*, 1993). For some tourists, tradition and historical accuracy are less important in determining authenticity than are product quality and good design, for they will accept and understand that artistic designs and techniques change over time (Littrell *et al.*, 1993).

- Fifth, when shoppers can determine if the artist has made the merchandise with his/her own hands and with great effort and care, the authenticity value is raised in their eyes as mutual respect is developed between the buyer and producer and as heritage is being shared (Borrus, 1988; Kim & Littrell, 2001; Littrell *et al.*, 1993; Shenhav-Keller, 1995). Artisans who are trained in authentic or traditional methods from previous generations are generally viewed as being more inclined to produce authentic crafts. According to Littrell (1996: 110), tourists also judge an item's genuineness based on the processes and types of materials (traditional) utilized by the craftsperson.

- The sixth criterion is the shopping experience, which entails meeting the craftperson and watching the craft being produced (Littrell *et al.*, 1993; Onderwater *et al.*, 2000). Tourists enjoy observing the production skills of artisans and purchasing items in the place they are made. 'Significantly, many tourists . . . purchase traditionally made, local handicrafts in the same locations in which they are produced, so that observation of production skills considerably heightens the authenticity of the tourist experience' (Markwick, 2001: 34). Being able to converse with artisans and perhaps purchase products directly from them is equally important. In the words of Hitchcock (2000: 9), 'the discourse between the purchaser and vendor provides opportunities to negotiate the meanings associated with the souvenir'. Halewood and Hannam (2001: 576) agree with this assertion and suggest that the practice of consuming where and while the goods are being produced verifies the authentic process. This is especially the cases when the object itself is seen to have been made, or is sold by the maker, and 'labels are not needed in this context, for the exchange value of the commodity has been seen and verified visually' (Halewood & Hannam, 2001: 576).

- Function and use are the next factor. Littrell *et al.* (1993) give the example of native colors that would have been used in the period a certain product would have been made and used. The present function is an important part of this as well, for when its utility is still native to the area and used by the indigenous people of the region, it is deemed more legitimate.

- Finally, a guarantee of authenticity through a form of certification is important to many tourist consumers. Documentation of legitimacy may be provided in the form of official paper work and certificates, photographs, artisans' signatures, and dates. Littrell *et al.* (1993) suggest that it is typically tourists with a need for status who often judge authenticity by external markers such as these. According to nearly half of the visitors in one New Zealand study, authenticity was important in their decision to buy an item of clothing. When asked if they would be more likely to buy clothing from New Zealand if design authenticity were included on the label, 46% said that they would (Asplet & Cooper, 2000: 310). The same study also noted that domestic tourists from New Zealand, as well as visitors from Australia and Asia, considered verification of genuineness on labels very important in their purchasing decisions, while visitors from Europe and North America were less concerned with the issue.

Kim and Littrell (2001) found that the more people travel to the same destination, the more their souvenir purchasing behavior changes in relation to authenticity. According to their findings, the more times people traveled to Mexico, the less likely they were to buy stereotypical souvenirs, although tourist-oriented souvenirs that were representative of an area were purchased by people on a first visit. This, Kim and Littrell note, is because as tourists begin to understand quality and uniqueness through greater levels of exposure to destination handicrafts, they will be more inclined to look for higher quality and more authentic items, while disregarding more the tourist kitsch associated with popular destinations.

Another study had similar conclusions. Love and Sheldon (1998) found a connection between the degree of travel experience and the type or level of authenticity assigned to souvenirs by travelers.

Novelty-seeking

Novelty is the need to be involved in something new and outside the ordinary range of activities (Crompton, 1979; Snepenger, 1987). In common with leisure shopping in general, tourist shopping is characterized by the need for novelty. With the standardization and globalization of consumer products, tourist shopping has taken on a more serious role as tourists begin to search for novel and unique shopping opportunities (Page, 1995: 94).

Novelty-seeking in shopping behavior may be manifest in various ways (Hirschman, 1980). For example, for many tourists visiting a supermarket or farmers' market is intriguing because it allows them to see the different array of products available in other regions or countries. In McCormick's (2001) study, 73% of travelers desired to visit different, rather than more familiar, stores. Product difference, or uniqueness, is a major driving force for people shopping away from home (Burns & Warren, 1995). For others, discovering unusual and interesting handicrafts may be an important motivation (Anderson & Littrell, 1995). Snepenger (1987) observed, however, that people who are interested in novelty rarely return to the same locale regardless of their previous experience there.

Aesthetics is an important part of the novelty association as well. Littrell (1996) found that many people, particularly women, purchase crafts during their travels because of their aesthetic qualities. Littrell calls this 'sensuous appreciation', which refers to multisensory attachments to souvenir items. Colors, designs, beauty, style, and softness are all adjectives that describe sensuous appreciation. So, like purchasing behavior at home in relation to clothes shopping, shopping for textile souvenirs is enhanced and directed by the same general descriptors (Kim & Littrell, 2001).

Functional needs

Shopping for utilitarian purposes and the products purchased can be seen from at least four perspectives. First, in line with the 'shopping for leisure' aspect of Jackson's (1991) leisure shopping model, people often shop before taking a trip for items that they will use during the journey. Bathing suits and sunblock lotion may be purchased for a beachfront holiday, hiking boots and a sleeping bag for a mountain adventure trip, and a camera, insect repellent, and hat for a trek through the rainforest. According to one travel poll done by the Travel Industry Association of

America (2000), nearly half (44%) of all adults who traveled in the previous year made pre-trip purchases, which statistically amounted to some 66 million American adults. Cameras, luggage, camping gear, hunting and fishing equipment, and mobile phones were among the most common purchases. Secondly, situations in the destination may require people to purchase items of a utilitarian nature, such as groceries if they are staying in a rented apartment, a toothbrush if they have left theirs at home, and a new jacket if the weather is cooler than anticipated. Thus, these products, with the exception of groceries, may overlap in their purposes – they are utilized in the destination and carried home to be used later. Very often, these types of purchases take place in establishments that are more geared toward local residents than to tourists (e.g. department stores and supermarkets). Third, some travelers purchase goods that are specifically for consumption only at home and not in the destination. Examples include cartons of cigarettes, unusual or difficult to find cooking utensils, certain apparel items, and so on. Very often, the purchase of these products is driven by lower prices in the destination compared to prices in the visitors' home countries (Keown, 1989). Finally, people purchase items in the destination that may fill more of a souvenir role but which may also be utilized on an everyday basis at home. This form of dual-purpose purchase fulfills both utilitarian and hedonic needs and might include things like coffee mugs, hot-pot holders, key rings, clothing, food products, pens, and stationery.

Regardless of the types of merchandise purchased or the opportunities that occur, it should be noted that, from a utilitarian perspective, tourists are also interested in time and money. Thus, getting good value for their money is a major concern for many tourists (Jansen-Verbeke, 1998; Turner & Reisinger, 2001). From a pragmatic perspective, tourists are also concerned about portability and whether or not something might be easily cleaned/maintained, so that size, weight, and material may also help determine the types of products that tourists will buy (Graburn, 1976).

Boredom/excess time

Perhaps the least common but still important reason people shop while on holiday is to fill excess time or as something to do because they are bored. The most important venue for this purpose is probably airports, where retail shops capture passengers' attention and take advantage of their spare time in transit. For many, shopping at a stopover point may be seen as a way of relaxing, stretching their muscles, and increasing circulation, which can lead to either planned or impulse purchases (Rowley & Slack, 1999). According to Sun's (1998) study of passenger shopping at Minneapolis-St Paul International Airport, approximately half of the travelers went shopping in the airport simply to kill time.

People also commonly choose shopping as a preferred activity during bad weather in a tourist destination. If sunbathing or other outdoor pursuits are not an option owing to a thunderstorm, for example, tourists will often choose spending time at a covered marketplace or shopping mall instead of waiting out the torrent in their hotel rooms.

Buying gifts for people at home

In tandem with buying items for themselves because they are useful and of personal interest and buying souvenirs as reminders of their trips, purchasing souvenirs or other items as gifts for people at home is one of the top three reasons tourists shop (Anderson & Littrell, 1995). In fact, in one study of tourists who shopped in Australia, 37% did not buy any items for themselves, just for people at home (Bureau of Tourism Research, 1990). Other studies have confirmed that tourists commonly make more planned purchases for other people than for themselves (e.g. Rucker et al., 1986, cited in Kim & Littrell, 2001).

It is interesting to note that, in several studies, gender was found to be a variable in determining who is more prone to purchasing souvenirs and gifts for others while on holiday. Women, according to the research studies that have examined gender differences in shopping, are more inclined to buy gifts for other people and they devote more time and attention than men to selecting gifts for others (Anderson & Littrell, 1995; Kim & Littrell, 2001; Mata & Stanley, 1995; Zalatan, 1998).

Another group of tourism-related shoppers that has not been examined before is destination residents who buy items to give as gifts to their visitors from abroad. This is a fairly common occurrence in places that have unique cultures and where tourism is an important part of the local economy. Israelis, for instance, comprise an important cohort of shoppers at Israeli souvenir stores. Many buy items for religious holidays, special events, and rights of passage but most buy souvenirs as gifts for foreign guests (Shenhav-Keller, 1993, 1995).

Altruism

Another less typical reason for tourist shopping is altruism. This motive drives people to shop for and purchase products that will benefit a specific cause, such as charitable foundations, conservation movements, non-government organizations, or religious associations. Shoppers at Canada's national parks and monuments gift shops, for instance, are sometimes motivated by a knowledge that part of the profits go to help protect parklands and sites (Mata & Stanley, 1995). Altruistic shoppers may also desire to buy items that will benefit indigenous peoples and less affluent destination residents.

When Jewish tourists purchase souvenirs in Israel, a link is created between themselves, the center of Judaism, and the cultural group to which they belong. This helps them express their loyalties and obligation to Israel and contributes to the continuation of the Israeli state and its identity as the Jewish homeland (Shenhav-Keller, 1995).

Culture, nationality, and tourist shopping

As argued so far, many variables (e.g. price, selection, need for mementos, a search for authenticity, functional need, etc.) affect tourists' purchasing behavior and the types of goods they buy. Other research shows that national and cultural background also have a considerable bearing on the shopping experience and other forms of consumption (Keown, 1989; McCracken, 1986; Mok & Lam, 1997; Popelka & Littrell, 1991; Thompson & Cutler, 1997; Wang & Ryan, 1999; Wong & Law, 2003). The propensity of certain nationalities (e.g. Japanese, Korean, Taiwanese) to shop with considerable devotion has earned them a reputation of being avid and reliable tourist shoppers (Boydell, 1987; Bureau of Tourism Research, 1990).

Nationality may be one determining factor in people's choice of handicrafts. According to Thompson and Cutler's (1997) research, craftspeople in The Gambia associate specific merchandise preferences with nationalities. German tourists, for instance, tend to prefer brighter colors and more abstract designs, and they are more apt to buy crafts that feature elephants and other large wildlife, even though these no longer exist in The Gambia. They also commonly buy miniature carvings of items that might have been an important part of traditional Gambian life (e.g. shields). Craft vendors noted that British tourists were more inclined to buy items that have a slightly utilitarian value, such as bowls and chess sets. They were also noted as preferring items that have little to do with The Gambia but favor novelty or humor, such as carvings of the see, hear, and speak no evil monkeys, children's toys, and sexually evocative figures. Scandinavian tourists preferred batik that incorportates more customary colors and designs. They also tend to favor clothing and other functional items, such as batik table cloths and tea towels. Scandinavians were also viewed as more likely to buy wood carvings that they perceived to be authentic, such as spears and large masks. In summary, Thompson and Cutler (1997) recap that Scandinavians prefer better quality and more authentic items with less concern for expense. German visitors favor abstract designs, western styles, and items that represent Africa in general rather than The Gambia specifically. The British have a preference for usable, miniaturized, and inexpensive products that do not necessarily reflect Gambian traditions.

In addition to product preferences, the entire shopping encounter may be influenced by nationality and culture. It also involves the major elements and motivations described earlier. The following paragraphs describe some of the ways in which culture and nationality influence the shopping activities among Japanese and Korean tourists.

An example of Japanese and Korean tourist shoppers

Japanese tourists are perhaps the best-known shoppers of all traveling nationalities. Shopping is one of the most popular pastimes among Japanese tourists of all ages and they typically spend thousands of dollars shopping on each trip, nearly three times as much as Europeans and North Americans (Bureau of Tourism Research, 1990; Rob Tonge & Associates, 1995).

According to a mid-1990s survey, prosperous Japanese visitors spent an average of US$3,000 per person on souvenirs and other merchandise when they traveled abroad, and less-affluent youth travelers typically spent US$1000 on gifts (Nishiyama, 1996). Table 4.4 demonstrates the shopping behavior of Japanese tourists in Hawaii.

Social practices and cultural traditions have long dictated much of Japanese social behavior, which are manifested in shopping activities (Table 4.5). The first practice is the desire for brand-name and high-quality merchandise. In recent decades, the Japanese have been influenced by advertising and consumer practices, which suggest that quality can only be found in specific brand-name products (Moeran, 1983). Therefore, one of the 'requirements' of travel abroad is to purchase brand-name commodities in their countries of origin (Jansen-Verbeke, 1994). In modern Japanese society, branded products posess a prestige that creates the impression of sophistication, international stature, and good taste (Hobson & Christensen, 2001). Thus, Japanese tourists traveling in Europe would desire to purchase Delft china in The Netherlands, Givenchy perfume in France, various Swiss watches in Switzerland, and brand-name shoes in Italy (Hobson & Christensen, 2001: 40).

The brand-name phenomenon leads into another important cultural element among the Japanese: prestige and social status. When high-quality and brand-name products are purchased abroad, the social status of an individual is reconfirmed and strengthened. 'The almost metaphysical levels that [social status] can reach in Japan seem to transcend those found elsewhere' (Hobson & Christensen, 2001: 40). For many Japanese, the elitist image of shopping at world-famous stores and world-famous destinations for their associated products is very significant. Boasting to acquaintances at home of shopping in these prestigious places is an important reward for making such a journey. Many Japanese tourists visiting New York City, for

Table 4.4 Japanese shopping behavior in Hawaii

Item	Response (%)
Time spent shopping	
1–4 hours	20
5–8 hours	32
9–12 hours	21
13–16 hours	11
More than 17	16
Allocation of total shopping budget by category	
Self	30
Family	25
Friends	20
Work colleagues	15
Others	10
Reason for buying in a particular store	
Price	53
Warranty/guarantee	25
Store reputation	12
Clerk's attitude	5
Store location	5

Source: Adapted from Keown (1989)

Table 4.5 Sociocultural traditions and issues that affect Japanese shopping behavior

• Desire for brand-name, high-quality items
• Prestige and social status
• Outward appearance is very important
• Gift-giving customs (*senbetsu* and *omiyage*)
• Non-individualism – the belief that individuals are part of a larger social community
• Limited knowledge of foreign languages
• Require high-quality service
• The belief that loyalty should be amply rewarded
• Tendency to travel in tight-knit groups with tight schedules

instance, will shop at Macy's and Tiffany's and, to satisfy their esteem needs, will purchase one or two extremely expensive items and continue carrying around the stores' shopping bags at home in Japan. This demonstrates their having shopped in high-class establishments abroad (Hobson & Christensen, 2001).

Probably the most influential cultural tradition that causes Japanese tourists to spend so much time and money shopping is the custom of gift-giving (Ahmed & Krohn, 1992; Graburn, 2000a; Iverson, 1997; Ko, 1999; Larke, 1994; Mok & Iverson, 2000; Nishiyama, 1996), which according to Rob Tonge and Associates (1995), probably stems from the long history of Buddhist and Shinto practices of gift giving at special times (e.g. birth, marriage, year-end, and New Year). One of the most prevalent forms of gift exchange in Japanese society is known as *omiyage* and *senbetsu*. *Omiyage* is the age-old tradition of buying gifts for one's family, friends, work colleagues, bosses, assistants, neighbors, and other acquaintances when traveling. Generally, the items purchased are representative or typical of the area visited and should have high value or at least a perceived high value. Usually, these purchases are a response to departing gifts (*senbetsu*) given by the same people in the form of money, cameras, and other travel supplies they received before departing (Graburn, 2000a; Hobson & Christensen, 2001). Souvenir-giving is an important method of fostering harmonious interpersonal relationships with, and demonstrating appreciation to, those with whom one works and lives and it may also be an important method of gaining favor with someone (Nishiyama, 1996: 98). *Omiyage* is a crucial element in enhancing social interaction. It is a means of communication, allowing one to bond with those who were unable to go on vacation, a reflection of the giver's social understanding and etiquette, evidence or proof of having been to a specific region or country, a way of pacifying a guilty conscience for going off and having fun all by oneself, and as a return gift for someone who gave *senbetsu* (Park, 2000: 85–87).

Much (perhaps most) of this gift-giving behavior is in response to obligations created when *senbetsu* is received from these same people (Park, 2000). This form of *omiyage* is known as *okaeshi*, or a return gift, and is given in reciprocation to a gift given by someone at an earlier time. When *senbetsu* is received before departure, sometimes at a bon voyage party, travelers are obligated to buy an appropriate souvenir in return (Hobson & Christensen, 2001). Most commonly, the value and type of the pre-trip gift and the relationship between the gift-giver and the traveler will determine what kind of souvenir will be returned. Japanese newlyweds who have received large amounts of money for their honeymoon from relatives are expected to purchase expensive, brand-name products for those who gave them money (Nishiyama, 1996).

An office clerk may receive money from several coworkers who actually request certain items. A young college student who has received a lot of money from his or her parents and grandparents may buy a token gift for each of them. A junior manager who has received some money from a senior manager should buy an expensive souvenir that costs more than the amount of money given to him. In a nutshell, receiving *senbetsu* creates a strong social obligation to buy *omiyage*. This is one of the most important reasons why Japanese visitors spend so many hours shopping on overseas trips. (Nishiyama, 1996: 99)

Failing to counter the original gesture would be a clear violation of the social custom of reciprocal gift-giving. The practice of receiving and returning gifts 'may continue almost indefinitely as long as both parties wish to maintain a cordial interpersonal relationship' (Nishiyama, 1996: 100). Another form of travel-related *omiyage* is *orei*, or a token of appreciation, which may be given to a neighbor or friend who has watched the house or the children during a period away but who has not necessarily provided a physical or monetary *senbetsu* (Hobson & Christensen, 2001).

These gift-giving behaviors stem from a fundamental principle of Japanese society and culture, which dictates that individuals are always part of a larger group or community (Hobson & Christensen, 2001). The basis of this verity lies in the related concepts of *on* and *giri*. *On* refers to the social obligation of the individual to the larger group or society, which is manifested among other ways in terms of *giri* – the responsibility of reciprocating social obligations. In the tourism context, an 'intricate balance [must] be kept in the relationship between those that travel and those that stay at home' (Hobson & Christensen, 2001: 39).

While Japanese tourists are eager to shop almost anywhere, owing to the cultural norms describe before, their preferred venues are well-known specialty shops (e.g. Calvin Klein, Benetton, etc.), souvenir stores, airport shops, duty-free shops, in-flight vending carts, and discount/outlet stores. Their preferences at souvenir shops are locally made articles that are well known for the area, although they are often content with inexpensive imported knick-knacks as well. Discount stores (e.g. Wal-Mart, Costco, K-mart) are popular too for the more economically minded visitors. Japanese travelers also generally prefer to use up leftover foreign currency at airport and in-flight shops – duty-free shops are a virtual 'must' on overseas trips (Nishiyama, 1996; Rob Tonge & Associates, 1995).

Another interesting point about venue discussed by Hobson and Christensen (2001) is the establishment of overseas branches of major Japanese department stores, such as Daimaru, Isetan, Mitsukoshio, Seiyu, Sogo, and Takashimaya, in popular overseas destinations like Australia,

England, Hong Kong, and Singapore. Hobson and Christensen (2001: 41) identified several reasons for this phenomenon. First, traditionally most Japanese have had limited foreign language skills and, therefore, have tended to travel in large tour groups with guides and interpreters. These domestic stores located abroad provide Japanese-speaking staff and printed literature to provide information on gifts and products. Second, shop staff are able to provide high-quality service demanded by the Japanese public. Valuable advice and knowledge about certain items before they are bought is required and information on the latest styles and colors will ensure that customers are buying the right merchandise. The third reason is that gifts must not only be of high quality, they must also be properly packaged. *Teisai* (outward appearance) is essential in Japanese culture and is reflected in the appearance of gift wrapping and packaging. In Japan, packages are carefully wrapped in intricate and lovely packaging at the store. To give a badly wrapped present would be regarded as a sign of sloppiness, poor taste, and disrespect. 'To present a gift that is not correctly wrapped would be a social disaster' (Hobson & Christensen, 2001: 41). Non-Japanese retailers are generally not accustomed to, or skilled in the area of, elaborate gift wrapping, which creates problems for Japanese consumers. Fourth is the provision of the personal and concrete rewards (*saabisu*) for shopping in a Japanese-culture store. Loyal customers, new customers, or high-spending customers can expect special gifts or discounts as a demonstration of appreciation for their loyalty and patronage. Taxi or bus coupons, free refreshments, videos, and free merchandise delivery are examples of *saabisu*. The fifth factor is that Japanese retailers are willing to pay a commission fee to tour operators and guides who bring groups to their shops (Yamamoto & Gill, 2002). Finally, Japanese tour groups generally follow a tight daily schedule, which allows only limited time for shopping (Rob Tonge & Associates, 1995). Their purchases can be made more quickly and in the preferred way in fewer stops than traveling from one store to another.

Koreans are also avid shoppers, who travel to places like Australia, Japan, the United States, China, and Europe in search of quality bargains (Prideaux & Kim, 1999). Korean gift-giving behavior is very much like that of the Japanese and the social responsibility issue surrounding the *yeohaeng* (similar to Japanese *senbetsu*) and *sunmul* (similar to Japanese *omiyage*) are nearly the same (Ko, 1999). The souvenirs given to friends and family members on returning from a vacation are known as *sunmul* in Korean. The primary distinction is that *omiyage* is used exclusively for presents brought home from travel, while in Korea, *sunmul* includes the meanings behind *omiyage*, as well as the general idea of giving presents at any time (Park, 2000: 83).

In both Japan and Korea, the routine of giving money to people going on a trip exists as a way of covering part of their travel expenses and there is just as much obligation in Korea to reciprocate with *sunmul* as there is in Japan. According to Park's (2000: 82) evaluation, Korean views of souvenirs and gift-giving include the following:

- *Sunmul* is an expression of affection and showing one's feelings.
- Giving *sunmul* is in harmony with social conventions and traditional etiquette.
- Souvenirs help meet people's expectations.
- *Sunmul* is an expression of gratitude.
- *Sunmul* is a standard of the traveler's evaluation of the one receiving the gift.
- *Sunmul* demonstrates specialty goods from the country or region visited.
- *Sunmul* represents economical and reasonably-priced products.

Tourist shoppers, behavior, and psychographics

The final element affecting tourist shopping as identified in the literature is the shoppers' characteristics. Psychographic attributes, behaviors, and other personal factors are influential in the ways people shop, the types of products they buy, and the venues they select to visit. These influential factors are generally acknowledged and examined in the form of tourist shopper typologies, which are developed as tools to understand various segments of the market and how their experiences play out in shopping locations.

In the context of textile souvenirs, Littrell (1990) identified five groups of tourist consumers (Table 4.6). The first is *shopping-oriented tourists*, who are keen on locating shops, craftspeople, bargaining, and using a foreign language. The bargaining/shopping experience, coupled with meeting the crafters themselves, adds considerable value to the trip and the buying experience. For this group, the interactions with the artists or sellers made them feel good about themselves and provided important memories about the items they bought.

The second group is comprised of *authenticity-seeking tourists*. As noted earlier in this chapter, the search for authenticity is an important part of many people's travel experiences. For them, the meaning of the souvenir stems from the knowledge that the item was not produced for tourists. Descriptors commonly used include 'genuine', 'indigenous', 'traditional', and 'part of the local heritage' to represent authenticity. The materials used, colors, motifs, design, and production methods are generally consid-

Table 4.6 Types and characteristics of textile souvenir consumers

Shopping-oriented Tourists
• Enjoy finding shops
• Enjoy mingling with craftspeople
• Enjoy bargaining
• Enjoy using foreign languages
Authenticity-seeking tourists
• Want items not specifically created for tourists
• Materials, colors and motifs are important in defining authenticity
• Want items they describe as genuine, indigenous, traditional, and local
Special-trip tourists
• Not as concerned about the link between the souvenir and the local culture
• Concerned with preserving memories
• Handicrafts remind of friends, places, sites, and activities seen and done on holiday
• Memories of special relationships formed while away are important
Textiles for enjoyment tourists
• Appreciate the intrinsic beauty found in the design, workmanship, and colors of handicrafts
• Display their souvenirs prominently at home
• Souvenirs give them aesthetic pleasure
Apparel-oriented tourists
• Buy cloth and clothing items to wear at home
• They tend to wear flamboyant clothes to reflect their personalities
• The product's meaning deepens with an understanding of where it was made

Source: Based upon Littrell (1990)

ered by this group to ensure authenticity. Another indicator is whether or not the local people are using the product themselves.

Special-trip tourists make up the third of Littrell's souvenir consumer groups. These people are not as concerned about the link between the souvenir and the culture visited as they are about the memories from the travel experience. Their handicrafts reminded them of travel companions, sites seen, and activities undertaken. Special-trip tourists emphasize the memories of special relationships formed and strengthened and take pleasure in establishing friendships with other people.

The fourth cluster is the *textiles for enjoyment tourists*. These tourists take pleasure in the intrinsic beauty found in the design, workmanship, and colors in the crafts they purchase, resulting in the items being displayed prominently in their homes and/or offices. To them, the items are beautiful, stunning, or unusual and bring aesthetic pleasure.

Group five, the *apparel-oriented tourists* enjoy obtaining cloth and apparel items to wear at home. They typically enjoy wearing showy clothing to reflect their flamboyant lifestyles. When the item of clothing has been specially tailored, the meaning attached to the product deepens.

Based on their assessment of tourists' perceptions of the importance of certain travel activities, the sorts of products purchased, and where purchases were made, Littrell *et al.* (1994: 8) recognized four tourist styles in buying souvenirs: ethnic, arts and people style; history and parks style; urban entertainment style; and active outdoor style. 'Ethnic, arts, and people' tourists are actively involved in tourism. They conform quite readily to Plog's (1973) definition of allocentric tourists in that they prefer to visit ethnic communities different from their own, participate in destination community festivals, and immersing themselves in community life with local residents. They are also inclined to be more interested in arts, festivals, and ethnic concerts than other tourist profiles. Tourists in this category are inclined to buy crafts, jewelry, local foods, books, and antiques. They are particularly prone to buying crafts made from clay and fabric; and they appreciate art works made by well-known local artists, appealing colors and designs, and product uniqueness.

History and parks tourists prefer natural areas, historic sites, museums, and outdoor living museums. Although they are interested in the outdoors, they are not active outdoorspeople and mingling with destination residents is not a high priority. In their shopping endeavors, these people look for local foods, collectibles, postcards, books, and crafts. Although they are similar to the first group in their preference for crafts and local foods, history and parks tourists are more interested in printed materials and collectibles owing to their interest in nature and history.

Urban entertainment tourists are generally active, always on the go, and even in need of stimulating diversions. Littrell *et al.* note that they may shop in the morning, attend a professional sporting event or visit a theme park in the afternoon, and go dancing at a nightclub in the evening. Tourists in this class buy souvenirs that symbolize their holiday destinations through recognizable names or logos, such as T-shirts, pens, bumper stickers, key chains, and ash trays, which they can wear, use, or display in a prominent location.

The active outdoor tourists are devoted to the outdoors. They prefer visits to parks and other natural areas where they can walk, hike, backpack, camp, sail, hunt, and fish. They also tend to be avid swimmers, skiers, and golf and tennis players. People in this group also prefer items with logos to mark the destination visited and they often buy items that are made from natural materials.

The final classification of tourist shoppers is that proposed by Anderson and Littrell (1996: 44–50) who were interested in group profiles of women travelers and their souvenir purchase behaviors and preferences. The first group, low-involvement travelers, are not very engaged in travel. They tend not to plan much in their trips, including shopping. Low-involvement tourists purchase the least of all other groups examined. Laid-back travelers comprise the second group and have traveled more extensively than the first group. These people were relaxed in their trip-planning but were more involved in shopping-planning. The third group is centrist travelers. These tourists are more regular travelers than the first two groups. These women were characterized by preplanned trips but unplanned souvenir purchases. Goal-attainment tourists, the fourth bunch, knew what they wanted to buy, set goals, and planned to fulfill them. Their trips are preplanned and they make both planned and unplanned purchases. Eclectic tourists are avid travelers and enjoy variety in shopping and other activities. Many are organized trip-planners, while others are not and this is reflective also in their tendency to make both planned and unplanned purchases.

Summary

Many studies show that shopping is the most omnipresent tourist activity in nearly all destinations. In fact, it typically accounts for the second largest category of on-site expenditures, after accommodations, although it is, in many cases the largest expenditure. Similarly, shopping is a natural fit with many other activities, such as sunbathing on a beach, skiing, sightseeing, attending fairs, and visiting museums and historic sites, and it is usually in conjunction with these activities that tourist shopping occurs.

Tourists appear to have an innate need to shop. This is likely owing to the fact that vacation environments and leisure states of mind create conditions that are conducive to higher levels of spending and more frivolous behavior. Additionally, researchers have identified several variables that create the need to shop in tourists or that influence the type of experience they have: the possession of keepsakes, a quest of authenticity, the search for novel experiences and products, functional needs, the necessity to kill time or alleviate boredom, obligations and desires to buy gifts for people at home, and cultural traditions and social mores.

Shopping is such an important part of the tourism economy that many places have adopted it as the center of their policy initiatives and as the basis of their promotional campaigns. This is particularly so in destinations such as Hong Kong, Thailand, Singapore, and Dubai. Additionally, several associations have been developed by private organizations, public agencies, and quasi-government groups to deal specifically with shopping as a tourist activity and to promote it through various media.

Chapter 5

What Tourists Buy: The Ubiquitous Souvenir

Introduction

It was established in the previous two chapters that tourists love to shop. Sometimes they are obsessed by it and, in extreme cases, it motivates them to travel overseas. From the utilitarian viewpoint, tourist merchandise ranges from grocery items on one end of the spectrum to clothing and toys on the other. According to the Bureau of Tourism Research's (1990) study, three-quarters of the tourists in Australia purchased clothing and footwear to carry home; almost half bought toys; and more than one-third purchased alcohol. In Hungary, the most popular purchases are food, cultural items, arts and crafts, glassware, and porcelain (Michalkó, 2002). The most popular merchandise among tourists in the United States is clothing and/ or shoes, souvenirs, books and music, specialty foods, children's toys, handicrafts, jewelry and accessories, home accessories and/or furniture, home electronics, sports equipment, cameras and camera equipment, art, luggage, and camping gear (*Arizona Republic*, 2001; Littrell *et al.*, 1994; McCormick, 2001; Travel Industry Association of America, 2001). Table 5.1 shows the most popular retail products among tourists in Hong Kong, Australia, and the United States, of which clothing has long been the most favored item.

Japanese tourists, noted in the last chapter as one of the most devout shopping groups, have certain product preferences, owing to the social obligations that exist in Japan and their own personal tastes. Foreign-made items are popular among the Japanese. Even when similar products produced domestically and of higher quality can be purchased, they still tend to desire foreign-manufactured merchandise for the prestige associated with it (Nishiyama, 1996; Rob Tonge & Associates, 1995). Some scholars hypothesize that this preference might be 'a reflection of the deep-seated inferiority complex that the Japanese have had toward Western civilization for centuries' (Nishiyama, 1996: 10).

Table 5.1 Most popular retail items among tourists in Hong Kong, USA and Australia

Hong Kong (1995)	United States (1999)	Australia (1994)
Clothing	Clothing/shoes	Clothing/shoes
Jewelry	Souvenirs	Toys[a]
Leather	Books/music	Sweets
Clocks/watches	Foodstuffs	Books
Cameras/optical	Toys	Alcohol
Cosmetics	Local handicrafts	Paintings/crafts
Souvenirs/crafts	Jewelry	Jewelry
Sound equipment	Home accessories	Perfume/cosmetics
Foodstuffs	Home electronics	Home accessories
Medicine/herbs	Sports equipment	Cameras & equipment
Alcohol	Cameras & equipment	Travel equipment
Perfume	Artwork	Music

[a] Includes some stuffed animal souvenirs
Sources: Haigh (1994), Heung and Qu (1998), Travel Industry Association of America (2001)

Table 5.2 Most popular purchases among Japanese tourists

Liquor	Neckties	Chocolate and candies
Cigarettes	Cosmetics	Food products
Perfume	Shoes	Furs
Jewelry	Leather goods	Floor rugs
Watches	Bags	Handkerchiefs/scarves
Cigarette lighters	Clothing	
Souvenirs/Crafts	Sports gear	
Pens	Fruit	

Sources: Keown (1989), Nishiyama (1996) and Rob Tonge & Associates (1995)

Researchers have found patterns and trends amid the most prevalent retail items purchased by Japanese tourists (Table 5.2) (Keown, 1989; Nishiyama, 1996; Rob Tonge & Associates, 1995; Shokeir, 1991). Liquor is the most popular item for Japanese tourists. The most prevalent liquors include expensive brandies and Scotch whiskeys, as well as various wines from well-known viticulture areas. The most popular wine destinations for the Japanese are France, Australia, New Zealand, Switzerland, Germany,

Italy, Spain, Canada, and the United States (Nishiyama, 1996). Brand-name cigarettes are important, for they add cachet to one's trip abroad. French perfumes and American cosmetics are popular with Japanese women, because they are expensive in Japan and more prestigious than locally made goods. Famous Swiss watches and eminent brands like Omega, Rolex, and Bulova are favored items, as are gold and platinum jewelry pieces with diamonds, rubies, opals, jades, emeralds, and sapphires. Similarly, cigarette-lighters and pens, especially if they bear a famous brand name like Cartier, are a must on any shopping trip abroad. Neckties and related accessories, leather bags (preferably with names like Gucci and Christian Dior), golf bags, and shoes are important to demonstrate respect for social status. Sports equipment and clothing should prominently display world famous logos. One of the simplest, yet most desirable, items is food. The highest demand is for fresh fruits, frozen beef from Australia and the United States, beef jerky, live lobsters from the US northeast and Canada's Atlantic provinces, crab meat, smoked salmon, nuts, coffee beans, cookies, jams and jellies, and maple syrup (Nishiyama, 1996).

Like the Japanese, Koreans have a propensity to buy many of the same items just described. However, they also buy several unique items that are not traditionally seen as being tourist commodities. For instance, in Australia, Koreans often buy royal jelly, Tasmanian honey, deer antlers, sheepskin products, aloe, wild boar bladders, opals, and kangaroo skin/fur products, owing to many of these items' importance in traditional oriental medicines and their high prices in Korea (Hobson, 1996).

It is clear then, that tourists buy a wide variety of products for utilitarian purposes and for gifts, thereby contributing significantly to various sectors of retailing. However, the most ubiquitous item and the one most commonly purchased by tourists throughout the world is a souvenir – an object which has received considerable attention in the research literature. This chapter examines the origins and meanings of souvenirs followed by the role of souvenirs in tourist shopping and how tourists' consumption patterns have led to changes in the forms, functions, and meanings of traditional souvenirs and handicrafts. These are important considerations in understanding tourists' shopping behaviors and tendencies and the various effects of tourism in destination communities. As all forms of tourism have impacts in destination regions, so does shopping as a primary force in the industry.

Souvenir Origins and Meanings

While the items discussed earlier are critical in the tourist retailing sector, perhaps the most interesting and widely noted product related to tourist purchases is souvenirs. Some of the earliest accounts of souvenirs date back to the ancient Egyptians, who brought mementos to friends and family from their foreign trading expeditions (Hudman & Hawkins, 1989). During the Middle Ages, as global exploration began to expand into Africa, Asia, and the Americas, voyagers, following extended periods overseas, arrived home in Europe with large quantities of arts and crafts from the societies they had explored and / or conquered (Stanley, 2000). Colonialists and explorers through their art expositions and tales of exotic and 'dark' places introduced the arts of 'marginal' peoples to the Western world (Horner, 1993).

During the 17th and 18th centuries, participants in the Grand Tour through the art cities of Italy commonly purchased paintings, small bronze replicas of classical sculptures, and other antiquities (Evans, 1998; Mars & Mars, 2000). According to Evans (1998: 114), the souvenir trade in Italy was flourishing by the 18th century. Travelers to Italy in the 18th and 19th centuries, who were primarily aristocrats and prosperous professionals, had many opportunities to purchase souvenirs, which reflected the interests of visitors.

Perhaps the most widely accepted origin of souvenirs is the religious pilgrimage. Pilgrims who traveled to sacred sites during the Roman Empire era and medieval times developed a passion for relics associated with places of special religious importance (Houlihan, 2000; Mars & Mars, 2000; Teague, 2000; Tythacott, 2000; Vukonić, 2002). Among the earliest Christian souvenirs were stones, soil, and water collected at holy places associated with Jesus Christ and his apostles in the Holy Land and around the Mediterranean. These items were commonly placed in small containers, sealed up and blessed. For many pilgrims, these items conveyed sacred power, and possessing them was thought to bring spiritual blessings, protection, and healing (Evans, 1998). Thus, these bits and pieces of sacred sites became popular keepsakes for pilgrims, and eventually resulted in concerns among guardians of holy places that too much of the sites was being looted or destroyed as pilgrim numbers increased. As a way of mitigating this problem, caretakers responded by producing mementos and tokens that symbolized the sacred nature of the location. This is often regarded as the beginning of the manufacture and trade in souvenirs purposefully made for travelers (Evans, 1998: 105). The earliest manufactured Christian souvenirs were drawings, metalwork, crosses, pilgrim badges, and pottery, which are still availabe for purchase at several Catholic pilgrimage sites throughout Europe for modern-day pilgrims (Houlihan, 2000; Shackley, 2001; Vukonić, 2002).

Although modern souvenirs derived from rather simple beginnings, today they are a major component of the tourism retailing system, employ

Table 5.3 Types of souvenirs

Pictorial images	Piece-of-the-rock	Symbolic shorthand
Postcards Books Posters Photographs	Rocks Shells Plants Wood Fossils Bones Pinecones	Replicas of famous attractions Miniature images Manufactured items that represent images of the place where they are purchased
Markers	**Local Product**	
Items no representative of the place but marked with words and logos Coffee mugs Coasters Shot glasses Spoon	Indicative of local merchandise Foods Drinks Cooking utensils Clothing Handicrafts	

Source: After Gordon (1986)

millions of people throughout the world in production, distribution and sales, and contribute significantly to the economies of destinations (Blundell, 1993; Cohen, 2001; Connelly-Kirch, 1982; Evans, 2000; Markwick, 2001; Morbello, 1996; Moreno & Littrell, 1996; Ryan & Huyton, 1998; Smith, 1996). According to estimates by Love and Sheldon (1998), souvenir sales in the United States alone account for more than $25 billion in spending every year. Souvenirs range from primitive handicrafts to mass-manufactured items made in countries far from the destinations where they are sold. Gordon (1986: 140–4) identified five souvenir types, which are useful in understanding the breadth of souvenirs (Table 5.3). The first are pictorial images – the most common type of modern-day souvenir (Stefano, 1976). These include postcards, photographs, posters, and books, all items that provide visual snapshots of tourist destinations. The second type is what Gordon calls piece-of-the-rock souvenirs. These include items that are literally part of the destination environment. Materials like rocks, plants, shells, wood, fossils, animal bones/teeth, and pinecones are examples of this type. In reference to this form of souvenir,

> an interesting thing happens to these inherently insignificant hunted and gathered objects when they are taken out of their ordinary environment. A rock sitting on a beach or a brick positioned in a building – in its ordinary context – is just one of many, and barely noteworthy. When it is taken away and brought into a living room setting, however,

it becomes transformed into a significant icon. It becomes sacralized in the new context, and is imbued with all the power of the associations made with its original environment. (Gordon, 1986: 142)

Symbolic shorthand souvenirs are the third type. These tend to be manufactured items that conjure up images and messages about the place where they were bought. Piñatas from Mexico, a miniature Statue of Liberty from New York, and plaster-cast replicas of the Coliseum from Rome are examples of symbolic shorthand mementos. Often these are functional items, which despite their miniaturized and stereotypical images, can be used at home (e.g. salt and pepper shakers in the shape of famous buildings). Markers are Gordon's fourth souvenir type. These, in themselves, have no real reference to a specific place, person, or event but are inscribed with words and logos that mark the destination in place and time. For instance, a coffee mug or shot glass may have little to do with Niagara Falls in its own right but when the words 'Niagara Falls' are printed on a glass that could just as easily have been for sale elsewhere, it becomes marked for Niagara and can help preserve memories and pleasant associations with that place. Another example is the ubiquitous souvenir spoon, which was pioneered in the United States in the late 1800s and still remains a popular generic marker of tourist destinations throughout the country (Evans, 1998).

Finally, local product souvenirs are items that are indicative of local merchandise. The most common include indigenous food and drink products (e.g. olive oil from Greece, tortillas from Mexico, cheese from Switzerland, wine from France), food-related accouterments (e.g. chopsticks from China, pasta bowls from Italy), regional clothing (e.g. Scottish kilts, Japanese kimonos, Middle Eastern turbans), and handicrafts (e.g. pottery, carvings, fabric, native arts).

Gordon's (1986) taxonomy is very much place-bound, which is not surprising since tourism itself is place-bound. However, there is also a type of souvenir, which initially is event-based and which may later become connected to a specific location as the place becomes better known. This type is termed here situational souvenirs and refers generally to disasters and wars. Stanley (2000) notes that war souvenirs during and immediately following a war are major objects of desire, even though this raises ethical and political issues. One example of this is in Bosnia Herzegovina, which has yet to recover from the devastating wars of the 1990s, where in places such as Mostar, souvenirs have been created from machine gun shell casings, pieces of shrapnel, and other munitions spoils from the war.

Natural disaster souvenirs are desirable possessions among travelers as well. Immediately following the eruption of Mount St Helens in Washington (USA) in 1980, souvenir collectors were on site filling jars of ashes and rocks, which they sold throughout the United States. It is common for people to capitalize on disasters as they are happening by printing T-shirts to commemorate the event. Within a matter of hours, such souvenirs can be manufactured and sold to onlookers or sent out via mail to online and telephone shoppers (Slivka, 2001). This occurred in the summer of 2002 in Arizona as that state experienced the worst forest fires in recorded history and in New York City immediately following the terrorist attacks of September 11, 2001.

In understanding souvenirs as subjects of tourist consumption, Shenhav-Keller (1995) rightfully acknowledges that the form of the souvenir itself is not as important as understanding how it is perceived by the people who are involved in its production, sale, and purchase. Indigenous arts and handicrafts have long been a conduit of identity and self-preservation. As contact with outside societies increased through the centuries, however, artwork became more symbolic of cultural identity and people began using crafts as a way of communicating their society's individual cultural and spiritual identity. Through handicrafts, indigenous societies were able to create positive images and portray their most esteemed attributes to the outside world (Crozier, 2000; Dougoud, 2000; Graburn, 1976).

Often handicrafts are symbols of spiritual consciousness or religious events. For example, the Tibetan *thangka* (a painted, embroidered, or stitched scroll or handwoven or printed tapestry) plays an important role in the creation and transmission of religious concepts and ideals. Tibetans traditionally have seen them as the embodiment of spiritual enlightenment (Bentor, 1993: 109). Artworks are also seen from the producers' perspective as a symbol and source of national pride (Grieco, 2000; Hanefors & Selwyn, 2000), as is the case with batik cloth in Indonesia, Kente cloth in Ghana, and Fijian *tapa* (Hitchcock & Nuryanti, 2000).

All souvenirs, whether carefully crafted by indigenous peoples or mass-produced on assembly lines, may be viewed as texts that can be read to reveal meanings and events behind their production (Shenhav-Keller, 1993, 1995). According to some observers, souvenirs are political in that they are deliberately crafted to portray an image or to influence consumers' views and perceptions (Cohen, 1995a; Edwards, 1996; Shenhav-Keller, 1993). For example, according to Shenhav-Keller (1993), souvenirs in Israel are dominated by the country's attitudes toward religion, the Arab–Israeli conflict, and the past. Cohen (1995a) studied the portrayal of Arabs and Jews in Israeli postcards and concluded that both groups are represented stereotypically but that Arabs were nearly always represented in more traditional roles, while Jews were depicted as more modern and futuristic.

According to Cohen (1995a: 219), such a portrayal places Jews and Arabs on an unequal footing culturally and politically but, as a way of disguising the profound conflict between the two groups, it also implies that Israel is a pluralistic society where different groups live harmoniously side-by-side. Such a notion was also recognized in the Australian context where postcards tend to show aboriginal people in stereotypical activities, such as making bark paintings, playing a didgeridoo, and hunting (Edwards, 1996; Ryan & Huyton, 1998). In fact souvenirs, in general, in many parts of the world purposefully depict the traditional and / or stereotypical elements of local society and culture. For example, bows and arrows, miniature teepees and totem poles, feathered headdresses, and Indian moccasins adorn souvenir shops across the United States and Canada, even in places where those types of accouterments were never used by the indigenous population. These stereotyped souvenirs have been almost universally adopted in North America, even in publicly-owned national and state / provincial parks.

In addition to the meanings held or assigned by the producers of souvenirs, the consumers themselves attach specific meanings to souvenirs (Kim & Littrell, 2001). In Levy's (1959: 118) words, 'People buy products not only for what they can do, but also for what they mean'. However, as Love and Sheldon (1998) point out, souvenir meaning is difficult to measure and some souvenirs may simply function as decorative objects at home with relatively little underlying meaning. Perhaps the most widely recognized meaning of souvenirs for tourists is that they make intangible experiences tangible. Souvenirs' physical existence assists in defining, freezing in time, and locating an ephemeral experience in extraordinary time in ordinary time and space (Gordon, 1986; Graburn, 1984). By bringing something home from the extraordinary place (the destination), home can become, in some small part at least, a part of the extraordinary, and experiences can be relived in routine time and space; a memorial function is, thus, created (Graburn, 2000a). Tourists cannot hold on to the non-ordinary experience, for it is, by nature, ephemeral but they can hold on to a tangible piece of it, an object that came from it, for Western culture tends to define reality as 'that which you can put your hands on' (Gordon, 1986: 136).

The esteem element mentioned earlier also manifests itself in the purchase of souvenirs with an element of superciliousness or ego enhancement. Souvenirs are key in boasting of places visited or lived and are symbolic of tourists' travel achievements, for they demonstrate the reality of one's existence in a particular place at a particular time. In this sense, Stanley (2000) believes that tourists in their pursuits of souvenirs are like the early colonialists, missionaries, and traders. Tourists value souvenirs because of what they tell about the societies or places visited or lived in, and they can 'prove' through tangible evidence that a unique place was visited (Gordon, 1986; Hitchcock, 2000; Kim & Littrell, 1999). By collecting and displaying souvenirs from other places in conspicuous locations at home or at work, people can satisfy a need for approval by seeking the recognition, and even admiration, of relatives, friends, and neighbors (Timothy, 1998). Even though these items may be characterized as inexpensive or 'cheap',

> they still held somewhat honored places on office desks or on living room shelves. It is likely that these objects were used as a means of communicating to others that the tourist had ventured beyond the bounds of the known and successfully negotiated an arduous journey into the less familiar . . . the [item] signal[s] that the tourist had chosen adventure over familiarity and was bringing back native items (e.g. an ashtray) to validate his or her claim. (Smith & Olson, 2001: 28)

Love and Sheldon (1998) identified a relationship between the types of meanings assigned to souvenirs and the extent of travel experience a consumer has. They conclude that experienced travelers are more inclined to assign souvenir meanings that focus on relationships, people, and events. They focus more on the sensations remembered from the trip and buy items that remind them of their sensory experiences, such as brightly colored products or food items they enjoyed while abroad. Less experienced travelers have a tendency to assign meanings that are more representative of their destinations. In this case, souvenirs represent the destination quite literally, such as Hawaiian shirts from Hawaii and chocolate from the world's chocolate capital.

Similar to this idea, Smith and Olson (2001: 27–30) proposed a three-phase model that demonstrates how tourist shopping becomes more sophisticated over time (Figure 5.1). In the first stage, when people are new to the host society, they undertake familiar forms of social consumption and take their first step toward acclimatizing to the customs, habits, and norms of the destination culture. In other words, shopping gives the tourist an 'easy' leisure activity and exposes him/her to cultural objects and symbols. Because the experience in the location is new, items acquired during the first phase are typically cheap souvenirs that are commercially symbolic of the country (Graburn, 2000b). By way of example, first-time visitors to Australia characteristically buy bush hats, diggeridoos, and stuffed kangaroos or koalas. They also purchase many other objects splashed with images of cultural significance, such as T-shirts, shot glasses, and ashtrays. The shopping activity associated with these acquisitions usually involves significant social interaction on the part of the tourist. The market place gives first-time visitors occasion to observe the customs of

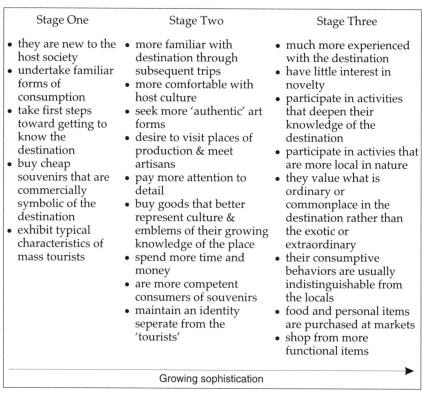

Stage One	Stage Two	Stage Three
• they are new to the host society • undertake familiar forms of consumption • take first steps toward getting to know the destination • buy cheap souvenirs that are commercially symbolic of the destination • exhibit typical characteristics of mass tourists	• more familiar with destination through subsequent trips • more comfortable with host culture • seek more 'authentic' art forms • desire to visit places of production & meet artisans • pay more attention to detail • buy goods that better represent culture & emblems of their growing knowledge of the place • spend more time and money • are more competent consumers of souvenirs • maintain an identity seperate from the 'tourists'	• much more experienced with the destination • have little interest in novelty • participate in activities that deepen their knowledge of the destination • participate in activies that are more local in nature • they value what is ordinary or commonplace in the destination rather than the exotic or extraordinary • their consumptive behaviors are usually indistinguishable from the locals • food and personal items are purchased at markets • shop from more functional items

Growing sophistication ➤

Figure 5.1 The sophistication process of tourist shopping (after Smith & Olson, 2001)

local residents and engage in various forms of social interaction. In this way, shopping serves as a crucial acculturating instrument and conduit for boosting a person's perception of his or her abilities to cope during a trip.

During the second phase, as familiarity with the place develops through subsequent trips, tourists identify components of the host culture they found to be personally relevant to their sense of identity and lifestyle. Also in this phase, tourists have a desire to differentiate themselves from the inexperienced or unseasoned traveler. Both of these factors influence subsequent shopping behavior. For instance, in seeking an 'authentic' art form, tourists may desire to visit the places of production and meet the original artisans. This will require more complex communications skills and travel *savoir-faire*. These more experienced tourists can be expected to pay greater attention to detail and invest more time and money into the shopping experience than the 'beginner' tourists. At this stage, through their prior travel experiences as novice tourists, they have learned to become more competent in their buying activities and they struggle to create an identity for themselves that sets them apart as experienced travelers. 'Several informants at this level actually seemed somewhat contemptuous of those tourists who bought souvenirs and would often refer to their inexperienced counterparts as "tourists", being careful to avoid using that term in reference to themselves' (Smith & Olson, 2001: 29). The purchases of these more acclimatized travelers represent cultural objects and served as emblematic displays of their knowledge, experience, and, hence, sophistication.

Finally, as individual travelers become even more experienced with a place, they enter the third phase. Tourists who accumulate the most experience with a single destination tend to be much less interested in novelty. Similarly, their need to communicate their travel and cultural expertise to others appears to abate. At this level, time, effort, and perhaps money are given over to activities that deepen the person's knowledge of the cultural elements with which they are already familiar through extended visits and shopping activities that are more 'local' in character. By this time, the tourist begins to value what is commonplace or ordinary in the local environment rather than being preoccupied with the exotic or extraordinary. These more experienced visitors undertake many consumptive behaviors that are indistinguishable from the routines of destination community members. Food and personal products are purchased at markets, for example. As opposed to their previously inexperienced selves in Phase 1, instead of being preoccupied with objects that are authentic or exotic in nature, these more experienced guests acquire items for their functional importance.

Handicrafts and Traditional Arts as Souvenirs

As noted previously, one of the most common types of souvenirs is handicrafts and art. Handicrafts are goods produced by hand with special attention to design, quality, and material used. They may have primarily a decorative function, a utilitarian function, or both (Littrell *et al.*, 1994). Among the most common in tourism are pottery, woodcarvings and figurines, baskets, blankets, clothing, fabrics, leather goods, and jewelry. In the context of the Americas, Feest (1992, cited in Evans, 2000) identified four types of art and handicrafts, which vary according to the artist's self-evaluation, his/her relationship with the consumer, and the art's function and meaning.

- *Tribal art* is/was made by tribal societies principally for their own use. There was no professional specialization, although expert producers were known for specialized products (e.g. Ashanti weavers, Inuit mask-makers, and Asmat woodcarvers). Usefulness was the primary purpose for production and aesthetics was not viewed in isolated from functionality.

- *Ethnic art* was produced by tribal societies primarily for use by other groups (e.g. Native American art produced for white Americans). Specialization became more commonplace even though indigenous crafters did not understand why their products were being purchased. Ethnic art became a source of income and, eventually much of it became symbolic of the crafters' ethnic identity.

- *Pan-Indian Art* is made by indigenous peoples who no longer feel bound solely to the customs and practices of their original tribal societies. Instead, they work for an external art market and, therefore, consider themselves as artists rather than craftsmen. While they commonly draw from their own cultural heritage, they are ever more influenced by the expectations and demands of outsiders and their perceptions of what the native arts should look like.

- *Indian Mainstream Art* is work created by artists who just happen to be Indians. Each artist has his/her own expressions and the theme of their work may be based in part at least on their ethnic heritage. Demand for such products is not limited only to tourists: they are also sold via mail order and shops in non-tourist areas.

Tourist consumption and changing art forms

In general, handicrafts were originally produced to fulfill ceremonial or practical needs but, as artisans became exposed to the outside world and as demand for local, indigenous handicrafts became more widespread, the very nature of handicrafts and traditional art forms began to change (Popelka & Littrell, 1991; Swanson, 1994). Arts and crafts, cooking utensils, shelters, canoes, clothing, weapons, furniture, baskets, and adornments, which once were produced for functional purposes (internal demand – see Graburn [1976] and Cohen [1993b]) and crafted from indigenous materials (e.g. bone, wood, stones, shells, etc.) became commercialized or commodified for tourists and other outsiders' (external) consumption (Halewood & Hannam, 2001; Holder, 1989; Markwick, 2001; Nason, 1984; Smith, 1996; Thompson & Cutler, 1997; Toops, 1993). In the process, their very forms, functions, and meanings changed. This course of change resulted in tourist kitsch (Cohen, 1992) or what Graburn (1976; 1984) disdainfully refers to as 'airport' or 'tourist' art.

Changes in the forms and functions of traditional arts and handicrafts have been brought about by many external and internal forces, not least of which is tourism (Gormsen, 1990; Parnwell, 1993). As modern-day tourism has grown, so has demand for souvenirs, primarily those of a handicraft and artistic nature, because tourists often perceive these as 'native', 'primitive', or 'typical' (de Vidas, 1995), and it is this expressed interest that has brought about many of the changes in destination arts and crafts. Native peoples have recognized tourist demand for something tangible to take home from their journeys, so the handicraft industry has expanded to service these demands, resulting in a wide array of changed and new items (Bunn, 2000; Crippen, 2000; Crozier, 2000; Evans-Pritchard, 1993; Ganslmayr, 1988; Graburn, 1976, 1984; Horner, 1993; Jules-Rosette, 1984; Popelka & Littrell, 1991).

Several examples can be used to illustrate this point. Until the mid-1900s, *sarapes* (shawls) were made for indigenous use and trade in the southern states of Mexico. After the completion of the Pan-American Highway and as tourism in southern Mexico began to grow, tourists became the primary consumers of the woven *sarapes*. By the late 1950s, the *sarapes* had lost much of their functional form and had started being designed with new and unusual patterns and for use as wall decorations (Popelka & Littrell, 1991).

Today in the Solomon Islands, woodcarving is done primarily to service the needs of tourists and has lost its traditional function and purpose. 'Many of the carvers are preoccupied with quantity rather than quality and may lack the expertise and dexterity of the traditional artist. As the need for cash increases among urban dwellers, many people, irrespective of their artistic skill, produce handicrafts for sale' (Horoi, 1980: 113), leading to the production of artifacts that represent little by way of tradition. Similarly, in Fiji, commercial woodcarvings are a direct product of tourism. In the words of Bolabola (1980: 95), 'tourists think it is traditional but it's really just "airport art", made specially to fit their expectations'. Some of the so-called 'traditional' carvings, which really did not become a part of the Fijian material culturescape until the 1960s and which depict items and events not found in Fiji (e.g. crocodiles and Maasai-looking warriors with spears), are manufactured by American-owned companies set up in Fiji to carve for the tourist trade (Bolabola, 1980).

A similar situation has occurred in Tonga, where traditional mats, baskets, *tapa*, and other handicrafts have been changed to meet the needs of tourists. By tradition, these items were made from local products for important family functions and ceremonies. However, tourist demand has led to an emphasis on quantity rather than quality here too, which has resulted in a loss of unique designs. Moreover, when Tongan women run out of prepared craft materials to sell, they cut up the family *tapa* and mats and use them to make items for sale to tourists. 'In doing so, these items seem to lose their value, for they are no longer carefully stored for special ceremonial occasions, but are sold to tourists who use them in any way they like' (Akau'ola *et al.*, 1980: 21).

Two broad types of souvenir-purchasing tourists can be identified: those who buy high-quality fine art and those who buy 'tourist art' or in other words, serious collectors and casual buyers (Graburn, 1976, 2000b; Simons, 2000). Cohen (1993a: 4–5) suggests that tourists place different meanings on handicrafts than local people do and it is these differences, which, through market mechanisms, lead to the adaptation of products to meet consumers' needs and preferences, which, in turn, commonly robs the depth of meaning from the artists. Cohen also suggests that differences in nationality, social class, and lifestyle create different demands for tourist arts – hence, the gaps between high-quality fine arts and cheap, immitation tourist arts. Similarly, there is a tendency among tourists to buy larger, more expensive items for themselves and cheaper items for their family and friends at home. This, in turn, results in the juxtaposition of cheap tourist art and expensive fine arts in most destinations. According to Gordon (1986: 139), vacationers who buy tourist kitsch do so simply because they are on holiday. It is a time where they are not serious and not as responsible, so money is spent or wasted on tourist art that has little meaning or real connection to the destination.

Obviously, tourism is not the only culprit in changing traditional arts to tourist arts. As Cohen (1992: 4) noted,

> a common misconception of ethnic arts is that they are historically stable, traditional cultural products, which have been rudely shaken by the acculturative influence of the expanding West. In fact, tribal and ethnic arts have been continually changing throughout history under the impact of internal forces and external contacts.

For instance, the earliest European colonizers and explorers 'discovered' unique elements of material culture in faraway lands, which they acquired through trading with indigenous peoples (Evans, 1998; Jensen, 2000). This has been well documented in Africa (Horner, 1993; Schädler, 1979; Shackley, 1997), Thailand (Cohen, 1989a, 1989b), among the Ainu people of Hokkaido, Japan (Wilkinson, 2000), and among the natives of Canada and the United States (Graburn, 1976; Wolfe-Keddie, 1993). Likewise, native arts were affected by the 'demonstration effect' where outsiders' art forms were adopted by indigenous societies (Cohen, 1993a; Moreno & Littrell, 2001). For instance, Native American women were influenced early on by 'white' women's magazines, from which they learned many skills such as beadwork and embroidery (West, 2000) – now treasured art forms among some Indian tribes in North America. A similar situation exists in East Africa. Many of the masks for sale in Kenya are only Kenyan by virtue of the fact that they were carved there. There is apparently no record of any ethnic groups in the country ever using masks for ceremonial purposes. In fact, the idea of carving masks and the concepts behind their design and form were originally based on photographs in foreign magazines (Jamison, 1999: 13).

Through time, as indigenous and outsider contact grew, demand for material icons of faraway and exotic places also grew, resulting in a thriving, albeit damaging, trade in antiquities and items of material culture. The illicit trade in valuable heritage heirlooms grew in many parts of the world, where graves and sacred sites were robbed and destroyed for their ancient riches, sunken ships were broken up and raided for their treasures, and statues, frescos, and mosaics were pillaged from ancient temples and monuments, so that unseen collectors could augment their collections (Evans-Pritchard, 1993; Littrell & Dickson, 1999; Shackley, 1997; Simons, 2000; Timothy & Boyd, 2003).

Another force for change has simply been modernization (Cohen, 1992; Hitchcock, 2000; Hudman, 1978). As contact with the outside world grew, indigenous peoples became ever more affected by industrialization and the arrival of modern conveniences, including radios, televisions, cars, and, more recently, computers and the Internet. These aspects of modernization have affected all parts of the world to some degree and introduced many changes to traditional art forms and material culture, particularly design and production techniques. Perhaps one of the best examples of this is the recent growth in computer-aided arts, such as batik-waxing in Indonesia (Hitchcock & Nuryanti, 2000).

Figure 5.2 demonstrates Graburn's (1984: 399–401) conceptualization of the process(es) of change in tourist arts. While the diagram is somewhat complex, his primary concern was to highlight three processes (see A, B, and C in the diagram). According to this model, the change from functional to commercial arts begins as tourists (or other outsiders) endeavor to purchase examples of functional embedded arts. This results in local people beginning to make replicas for sale. Most reproductions will adhere to near traditional designs that satisfy aesthetic traditions. Replicas of masks in Africa are an example of this form of change. In this process, change usually takes place within the following set of conditions: continuity of traditional artistic value, preserved role of the artist, the ability of the crafters to distinguish between sacred and secular art forms, a continuous supply of original materials, a market affluent enough to afford the handiwork, and buyers who know and care enough about traditional art to demand some level of 'authenticity'.

The second process is the transformation from commercial arts to souvenir arts/novelties. This is usually characterized by a departure from

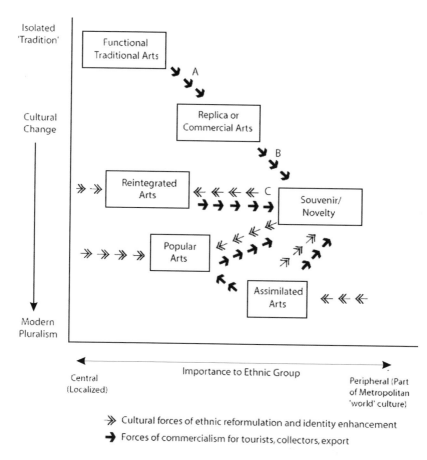

Figure 5.2 Processes of change in tourist arts (after Graburn, 1984)

tradition and changes in production processes and materials. While the basic patterns and designs may be maintained, the size and intricacy of detail may diminish. Miniature pots of non-traditional designs among Native Americans of the US Southwest are examples of this kind of change. Conditions for this type of change include: a mass tourist market; willingness among producers to stray from tradition, usually for economic reasons; a cessation of the customary role of the artists, allowing others to enter and compete; a depletion of traditional materials; new materials and techniques become cheaper, more abundant, or faster; and there is a large market that does not particularly care for 'authentic' handicrafts (Graburn, 1984: 400).

Process C entails re-integration into souvenir arts. These are arts introduced from some previous historic era re-introduced either through tourism or other forces of cultural change. Examples include the Kuna molas of Central America and the Hopi Kachina dolls in the United States. Often such items are priced highly and demonstrate considerable detail and fine workmanship (Graburn, 1984: 401).

The remaining processes (popular and assimilated arts) depict changes more from within traditional societies and minority groups as they become more acculturated and formally educated. Through acculturation and education, they become aware of the outside value of their traditional works (through interaction with the dominant society) and begin to purchase and collect such arts for their own appreciation (Graburn, 1984: 401).

Similarly, Cohen (1993a: 4) intimates a process where tourist arts commonly experience

> a period of creative innovation, immediately following their commercialization for an external public. However, after some time, as the market for the new art products becomes established, routinization tends to set in, as products become standardized and mass produced for an ever large, less discerning public.

According to Cohen, routinization in production becomes particularly pronounced when an art is targeted not just for mass production but also for the export market. This is especially the case when color catalogues are produced, which specify precise measurements, colors, and qualities of art products (Cohen, 1993a: 4).

Results of tourism-induced commodification

Many changes are wrought because of what tourists think the crafts 'ought' to look like, based on their stereotyped perceptions. This typically results in simplified visions of community life in destinations (Graburn, 2000a). Henrici (1999) points out how Pisac craftspeople paint stereotypical images of themselves on ceramics in order to sell them. Likewise, Toops (1993) noted that designs of some Uighur carpets from western China have been altered to appear more Persian, because this is what the tourists expect to find in a rug-making region. As alluded to earlier, 'native' souvenirs are widely sold in Canada and the United States, including replicas of familiar Indian symbols, such as drums, bows and arrows, feather headdresses, tomahawks, and totem poles – not because this is how natives live their lives (some never did) but because this is how tourists perceive Indian traditions. Native Americans are often depicted as 'colorful exotics, as children of nature, and . . . not in the contemporary world but in an eternal past-in-the-present' (Blundell, 1993: 73). Stereotyped images also often lead to the appropriation of elements of indigenous art forms as icons or logos for modern nations in the world of tourism (Graburn, 2000b: 346).

Similar to stereotypes is inauthenticity. While authenticity is socially constructed and may have different meanings in different societies (Cohen, 1988a; Markwick, 2001; Moreno & Littrell, 2001; Timothy & Boyd, 2003), Bunn (2000: 172) suggests that the Western idea of authenticity in craftsmanship requires that authentic goods be made by the members of a given society, made for the people of that society, using materials found or produced in that society, and used by members of that society. Such a definition does not allow for much leeway in determining authenticity and, indeed, would suggest that few tourist souvenirs could be considered authentic. Nonetheless, this definition is gaining widespread acceptance and, in many places, authenticity has received official attention and assigned official definitions. In New Zealand, for instance, the Aotearoa Maori Tourism Federation, in an effort to prevent the misleading of tourists by false claims to Maori authenticity, authentic Maori artwork is defined as (1) from the mind of a Maori, (2) by the hand of a Maori, and (3) a genealogical and/or spiritual connection to a tupuna Maori (Asplet & Cooper, 2000: 308).

In Canada,

> while [souvenirs] depict aboriginal cultural forms, such commodities are rarely produced or sold by aboriginal peoples or by companies that employ them . . . and . . . many of these souvenirs depict aboriginal peoples in distorting, stereotypical ways (Blundell, 1993: 65)

and are commonly promoted and sold as 'authentic' souvenirs of Canada. According to Blundell (1993: 69),

> Some tags claim that items are made of 'stone' or that they are 'carved,' when they are manufactured from synthetic materials. Designations such as 'handmade,' 'handcrafted', 'authentic', and 'original' appear on tags attached to mass-produced, non-native made objects. One producer of a widely available line of moldmade 'Inuit style' figures labels each as 'Wolf original', while another producer of such figures includes the words 'hand carved' in quotes on its tags, although the objects are clearly machine-tooled.

Thus, Blundell (1993: 72) argues that labeling is often used purposefully to deceive, because depicting signs and symbols of nativeness may lead some consumers to believe that there was some level of native participation in making the souvenirs when this is clearly not the case. Another key part of the authenticity debate in this context is tradition. Whether or not an artifact is seen as traditional commonly determines its degree of authenticity in western societies. In Kenya, wood carvings of Maasai figurines and wild animals are popular souvenirs, often promoted by sellers as, and believed by buyers to be, authentic Maasai handicrafts. However, as one Maasai informant in Jamison's (1999: 13) study commented, the wood items are very popular but 'we don't keep carved animals in our houses'.

Related to all this, Bunn (2000) and Teague (2000) raise a good question: How long is tradition? Society generally believes that something authentic must be ancient or at least very old. However, contrary to many people's beliefs, when an indigenous society adopts modern conveniences and innovations and they become a part of that group's everyday life, are they not then authentic or traditional as well? Some observers answer this question indirectly by noting that all tradition contains some portion of invention and adaptation (Horner, 1993; Moreno & Littrell, 2001). Cohen (1992) observed a similar notion, that over time, even contrived or inauthentic art forms may become recognized as authentic, even by experts – a process he calls 'emergent authenticity'.

An interesting, albeit under-researched, trend is the manufacturing of souvenirs in other countries for consumption in tourist destinations (Asplet & Cooper, 2000; Hobson, 1996; Markwick, 2001). Most of these souvenirs correspond with Gordon's (1986) 'markers' category, although many denote local traditions and lifestyles, even if they are manufactured abroad. For instance, in the United States, it is not at all uncommon to find Native American figurines and other popular icons of American culture that are made in China or the Philippines where labor and materials are much less expensive. Even many of the 'Indian crafts' for sale on Native reservations in the western United States are mass manufactured in China, Indonesia, and Mexico. In relation to this phenomenon, Evans (2000: 132) notes that 'Native Mexican replicas can be found in British craft shops, manufactured in Indonesia – post-Fordism has arrived as one indigenous group undercuts another, to the benefit of Western buyers'. Selling souvenirs made abroad can actually decrease shoppers' satisfaction levels, particularly when cheap, foreign-made products outnumber locally-made items in souvenir shops (Department of the Arts, Sport, the Environment, Tourism, and Territories, 1988; Hobson, 1996).

Types of change

There are many ways of understanding the types of changes that occur to ethnic arts as a result of tourism. For instance, as noted previously, changes commonly occur as artisans attempt to cater to what outsiders think the handicrafts ought to look like. Often this is a result of stereotypical images and this form of change can continue to sustain existing labels. For instance, Native Americans will most likely continue to produce commodified and hybridized forms of art as long as non-natives continue to buy them.

Based on a review of the cultural commodification literature, Cohen (1992: 20–4) identified eight types of changes that occur in tourist art products throughout the process of commoditization:

(1) *Traditionalism* versus *innovation in motifs and designs*

Patterns and designs are highly important ethnic markers and, in the early stages of commercialization, there is an inclination to reproduce neo-traditional motifs and designs that were current at some point in time. Traditionalist trends consist of a return to earlier, sometimes even archaic, designs. In some cases, these are re-introduced to the native society by outsiders. Innovation includes adaptations of existing styles to suit the demands of external audiences, making objects more attractive through the creation of new artificial styles, and introducing new styles and motifs altogether. It is common in many parts of the world for an entirely new craft form to emerge in response to tourist market opportunities (Cohen, 1989b, 1993a). Markwick (2001: 32) terms this process 'sponsored innovative commercialization'. While artisans may conceive of the new motifs themselves, they are more often influenced by media forces, popular culture, and other outside agents (i.e. tourists).

(2) *Naturalism* versus *abstraction motifs*

Within the context of tourist arts, two trends can be identified. The first is a change toward naturalism, which, according to Cohen, results in the destylization of handicraft products. While the symbolic significance of customary motifs may be weakened in this process, motifs become more readily recognizable and, hence, accessible to tourists. Second, there is an opposing trend that is a stylization of more naturalistic designs, sometimes resembling modern, westernized styles. For example, some African tourist arts are made after the style of Picasso.

(3) *Standarization* versus *individualization of products*

By tradition, tribal or ethnic craft-makers created similar but not identical articles, which were easily recognizable but not standardized like mass-produced merchandise. Commoditization of arts into tourist products brings about two divergent trends. The first is standardization, wherein arts become homogenized through mass production. This trend is especially apparent in small, inexpensive items for sale as souvenirs or as exports. The second trend is progressive individualization where artisans become responsive to the individualistic nature of Western art forms and seek to put their personal imprint on their work and become well-known artists.

(4) *Simplification* versus *elaboration of motifs and designs*

In this case, designs and patterns tend to become simplified and coarser compared to baseline ethnic arts. As crafts begin to be mass-produced and because they are for an outside audience, crafts lose many of the subtle details that were originally important for the cultural group in their artforms. In Cohen's (1992: 22) words, 'complex motifs are parried down to a few recognizable marks'. The reverse tendency is to make designs noticeably elaborate. Having access to new materials and colors and being free from traditions and ritual meanings, crafters seek to meet competitive demand by supplementing the intricacy of patterns, colors, and designs by adding ornamentation and embellishments to their products in an effort to make them more attractive.

(5) *Restraint* versus *exaggeration*

In some cases, where traditional arts are seen as too ornate or colorful, there is a propensity to subdue the flamboyancy of tradition and adapt colors and designs to meet the subtler tastes of Western artforms (Bunn, 2000; Cohen, 1988b, 1993a). Sometimes the opposite is true, however. In this case, art forms change because visitors demand exotic, grotesque, and exaggerated works that are often unrelated to the artisans' culture.

(6) *Gigantism* versus *miniaturization*

Gigantism refers to tourist art products that are made much larger than original artworks to satisfy some tourist demand. Miniaturization, however, is more common, i.e. where objects are made considerably smaller than their original forms to facilitate higher levels of mass production, to reduce costs, and to allow visitors to transport them home in their luggage (Dougoud, 2000; Moreno & Littrell, 1996; Smith, 1996). The fledgling tourism industry in Kyrgyzstan has already brought about some changes in the forms of popular Kyrgyz felt material. Most Kyrgyz felts are large, often bigger than four metres in length but tourists are unable to carrying them home, so artisans have begun to make smaller versions, which tourists can pack home in their suitcases (Bunn, 2000). Sizes are sometimes altered to physically fit the tourists. Because the textiles and clothing of many indigenous groups of Mexico are attractive to tourists, many visitors want to buy them as wearable souvenirs. As most outsiders are larger than the natives, 'indigenous Mexicans have to modify their huipil shirts to accommodate the very large arms and bodies of Caucasian tourists' (Graburn, 2000b: 348).

(7) *Introduction of novel materials* versus *return to native materials*

There is also a move from the use of indigenous materials (e.g. bones and shells) to new industrial materials. This has come about as a result of convenience of production, exhaustion of native resources, preservation of natural products, and the growth of new types of art forms that can be made better with newer non-indigenous materials. However, there is an opposite movement as well, which results in a return to native materials from artificial and non-local material.

(8) *Product for show* versus *use*

As highlighted earlier, ethnic crafts were originally functional arts but early outsiders collected them for show in exhibitions and museums. Modern-day tourists usually do not collect objects that are not authentic representations of a culture. Instead, they often purchase items to put on display as decorations in their homes (Cohen, 1988a, b, 1990). Armed with this knowledge, artisans commonly change their art forms for this purpose. Clothing designs become wall hangings and sand paintings are framed as pictures. Thus, traditional fabric designs, for instance, are now created for tourist uses at home, and new ones are invented. As Cohen (1992: 23) notes, 'ironically bookmarkers and tablecloths are produced by Southeast Asian tribal people, who have neither books nor tables'.

Summary

While tourists shop for many utilitarian items and everyday products (e.g clothing, toys, food, stationary, etc.), the primary interest of this chapter and, indeed, of tourism researchers, in general, is the ever-present souvenir. Souvenirs have undergone considerable changes since their ancient foundations as physical pieces of destinations marked with special meaning to the point where, today, many are inconsequential and mass produced in countries far from the attractions or destinations they are meant to commemorate. Researchers have identified several types of tourist souvenirs, each with its own allure and subjective set of meanings.

Among the most popular forms of souvenir are handicrafts and artworks, most of which were originally created by native peoples for practical purposes. However, as tourist demand for something to take home increased, art forms began to change to meet the needs and specifications of tourists and the tourism industry. This commodification of material culture has resulted in various forms of stereotypical images, inauthentic reproductions, and mass-produced tourist art that possesses little meaning or attachment to place.

Chapter 6

Shopping Venues and Contexts

Introduction

The earliest forerunners of shopping took place in the form of trading and bartering at markets and periodic markets. As people became less dependent on products that they themselves produced, trade began to expand, and itinerant sellers began going from place to place selling merchandise they had either produced themselves or paid wage laborers to produce.

Since ancient and medieval times, new types of shopping venues have developed but, as noted in Chapter 1, department stores and shopping centers only began to appear once a 'leisure class' had emerged. As leisure consumption became more important to western societies, the variety of shopping venues began to expand, resulting in the foundation of malls, outlet centers, and do-it-yourself stores. Parallel to the growth of leisure shopping, tourist shopping grew along with tourism in the early 1900s and later following the Second World War, although global travelers have always purchased local handicrafts directly from artisans. With the expansion of tourism in the 20th century, however, souvenirs became mass-produced commodities for tourist consumption and, as a result, souvenir shops began to crop up around famous attractions such as Niagara Falls and the Roman ruins of Europe. Likewise, as air travel became popular in the 1940s, airports began expanding their services to include retailing for travelers. The description of this trend could go on and on but suffice it to say that as the world's population became ever more inclined to travel and seek out leisure opportunities, new shopping venues began to develop.

As has already been noted in earlier chapters, leisure and tourist shopping is a highly social and psychological undertaking, which can be strongly influenced by place, location, surrounding environments, and store characteristics. These facts, coupled with the growth of new shopping venues, as noted earlier, highlight the importance of understanding the locations and settings within which tourist and leisure shopping take place. This chapter, thus, aims to describe and assess the most common opportunities and sites for shopping and the issues that pertain to each type of venue in the context of leisure and tourism.

Souvenir Shops

Many types of souvenir stores are found in tourist destinations and in transit. Antique shops sell a range of local antiquities and imported goods that appeal to collectors. Galleries and shops are popular where special forms of art depict local creative styles and fashions. However, perhaps the most common form of souvenir store is the ubiquitous curio shop, which abounds wherever tourists congregate. Everything from locally made handicrafts to imported trinkets is sold. Generally, the items for sale are indicative in one form or another of the region where they are located, although many shops deal in non-destination-related items as well.

Souvenir shops are typically clustered near major attractions (Pearce, 1998, 1999; Prentice, 1993; Timothy & Boyd, 2003) and the right kinds of shops can enhance the attractiveness of a place for tourists (Irwin *et al.*, 1996; Jansen-Verbeke, 1991; Law, 1993). Often, the items offered are thematic in accordance with the type of attraction they are near. For instance, shops near churches, synagogues, cathedrals, and pilgrimage sites tend to focus on religious paraphernalia. Likewise, items on sale near ancient monuments tend to be related to the monument itself or other similar attractions close by.

> In the vicinity of the holy places and along the crowded streets which connect them lay scores of shops – some only the size of a small sitting room and others nearly that of a typical British corner grocery store – filled with items arranged to catch the eyes of passing pilgrims and tourists . . . Inside the windows . . . would be dozens of often dusty articles for the tourist trade – pieces of what appeared to be local jewelry (much of it made in Taiwan), swathes of embroidered cloth, small brightly colored cotton throw rugs, candles with transfers of Jesus or Mary stuck on them, reproduction icons, olive wood carvings of holy figures (both Judaic and Christian), T-shirts emblazoned with 'Israel is Real' or 'Israel we Love you', small metal castings of the word 'Shalom' and so forth. (Bowman, 1996: 88–9)

Supermarkets/Grocery Shops and Clothing Stores

Supermarkets and other food stores are a critical part of the tourism shopping supply (Hudman & Hawkins, 1989; Pearce, 1989). This is particularly the case in destinations where self-catering accommodations are popular (e.g. timeshare resorts and apartment complexes). Many budget-conscious travelers find grocery stores, supermarkets, and farmers' markets a valuable asset as they purchase fruits, vegetables, meats, breads, and cheeses rather than dining out in restaurants for every meal. Clothing stores are an important component of the retail mix in tourist destinations. According to the Travel Industry Association of America (2001), clothing is the number one item purchased by tourists in the United States. Tourists may desire to shop specifically for recreation/tourism-related apparel, such as bathing suits, sarongs, and souvenir T-shirts, and simply for good bargains on everyday wear, such as trousers, skirts, shirts, and dresses.

Department Stores

In the late 1700s and early 1800s, there were only a few cities in North America with populations large enough to support shops that could specialize in only one kind of merchandise (e.g. shoes, hardware, stationary, etc.). As a result, most people shopped in one store, a general store, for all their needs. According to Nelson (1998: 29), the idea of the general store originated in medieval Europe where shops that specialized in one primary product were also permitted by the craft guilds in some cases to deal in limited quantities of products they did not produce directly. By the mid-1800s, general stores selling a wide range of products were commonplace. Later, the general store evolved into supermarkets and department stores. These shops with a wide range of merchandise under one roof became popular in city centers for one-stop shopping. Like their general store prototype, they sold clothing for adults and children, dry goods, home furnishings, and household wares but on a much larger scale. So much merchandise was involved that it 'had to be organized into departments, hence the term department store' (Nelson, 1998: 32).

The primary features of department stores include low product prices, lower markups, central locations, relatively cheap rents, high sales as a result of rapid stock turnover, and a wide variety of goods under one roof (Chaney, 1983; Coles, 1999b; Michman & Greco, 1995). Department stores are popular shopping venues for tourists for several reasons, including some of those already listed. One is their depth of merchandise selection, which is important for visitors who desire to buy large quantities of items for themselves or friends and family. Breadth of merchandise is also important, because tourists can do one-stop shopping to meet all their needs and find products that might not be available at home. Department stores are usually set up in a way that makes finding certain items quite easy. This is a desirable characteristic for shopping tourists, particularly those who might be in a hurry. Finally, department stores offer a variety of goods in a broad range of prices, so that even the most budget-conscious shoppers can find what they need (International Council of Shopping Centers, 2000: 46).

Malls

By the late 1800s, multi-store retail centers started to appear alongside department stores and, by the mid-20th century they had become a standard feature of the ex-urban retail landscape (Sack, 1988). The most common location of retail services in towns and cities has traditionally been the downtown area, or High Street, usually referred to in conjunction with the central business district (CBD). However, limited CBD space, recent zoning regulations, suburbanization processes, and other forces have pushed the development of shopping malls and large centers to the urban fringe (Garreau, 1991; Rathbun, 1986), made possible by the popularization of the automobile and the development of highway systems (Angle, 1974; Reynolds, 1993). While most planned shopping centers began to move to urban peripheries with suburban development in the mid-20th century, some were established earlier. One of the first ex-urban multi-shop retailing centers was opened in London in 1873 and was known as Brent Cross. A dozen years later, similar regional shopping centers were built at Gateshead (Metro Centre) and Dudley (Merry Hill Centre), United Kingdom. In the United States, the first out-of-town shopping centre was built in Kansas in the 1920s. Today these centers are now commonplace throughout North America and Europe (P. Jones, 1991). At the close of the Second World War, there were only a few hundred shopping centers in the United States. The number grew to nearly 3000 in 1958, 7100 in 1963, and 22,000 in 1980. At the turn of the 21st century, there were nearly 45,000 malls and shopping centers in the United States (Satterthwaite, 2001: 52).

The original idea of shopping malls was to provide consumers with an indoor (or outdoor in some cases) collection of shops, which together would offer a variety of merchandise and prices. In this way, consumers were not required to travel around to individual shops for specialty items; a one-stop shopping environment was created. While the contemporary mall continues this traditional purpose, several new trends in malls and mall shopping can be identified (see Table 6.1). These include the provision of more intense recreational experiences, making malls complete vacation destinations, the development of themed environments, growth of 'festival malls', and the provision of broader community services.

Perhaps the most obvious and widespread trend in malls is the provision of a shopping-recreation combination (Balke & Rausch, 1990; Howard, 1990b; Killick, 1998; Simmons, 1991; Vester, 1996). In the process of offering additional amenities for consumers, shopping malls have

Table 6.1 Leisure trends in shopping malls

Provision of recreational activities		Themed designs
Restaurants	Bowling	Period themes (e.g. old west)
Mini-golf	Ice-skating	Places/countries (e.g. Mexicoland, Paris)
Zoos	Fitness clubs	Nature and natural surrounds
Casinos	Swimming pools	Festival malls (carnival atmosphere)
Arcades	Cinemas	
Children's playgrounds		
Shows and special events		
Malls as tourist destinations		**Provision of general community services**
Recreational facilities and services		Churches and chapels
Hotels		Medical and dental clinics
Food services		Law offices
Airport connections		Travel agencies
Tour agencies		Laundries
Car rental agencies		Real estate offices
Timeshares		Post offices and couriers
Souvenir shops		Banks
Currency exchange		

become recreation centers. In the words of Nelson (1998: 63), 'the mall [is] not just for shopping any more. The cutting edge is entertainment retail'. Leisure facilities typically include restaurants, bowling alleys, mini zoos, exhibition centers, fitness clubs, casinos, ice-skating rinks, sports centers, swimming pools, arcades, cinemas, food courts, and childrens' playgrounds (P. Jones, 1991; Killick, 1998; Lengfelder & Timothy, 2000; Wakefield & Baker, 1998). These recreational amenities have come to the fore during the past quarter century and are key in getting people to the mall and keeping them there (Belsky, 1992; Creno, 2001; Uzzell, 1995).

In addition to these permanent recreational features, a number of events also take place in malls as a way of appealing to recreationists and other users. These include among others, car and boat shows, sports registration, fashion shows, education weeks, antique sales, blood doner and health clinics, holiday shows, service club displays, charity bazaars, raffles, craft shows, auctions, and talent contests (Boudreau, 1983).

A second important trend, and related to the previous one, is the deliberate pursuit of out-of-town visitors by transforming malls into complete vacation destinations (International Council of Shopping Centers, 2000). In addition to providing leisure facitilies and recreational activities, mall managers have begun to promote malls as complete holiday destinations. Large malls cater specifically to the needs of tourists by providing hotels, food services, airport shuttles, tour agencies, and car rentals. Simon DeBartolo Group, the United States' largest mall owner, is now considering offering timeshares at its most popular malls (Wakefield & Baker, 1998). Some malls have recently started offering currency exchange booths, where foreign visitors can acquire more spending money (Elliot, 2001; Painton, 1994), and courtesy telephones that will allow visitors to confirm flights, book hotel rooms, and arrange ground transportation. For marketing and promotion purposes, the Mall of America, the largest shopping mall in the United States, even has its own Tourism Department and contains six Mall of America Gift Stores, where visitors can pick up souvenirs of the mall itself (Goss, 1999: 52).

The third fad in mall design and shopping center development is theming. Many types of themes are selected to appeal to tourists and other consumers, including period themes (e.g. the roaring '30s and the rock 'n' roll '50s) and other more unusual topics (e.g. dinosaurland). However, perhaps the most common theme is places or countries. A good example of this is El Mercado mall in San Antonio, Texas. Here shops are filled with products from Mexico and South America (e.g. piñatas, blankets, silver jewelry, sombreros, and pottery), and buildings are designed in the stereotypical Spanish colonial style (Butler, 1998). One of the most popular resort communities in the US southwest, Sedona, Arizona, is also home to a Mexico-themed indoor/outdoor mall, which is highly popular among visitors. This Mexicoland theme is popular in the United States, for it allows Americans 'to visit Mexico without going there' and offers them Mexican crafts, 'free of the Mexican experience' (Arreola, 1999: 12, 27).

Smaller shopping malls are able to gear themselves toward a specific theme better than large and diverse malls. For example, in the Park Meadows shopping mall outside of Denver, Colorado, a theme of nature and national parks is portrayed as security guards are dressed to resemble park rangers, customers can relax in front of a fireplace as though they were in a park lodge, and the air is perfumed with the smell of pine trees (Wakefield & Baker, 1998: 516). The larger malls generally find more success in segmenting themselves spatially by various themes. The Mall of America, for instance, is divided into areas resembling different settings, including 'a bustling European marketplace', 'a European landscaped garden', a luxurious South Avenue district, and a bright American city theme (Goss, 1999: 52).

Commonly associated with theming is the development of 'festival malls'. This specialized form of mall is generally smaller in scale and focused more directly on recreational shopping than some of the larger establishments. Union Station in St Louis, Trolley Square in Salt Lake City, and Faneuil Hall in Boston are good examples of this phenomenon in the United States. The developers of these specialized malls aim to create a carnival-type ambiance by mixing arcades, restaurants, boutiques, and specialty shops with live music, juggling, magic shows, and acrobatics to entertain shoppers (Judd, 1995: 175). While festival malls clearly possess a recreation focus, retailing is still their primary concentration.

Finally, malls now typically cater to the broader community in addition to tourists, recreationists, and retail consumers. It is common for malls to contain churches/chapels, dental, eye and medical clinics, legal services, travel agencies, laundries, real estate offices, post offices, and several other types of services that the broader community may need. In this sense, mall managers have sought to become virtual indoor cities. In fact, they have become multifunctional environments providing much more than retail (Uzzell, 1995).

Outlet Centers

Similar to malls, and sometimes taking the form of malls, are factory outlet centers. Outlet shopping has become a highly prized tourist and recreational activity throughout much of the developed world, particularly in North America and Europe, although the idea is spreading in Asia as well (Cramer, 1995). The notion of factory outlet shopping originated in the 1800s in the textile mills of the northeastern United States, where factory owners sold excess inventory, imperfect goods, and damaged products in an effort to clear floor space (Lowe, 1998: 98). The primary locations of outlet malls have traditionally been industrial cities where apparel and specialized accessories were produced, as well as smaller towns and cities lying near enough to major markets to be convenient but not so close that competition was created with major retail centers (Patton, 1986: 10). This practice has continued into the present day where items are sold at considerable discounts as retailers eliminate the high mark-ups and amenities associated with traditional retail operations. Such discounts lure consumers who willingly overlook the product's potential flaws to save money (Gilpin, 1952; Patton, 1986), ranging from 5 to 50% savings compared to non-outlet retail centers (Bly, 1998).

Outlet malls developed in response to the needs of producers, retailers, and customers. They especially reflect the struggle between producers and retailers. In essence, producers lost a great deal of control of their products to large retail monopolies, as retailers increasingly had the power to dictate the scheduling of production and delivery and to insist on certain price levels. Outlet shops are, in most cases, an attempt by producers to gain back control and to profit directly, since, in this context, the retailer is also generally the producer. Prices are sometimes kept low by acquiring stock from foreign plants in Mexico, Asia, and the Caribbean. The outlet phenomenon also developed in response to consumer demand. Designer label desirability drives many shoppers to outlet malls, where most stores carry a famous brand name (e.g. Mikasa, Reebok, Nike, and Ann Taylor) (Hathaway & Hughes, 2000: 190).

During the 1980s and 1990s, outlet centers became an important part of the new retail and tourism landscape. The first multi-store outlet mall opened in Reading, Pennsylvania, in 1974. Presently there are over 300 outlet malls and 14,000 factory stores throughout the United States (Hathaway & Hughes, 2000; Outletbound, 2002) and many more in Canada, Europe, and Asia. Factory outlet malls are, according to Hathaway and Hughes (2000), the fastest growing segment of the shopping center retail industry. In fact, outlet shopping has become so popular that it surpasses the availability of second-quality and discontinued merchandise. To keep up with rising demand, manufacturers now produce goods in large quantities purposefully for direct sales at outlet shops, some of which may be of lower quality than those sold at more expensive retail establishments (Bly, 1998; Lowe, 1998).

The role of factory outlets as tourist attractions cannot be overstated. Areas of high outlet concentrations have long been targeted as potential tourist attractions, transforming many small towns and suburban areas into significant destinations (Lowe, 1998; Patton, 1986; Ritzer & Liska, 1997). The outlet malls near New York City, for instance, are important attractions for Japanese tourists for whom the center 'is hallowed ground, a must-do destination for even the most abbreviated trip to New York' (Foderaro, 1998: 15). The Potomac Mills outlet center, just outside of Washington, DC, is one of the most popular attractions in the Washington area, drawing in some 25 million shoppers a year – more than George Washington's home at Mount Vernon, Colonial Williamsburg, and Monticello, the plantation of Thomas Jefferson (Beddingfield, 1999). Similarly, Woodbury Common Premium Outlets, which is located approximately an hour's drive from downtown New York City, receives as many tour-bus-based customers as the Empire State Building each year (Bly, 1998: 4).

According to the Tourism Industry Association of America, approximately 40% of all tourists in the United States visited a discount mall in 1997 (Bly, 1998; Lowe, 1998). In 1998, some 37% of US travelers shopped at an outlet mall and 10% of shoppers cited the outlet 'experience' as the main

Table 6.2 Major factory outlet centers in the United Kingdom, 1996

Center	Description	Size (m²)	Developer
Bicester Village	51 shops, café	9951	Value Retail
Cheshire Oaks Designer Outlet Village	60 shops, cafés, fast food	167,740	BAA
Clarks Village Street	35 shops, cafés, footwear museum	7530	C&J Clark
Freeport Shopping Village	40 shops, marina, restaurant	7990	Freeport Leisure
Hornsea Freeport Shopping Village	29 shops, cafés, leisure park	3720	Peter Black / Freeport
Jackson's Landing	28 shops, café, marina, museum	6975	Guinea Properties
K Village	9 shops, restaurant	1767	C&J Clark
Lightwater Village	10 shops, coffee shop, restaurant	3800	Lightwater- Holding
Merchant Quay	27 shops, pubs, restaurants, cinema	3720	Brighton Marina Co.
The Galleria	40 shops, cinema restaurants	15,000	Lansfastighter Property

Source: Based on Mintel (1996a)

reason for their trip (Beddingfield, 1999). The line of thinking behind the success of these specialized malls among tourists is that the savings supposedly realized there offset much of the money spent on the holiday trip (Patton, 1986). This attitude has resulted in the success of many outlet centers and in the development of dozens of new ones during the past 20 years. Table 6.2 shows several of the largest outlet centers in the UK in 1996. About such popularity, Fisher (1996: 5) facetiously mused, 'the second largest town in Middlesex County during the Labor Day weekend was the new Clinton Crossing factory outlet center'.

The growth in popularity of discount malls has brought about several recent trends in their structure, operation, and locations. First is the tendency to combine stores that offer a single manufacturer's own products at reduced prices (outlets) with stores selling discounted merchandise from a wider variety of manufacturers (offprice) (Lowe, 1998: 98). Second, while outlet malls have traditionally been no-frills operations where people go to seek bargains, they have begun to offer recreational opportunities (e.g. food courts, carousels, playgrounds, cinemas) as additional amenities in the same way large shopping malls have done (Cramer, 1995). Third, some factory outlet centers are turning to themes of nature and nostalgia to attract increasingly selective consumers. In the context of one outlet center, Goss (1999: 68) claims that

> the village-like setting helps set it apart from what may be seen as chaotic and dirty downtown shopping areas and from the placeless aura of generic suburban shopping malls. A component of the nostalgia theme at Prime Outlets at Grove City is their Victorian appearance.

Such characteristics, Goss argues, creates a sense of simpler virtues, a stable identity, and a more peaceful life of America's bygone days. Thus, even outlet shopping malls are beginning to play on people's sense of nostalgia, which is becoming more pervasive in a multiplicity of contexts (Timothy & Boyd, 2003). Fourth, more outlet centers are catering more specifically to tourists by forming associations with the accommodation and restaurant sectors and marketing themselves more closely in conjunction with other regional attractions. Some outlet centers are even beginning to provide transportation for shoppers to and from airports and establishing shopping tours that take in cultural and natural attractions as well (*News for You*, 1996; Patton, 1986). Finally, outlet complexes are more often being located in desirable locations – near beaches, amusement parks, historic landmarks, and unique cultural areas (*News for You*, 1996). For instance, two large outlet malls with 170 stores were built in the 1980s and 1990s within a distance of 3 km from Lancaster, Pennsylvania (Lowe, 1998). Both malls emphasize their unique selling proposition in terms of their location in 'Amish Country', drawing thousands of shoppers each month from New York, Philadelphia, Washington, and Baltimore (Hovinen, 1995).

Airports

For obvious reasons, one of the most common and popular venues for tourist shopping is airports. Large airports typically house two distinct shopping areas in passenger terminals: landside and airside. The landside area is usually open to all passengers, visitors, greeters, and airport employees and is located before security checkpoints. Airside shopping refers to the area attached to departure gates, past passport control and security, and which are accessible only by ticketed passengers and airport employees (Kim & Shin, 2001). In 1996, airside retailing comprised some US$3.5 billion (49%) of the total spent on tax-free goods in the European Union and represented nearly 70% of all commercial sales in airports (Freathy & O'Connell, 1999). Airport retailing ranges from food services to duty-free shopping, including luggage shops, magazine stands, post offices, handicraft shops, and fine clothing stores. Kim and Shin (2001) classify this range of airport concessions as one of three types: duty-free shops, retail and convenience stores, and food and beverage services.

Nowadays, airports are not only transit points or travel hubs: they have also become shopping centers. During the past 25 years, owing to increasing passenger traffic, increased pressure on airport infrastructure, airline deregulation, reduced state involvement in the airline industry, and the elimination of duty-free shopping within the EU, many airport authorities have been forced to reconsider the methods they use to generate revenue. This has led many to branch further afield from the traditional and exclusive income sources of landing and take-off fees, parking, and airport taxes to include more retailing (Freathy & O'Connell, 1999). Many airports see themselves as part of the world of high-end retailing, competing with other major airports, and malls in some cases. Several international airports have become major shopping destinations in their own right and are widely known for their variety and quality of products. The best examples include Dubai International Airport, Changi Airport in Singapore, and Amsterdam's Schipol Airport (Hobson, 2000), which are popular for gold and jewelry, perfumes and candies, tobacco products, furs and clothing, and travel accessories. Some of the larger airports have even established grocery and department stores, and several have set up shopping information booths where consumers can find facts about what to buy and where to buy it (Graham, 2001; Hobson, 2000).

One of the largest airport retail companies is BAA Plc. (BAA) (formerly known as British Airports Authority), which, in addition to managing normal airport functions, also operates shops in major airports throughout the world, primarily in Europe and North America. Traditionally, retailing has been somewhat marginal to the operations of the BAA but, in recent years, it has concentrated on developing airports as major retail centers (Graham, 2001; Hobson, 2000; Mintel International, 1996b), owing to the lucrative economic opportunities this can provide. In 1994–95, for example, BAA earned £362 million from its airport retail sales (Mintel International, 1996b). By the late 1990s, airport retailing had become so important to BAA that it accounted for more than 52% of all revenue, followed by parking and traffic charges (30.2%), property rentals (14.7), and other revenue (2.9%) (Hobson, 2000) (Table 6.3). According to one study, over 70% of air passengers bought some kind of product at an airport in the mid-1990s, not including food and drinks. Some 62% bought a newspaper, card, book, or confectionary item (Mintel International, 1996b). In light of the economic potential of airport shopping, the company was quick to begin developing more retail outlets and expanding its geographic coverage.

Table 6.3 BAA's main sources of retail income, 1997–98

Duty and tax-free merchandise	Millions of pounds sterling
Perfume	146
Gifts	101
Liquor	100
Tobacco	82
Subtotal	429
Other retail	
Tax-paid shops	10
Car parking	80
Car rentals	19
Currency exchange	31
Catering	23
Bookshops	23
Advertising sites	16
Other revenue	23
Total	654

Source: After Hobson (2000)

Many people are involved in the everyday airport functions, so many forms of retail consumption exist at airports. Several different categories of airport shoppers can be identified:

- Business travelers are one of the most ubiquitous groups of consumers. Hobson (2000) argues that business shoppers have a high tendency to buy at airports, since they spend so much time there. As a result, some airport retailers have begun to offer frequent shopper programs, which travelers can trade for discount vouchers.
- Leisure travelers often shop for souvenirs and travel-related merchandise, such as swimwear, toiletries, and sunglasses. In most cases, leisure travelers (and business travelers too) are required to check in at least two hours before their flight departs. This provides extra time to shop before passengers board the plane and airport retailers are very aware of this fact (Mintel International, 1996b).
- Meeters and greeters are the people dropping off and picking up passengers. This group also uses airport-retailing centers to buy welcome

or departing gifts. In this case, meeters and greeters are nearly always limited to landside outlets (shops located before passport control), while passengers are able to shop in both landside and airside stores (Mintel International, 1996b).

- Airport and airline employees also purchase goods and services at airports (Mintel International, 1996b). Food and drink vendors fare particularly well from employee spending, although this segment is important for souvenir shops, newspaper stands, and other stores as well. Many retailers even offer airport employee discounts as a way of capitalizing on their need to spend.

- Airport recreationists are people who simply visit the airport on a leisure outing, perhaps to watch the planes take off and land, observe passenger traffic, or, as Mintel International's (1996b: 10) study suggests, specifically to shop owing to the wide range of shopping opportunities now available in major airports.

In addition to stores, many airports have started to adopt the mega-mall model described earlier, albeit on a smaller scale. To maximize revenues, some airports (e.g. Schipol and Changi) have started providing casinos, virtual golf facilities, karaoke bars, swimming pools, and bathing rooms. These new commercial facilities have begun transforming airports from 'government organizations to commercially oriented enterprises capable of generating substantial profits' (Kim & Shin, 2001: 149).

This change in management orientation, and the widespread internationalization of some airport management companies (e.g. BAA's expansion into North America, Australia and Africa) has led observers to suggest that some airport operators have monopolized the retail sector and 'nothing could better illustrate the lengths to which BAA, which runs Heathrow, Gatwick and Stansted, has strayed simply from running airports' (*The Economist*, 1996: 52). Although each airport differs in management structure and organizational culture, four broad types of trading relationships that govern airport retailing were identified by Freathy and O'Connell (1999: 125–8) (see Table 6.4). The first type is concessions-based retailing. This arrangement occurs when responsibility for merchandise sales lies completely with third parties, who have contracted with airport authorities to sell in the airport terminals (Kim & Shin, 2001). Under this framework, airport operators function as landlords and are responsible for the building, the physical facilities, and contracted services (e.g. water, heat, and light). However, they are not involved in the sale or purchase of products, although there might be an obligation to market the airport as a whole. The advantage of this arrangement for airports is that they are able to rent out vending space – a significant income earner for airport authori-

Table 6.4 Airport Retailing Management Models

Concessions-Based Retailing	Authority Managed Retailing
• Airport authority is the landlord	• Authority has direct control of retailing
• Third parties responsible for merchandising and selling	• Buying, selling and marketing are the responsibility of the airport authority
• Airport authority owns building and responsible for maintenance	• Income remains with the airport authority
• Airport authority responsible to promote airport as a whole but not individual shops	
Management Contract Retailing	*Joint Venture Retailing*
• Trade groups are responsible for retail management on behalf of the airport authority for a contract fee	• Airport authorities are essentially developers in cooperation with governments and other companies in other countries
• Authority has less input into decision making and control	• Alliances are formed and airports co-owned and managed

Source: Compiled from information in Freathy & O'Connell (1999)

ties. For merchants, the advantage is to have a location in the midst of large passenger flows. In most cases, brand-name stores located in airports have a much higher revenue return than those located in shopping malls or high street areas, owing to the captive airport audience that sees shopping as a way of killing time, picking up last-minute gifts, and spending leftover foreign cash. In most cases, concessionaire contracts last from five to seven years, at which time other retailers have opportunities to bid on rental space.

The extent to which operators control the product market varies. Some airports, including Amsterdam's Schipol Airport, one of the world's leading airport shopping centers, have a strict policy against pricing and merchandise competition between merchants. At Schipol, different concessionaires are required to carry different merchandise to avoid pricing competition on similar items. This concessions-based management model also means that airport managers have little direct control over the types and ranges of products stocked within each store. Although some rules exist to ensure that no two stores stock similar merchandise, airport authorities have little control over the actual choice of merchandise (Freathy & O'Connell, 1999: 125).

The second model of airport vending is 'authority managed retailing'. Under this genre of management, direct control is assumed for all or most of the retailing by the airport authority itself. The authority's responsibility, therefore, goes beyond being a landlord to include being an active participant in the commercial undertakings. With authority-managed retailing, parking and catering are included in the airport's fiscal endeavors. The venture generally emphasizes duty-free products, although it will also run shops and vending areas before departure inspections. The buying and selling of products, merchandising, marketing, and stock control all become the responsibility of the port management organizations (Freathy & O'Connell, 1999: 126).

The primary benefit of this model is that all income remains with the authority which, owing to increasing levels of air travel in recent years, has become a highly lucrative source of revenue. Another advantage is that airport managers maintain direct control over the products stocked and the way they are exhibited and sold in the stores. A third benefit is higher levels of consistency as all shops are owned and operated by one authority. This is particularly advantageous in advertising, customer service standards, merchandise, and pricing. Despite these important advantages, there are at least three notable disadvantages. First, the airport authority has significant financial obligations for staffing, merchandise, warehousing, infrastructure, and utility services. Second, there is a greater level of risk since responsibility is not spread between various concessionaires. Finally, because airport authorities are more in the business of running airports, they may not have the necessary expertise or diversity of skills for retailing or understanding customers' shopping behaviors, particularly in specialty shops like florists and apparel (Freathy & O'Connell, 1999: 126–7).

Management contract is the third type of retail relationship at airports. This entails an existing trade group being contracted to take responsibility for concession management on behalf of the airport authority for a prearranged set of fees. This does not always, however, exclude the airport operator from having some degree of input. BAA has made this arrangement in its American airports in recent years wherein the operation of all stores became the responsibility of its management partner, although BAA itself retained all sales revenues and took responsibility for physical maintenance. BAA's operation at Pittsburgh (USA) airport is an adapted form of management contract wherein the airport authority leases out its entire retail space to a single third party, who is then responsible for building, developing and managing all concessions operations. In return, BAA is paid a guaranteed fee per passenger going through the terminals (Freathy & O'Connell, 1999: 128).

The final management arrangement is 'joint venture retailing'. Recent years have brought about an interest in airport operators to invest in, manage, and operate the commercial and aeronautical activities of airports outside their own countries. As well, there has been an increase in airlines, state development agencies, and specialist duty-free merchants seeking to augment their earnings by spreading out into airport retailing. These recent changes have resulted in a variety of joint ventures, alliances, and partnerships (Kim & Shin, 2001). Several Western European airport management companies have reached into Eastern Europe, North America, Asia, and the Middle East in partnership with operators in the host country (Freathy & O'Connell, 1999: 128).

Regardless of the type of administrative structure employed in an airport, there are several management factors that influence the level of revenue earnings and which managers must consider in their planning and partnership efforts (Kim & Shin, 2001):

- the level of traffic going through the airport;
- the amount of space allotted for commercial activities and the location and design of these spaces;
- the buying preferences and characteristics of air passengers – passengers' purchasing patterns will be influenced by the level of taxes on key merchandise in passengers' home countries, their religious and social customs, and the value of their home currency relative to the currency of the country where the airport is located;
- the level of involvement of the airport authority in operating concessions;
- the airport's marketing strategy;
- the types of contracts and rental fees; and
- concessionaires' pricing strategies.

Railway Stations and Harbors

Like the situations at airports, retail shops are an important part of the service environment of railway stations, harbors, and ferry terminals as well. Railway station shops cater primarily to short-distance commuters and people making long journeys between cities. Print media (i.e. books, magazines, and newspapers), confectionaries/snacks, and drinks are particularly important merchandise. Some stations, especially those whose primary role is to facilitate commuters, also carry various toiletries, hosiery, and other items that people can purchase quickly on their way to and from work. People waiting for trains can be enticed to purchase refreshments and print media if managers stock shelves and window displays in a way that encourages passengers to buy on impulse. Other services commonly utilized in train stations that can contribute to the retail environment include bars, dry cleaners, copying services, and shoe-shining booths (Mintel International, 1996b).

Harbors and ferry terminals that cater specifically to commuters will usually demonstrate many of the retail features found in railway stations. Ferry terminals tend not to have a great variety of shopping opportunities, as most passengers have opportunities to shop onboard, which is generally seen as part of the onboard entertainment (Mintel International, 1996b: 11). However, when these terminals are gateways for cruise-based tourism, they tend to have a wider array of merchandise and a different orientation in retail sales. Souvenir shops, liquor stores, jewelry and clothing boutiques, and dining establishments are among the most common features of the cruise port infrastructure. Even when passengers have opportunities to shop onboard the ship, they tend to want to purchase some items on shore. This is because the ports of call are one of the primary highlights of cruises and people generally want to buy items from the places they visit. As same-day visitors, cruise passengers have limited amounts of time in the ports of call. Therefore, destination residents and officials are eager to offer a wide range of souvenirs and other merchandise, ranging from Hard Rock Café T-shirts (even if there is not a Hard Rock Café in that location) to local handicrafts, foods, and jewelry.

Duty-free Shops

Almost all international airports, harbors, and land border crossings provide duty-free shopping for travelers once they have cleared departure inspections and, on many vessels, (e.g. aeroplanes and ships) duty-free shopping can commence once in international airspace or waters. On land, duty-free shops are generally located between the customs offices of each country. The notion behind duty-free shopping is that items can be purchased free of duties and import tariffs at the point where people depart a country since the goods will not be consumed in the country where they are bought. By purchasing merchandise after leaving the effective control of one country but before entering the next country, travelers can avoid paying import duties on highly taxed and deluxe items (Anthony, 1992; Lyons, 1991; Timothy, 2001). This does not mean, however, that shoppers are exempt from paying import duties on the merchandise they purchased by the country they are entering. Duty-free shopping, as Anthony (1992) points out, is not goods offered at a discount but rather that there are simply no taxes or fees added to the prices. Thus, there is no guarantee that visitors will always find a bargain.

This traditional model of duty-free shopping is changing. Some countries are beginning to allow tax-free purchases on arrival (Bia, 1996; Bureau of Transport Economics, 1979); Australia and some countries in Asia and Africa are recent examples of this. Tax-free shopping is also not limited to international gateways. For instance, the state of Louisiana (USA) adopted a sales-tax-free shopping program in 1990 for international visitors – the only one of its kind in the United States. Most of Louisiana's visitors know of the tax refund program and almost 82% of them used the program for sales-tax refunds in 1998. While the success of this program has yet to be fully determined, government leaders and tourism promoters anticipate an increase in tourist numbers to the state (Dimanche, 2003).

In 1947, the Irish Parliament passed the Customs Free Airport Act, which, to all intents and purposes, brought about duty-free shopping, as it is known today. The world's first duty-free shop opened in Ireland at Shannon Airport the same year and sold tax-free alcohol and tobacco to transit passengers on their way to and from the United States. Inflight duty-free sales are thought to have started with Air France in 1955 and Lufthansa in 1960. By 1960, the idea and practice of duty free had spread to airports in Brussels, Düsseldorf, Osaka, Oslo, London, Frankfurt, Miami, Amsterdam, and Tel Aviv (Bia, 1996: 38).

Duty-free shopping is a highly important tourist activity, estimated to be worth tens of billions of dollars each year. According to Bia (1996), approximately 30% of all spending by travelers on each trip is comprised of some kind of duty-free shopping. The most popular items are wines and spirits, perfumes and cosmetics, sweets and chocolates, jewelry and watches, and tobacco products, although the single most common item purchased in the mid-1990s was women's perfume (11% of total purchases), which was a change from earlier years, when cigarettes were the most commonly purchased item. The fastest growing items are confectionaries and clothing accessories (e.g. ties, purses, scarves, etc.). Bia (1996) argues that duty-free shopping is a unique form of tourist shopping because it focuses on prestigious brands and products, has a different pricing system, caters to a captive audience, and is regulated by special rules and regulations.

While Europe traditionally has been the largest area of duty-free commerce, the abolition of duty-free sales within the European Union (EU) in 1999 created a complex situation. The most recent policy on duty-free in the EU states that, when people travel between EU member countries, they may purchase certain items tax-free (e.g. some perfumes, cosmetics, sweets, and gifts), while other items (e.g. tobacco and alcohol products) can be bought at taxed prices and tax-free when traveling outside the EU. This is regulated by requiring passengers to show their passports and boarding passes to shop personnel. Before 1999, there was considerable opposition to the abolishment of duty-free sales within the EU, particularly by retailers and distributors of tax-free merchandise (Graham, 2001). The following arguments were identified for not abolishing duty-free retailing:

- Duty-free is an essential part of the travel experience.
- Duty-free positively affects the balance of payments and provides opportunities for exports.
- Duty-free can result in lower travel prices.
- This is a major retail forum for high-quality products.
- It is a crucial source of funding for the development of airports, ferries, airlines, and tourism in general throughout Europe.
- Duty-free offers souvenirs of the destination country, supporting local crafters, and major international brands.
- The European Union accounts for over half of all worldwide duty-free sales, resulting in billions of US dollars in the EU economy and supporting thousands of jobs.
- Duty-free was invented by Europeans, so it should continue its important role in the EU economy.
- Retailers themselves are able to enforce duty-free allowances and rules.
- The value of fees collected by airports on duty-free sales is larger than revenue earned from more traditional duty-included business (Bia, 1996: 53).

The majority of duty-free sales are concentrated in Europe, followed by the Americas and the Asia-Pacific region (*Travel and Tourism Executive Report*, 1997). The United Kingdom traditionally has profited the most from this form of shopping, with the United States coming in second (Bia, 1996). There are dozens of duty-free companies throughout the world, although the majority of sales is concentrated within the top 20 (Table 6.5).

In addition to on-ground sales, in 1995, over 200 international airlines offered inflight duty-free sales, which amounted to nearly two billion US dollars and made up 8.6% of all duty-free sales (Bia, 1996).

Highway/Motorway Service Centers

Motorway service centers are ubiquitous in the travel landscape and a significant part of the retailing side of tourism (Jansen-Verbeke, 1998). These centers cater primarily to people traveling long distances who want

Table 6.5 The world's 15 largest duty-free shop operators, 1995

Rank	Name of company	Sales (US$ millions)	Share of global sales (%)
1	DFS Group, USA	2,800	13.7
2	Allders International, UK	834	4.1
3	Gebr. Heinemann, Germany	800	3.9
4	Weitnauer, Switzerland	744	3.6
5	Duty Free International, USA	515	2.5
6	Stena Line, Sweden	493	2.4
7	Alpha Retail Trading, UK	481	2.4
8	Silja Line, Finland	402	2.0
9	Nuance, Switzerland	361	1.8
10	Aer Rianta International, Ireland	355	1.7
11	Duty Free Philippines	336	1.6
12	Aldeasa, Spain	326	1.6
13	Viking Line, Finland	314	1.5
14	King Power, Hong Kong/Thailand	314	1.5
15	Lotte Group, South Korea	307	1.5

Source: After Bia (1996)

to stop for a snack, a meal or a drink, and fill the car with petrol. However, other types of shops have found a degree of success in motorway service areas. These include, among others, shops selling for travel-related merchandise (e.g. car accessories, music CDs/tapes, maps) and regional souvenirs. In the early and mid 1990s, sales at retail shops annually comprised some 28% of the income of highway service areas, which may suggest that shopping facilities could be developed further along motorways (Mintel International, 1996b: 11).

Museums and Heritage Sites

Research studies commonly find that heritage/cultural tourists are more inclined to have high levels of disposable income and a tendency to spend more money during their vacations than other types of tourists (*Hotel Online Special Report*, 1998; Kim & Littrell, 1999; *Lodging Hospitality*, 1999; Silberberg, 1995). As a result, the heritage industry has begun to broaden its economic horizons by expanding into the retail sector (Butcher-Younghans, 1993; Prentice, 1993; Roberts, 1987; Smith, 1989; Thomas, 1989; US Department of Commerce, 1999), largely as a means of funding conservation projects and daily operations in light of major cutbacks in public funding in recent years (Borrus, 1988; Marsh, 1991; Timothy & Boyd, 2003). In the early 1990s, a Museums Association survey found that nearly 80% of museums had some form of retail point (Marsh, 1991) and this number is likely to have gone up in the intervening decade. Edwards (1989) found that heritage-site visitors have a relatively high propensity to shop and most desire to purchase souvenirs to document their travels. Several retail items at museums and historic sites are especially popular, including guidebooks, miniature replicas, photo albums, postcards, posters, camera film and batteries, candy, T-shirts, calendars, salt and pepper shakers, coffee mugs, wood carvings, pencils and pens, and handicrafts or skill works that are unique and representative of the place (e.g. model ships at a dockyard, copper pots at a coppersmith's shop, and souvenir bricks at a brickyard) (Crippen, 2000; Obeyesekere, 1988; Timothy & Boyd, 2003). Some locations have become quite creative in their retailing efforts. For instance, in 1988, Ironbridge Museum in the UK introduced its own token coinage, which represented the older system of coinage that was used in Britain before 1900. The exchange rate was 40 modern pennies for one old penny and shop prices were set to be at 17th-century prices. The coinage had the appearance of the old currency and, thus, was an interesting education tool but what was remarkable economically was that over 45% of the coinage went home with tourists as souvenirs (Smith, 1989: 26), thereby generating an enormous profit on something that costs little to produce (Timothy & Boyd, 2003).

Wineries and Distilleries

Wine tourism is growing quickly in many parts of the world, most notably in the United States, Canada, Australia, New Zealand, Spain, South Africa, France, Germany, and several other European locations (Dowling & Getz, 2000; Hall & Macionis, 1998; Telfer, 2001). One of the primary motivations for visiting wineries and distilleries, aside from tasting and observing the production process, is to purchase wine or whiskey. As a result, wineries have become an important part of the retailing sector of tourism. Many additional products, besides wine, are sold at wineries, usually with a focus on the winery theme (Table 6.6).

'Boutique' wineries, which produce signature wines on a smaller scale than the traditionally larger wineries, have become particularly involved in tourism recently. These nearly always have shops on the premises. At Australia's 900 or so wineries, the most popular items for sale, in addition to wine, are produce, souvenirs, and crafts (Hall & Macionis, 1998). In Canada's Niagara wine region, on-site wine sales comprise a large part of

Table 6.6 Typical merchandise for sale at wineries

Wine-related	Food	Clothing	Books	Crafts	Other items
Wine	Jams	Jewelry	Wine guides	Cups	Spoons
Wine glasses	Jellies	Ties	Regional books	Plates	CDs
Wine racks	Cheese	T-shirts	Magazines	Candles	Cigars
Wine bags	Chutney	Hats	Cook books	Pottery	Table cloths
Bottle openers	Gourmet foods	Sweatshirts	Souvenir books	Candleholders	Napkins
Decanters	Cookies	Aprons		Gift baskets	Postcards
Coasters	Crackers				Posters
Other accessories	Juices				

Source: After Telfer (2001)

the retail sales of wines. In Telfer's (2001) study, over half of the wineries surveyed claimed to sell 50% of their wine at the winery; some of the smaller enterprises indicated that they sell up to 100% of their wines on site.

In common with wineries, whiskey and rum distilleries in places such as Scotland and Jamaica have become key tourist attractions. Visits to whiskey distilleries in Scotland and Ireland have become popular tourist activities in those countries over the past 25 years (Boyd, 1999; McBoyle, 1996). By the middle of the 1990s, nearly a third of all malt distilleries in Scotland had constructed visitor facilities (including retail shops) aimed at meeting the purchasing needs of over a million visitors per year (McBoyle, 1996; Timothy & Boyd, 2003).

Special Events and Theme Parks

Festivals and events are another of the most popular tourist attractions and shopping venues. Communities of varying sizes have instituted festivals based on their notoriety from history, the dominance of a specific agricultural or food product, the settlement of a distinct cultural or ethnic group, and dozens of other criteria that set the community apart from others. These festivals draw people from local areas, some from distant communities, and even from abroad. Some events are founded on purchasing behavior (e.g. arts and crafts shows), while others have a different focus but, nonetheless, provide opportunities to spend on food, souvenirs, clothing, artwork, and even animals (Janiskee & Drews, 1998).

In their study, Irwin *et al.* (1996: 35) found that retail shopping was among the largest expenditure categories reported by sporting-event visitors. This led them to recommend that event organizers and managers should focus on providing shopping opportunities to increase earnings. They also suggest that event organizers should disseminate information ahead of the event to potential participants regarding the types of attractions and shopping opportunities that will be available at the event location.

Merchandising within theme parks is another indication of the importance of shopping in tourism. In many cases, retail revenue exceeds that gained from entrance fees (Dudding & Ryan, 2000) and ever more parks are diversifying their product base to include T-shirts and hats, souvenirs, trinkets, stuffed animals, toys, postcards, books and other types of memorabilia. The Disney them parks are probably the best examples of this phenomenon, where nearly every visitor purchases something related to the Disney theme.

Craft Villages

Historically in the developing world, individual villages were centers of production for specific types of handicrafts – crafts that were primarily for local use but which could also be traded with artisans and consumers in other villages. As a result, specialized handicraft villages developed. Some excelled in producing pottery, which could be used to cook beans or carry water; others perfected the skills necessary to weave cloth; and still other villages became centers of ceremonial clothing and jewelry production. As tourism developed and outsiders' consumer demand for pottery, local fabrics, and jewelry increased, villagers began to produce merchandise more abundantly and in varying forms to meet the needs of visitors.

With the change from being simply a production center for regional use to centers of tourist craft production, the primary role of these villages in places such as Indonesia and Thailand today is to manufacture items for tourist consumption. Once they are made, the artwork is shipped off to various tourist destinations where it is peddled by street vendors or sold in official souvenir shops (Timothy & Wall, 1997). In some cases, the villages themselves have developed into large marketplaces where tourists can go to shop. Perhaps two of the best examples on the island of Java in Indonesia are Kasongan and Kota Gede – both in the province of Yogyakarta. Historically, the village of Kasongan produced pots for local consumption, and it became known throughout central Java for this skill. Now it produces more decorative pottery, animal and human figurines, large clay statues, and various other ornaments that are perceived to be of interest to tourists (Sulaiman, 1992). These are sold in the nearby tourist cities of Yogyakarta and Surakarta, as well as throughout Indonesia. The village of Kota Gede, on the outskirts of Yogyakarta City, was known in its earliest days as a center for silver works – jewelry, pots, and ceremonial items. Today, the village is being promoted to visitors as a center for handicrafts, and many tourists are taken there to watch the silversmiths demonstrate their trade and to purchase silver items in one of the community's shops (Timothy & Wall, 1995; Wondoamiseno & Basuki, 1986).

Many of these handicraft villages take the form of ribbon development, which alludes to the location of shops alongside major roads to cater to passing trade (Cohen, 1995b). Originally, as described earlier, craft production places were often located a considerable distance from the large cities and towns that tourists began to frequent. They sold their products to local traders who then distributed them to the tourist market. However, as road access improved outside urban areas, tourists were able to expand their range into the previously more isolated regions, stimulating the development of a wide variety of roadside tourist craft outlets (Cohen, 1995b: 226–7). This pattern is not found only in Southeast Asia but is endemic to many less-developed parts of the world, including Africa and Latin America.

Tourist Shopping Villages

Handicraft villages represent one form of what Getz (1993b) terms 'tourist shopping villages' (TSVs) – small communities that attract visitors and whose appeal lies in their recreational/tourism retailing opportunities, usually in attractive settings surrounded by natural or cultural amenities (Getz *et al.*, 1994: 2). In most TSVs, heritage resources are the initial attraction but more recent tourist-oriented shopping and other services provide the appeal for repeat visitation (Getz, 1993b: 26).

Most of the businesses that fall into this category have distinctive looks about them, offer tourism-related goods (e.g. souvenirs), and are commonly associated with historic buildings and themed designs. It is also the concentration of specialty shops together with entertainment and dining services that defines the TSV (Getz, 1993b).

In their research on TSVs near Calgary, Alberta, Canada, Getz *et al.* (1994) found three types of businesses that tend to personify TSVs: local services, tourist services (e.g. lodging, tea rooms, icecream parlors, clothing, candy, books, antiques, pottery, bakeries, souvenirs, restaurants, toys, etc.), and festival-oriented services (e.g. gift shops, food and beverage services, antiques, art galleries, and bakeries). In the developed world, TSVs are often located near larger urban centers and benefit from suburbanization, which creates demand for people to get away into the country – but not too far. Natural or cultural heritage themes, an attractive small-town setting, and the provision of amenities and services such as parking, toilets, eating areas, food services, and interpretive signs are all an important part of the success of TSVs. They often are also known for special events and festivals that appeal to the visiting public (Getz *et al.*, 1994; Hinch & Butler, 1988). There also tends to be a variety of souvenir shops, craft markets, and other specialty shops, together with generalized merchandise retailers and, in some cases, factory outlet stores.

One of the most commonly cited examples of a TSV in North America is St Jacobs, Ontario (Canada) which was originally a small farming community in the midst of the province's Mennonite cultural area (Dahms, 1991a, 1991b; Getz, 1993b; Johnson, 1992; Mitchell *et al.*, 1998). The village itself, owing to its appeal as a trade center for Old Order Mennonites, became a tourist destination offering a variety of traditional and locally produced handicrafts in a small town environment. The village is located only a few kilometres from the city of Waterloo (population 300,000) and two hours from Toronto and has developed into an important tourist and day-trip destination. Some observers estimate that more than a million people visit St Jacobs each year from across Canada, the United States, and overseas, bringing between CA\$15 and 20 million into the village's economy (Mitchell *et al.*, 1998).

The physical appeal of St Jacobs lies in its unique cultural landscape, which derives from the dress, modes of transportation, foods, farms, and homes of Old Order Mennonites. It also possesses a scenic river and several interesting heritage buildings that appeal to visitors and which have been recycled into shops and restaurants (Getz, 1993b; Johnson, 1992; Wall & Hohol, 1989). In addition, a farmers' market and an adjacent factory outlet mall are located on the outskirts of town, adding yet additional tourist appeal. Tourism in St Jacobs is a relatively new phenomenon, as most of the shops and restaurants did not come into existence until the mid-1970s and early 1980s. At that time, many of the old buildings (e.g. the flour mill and grain silo, an abandoned grocery store, barns, etc.) were refurbished into gift shops, antique markets, bakeries, and restaurants (Dahms, 1991b; Mitchell, 1998).

Street Vendors

Hawkers, or street vendors, are among the most ever-present retail intermediaries in tourist destinations throughout the world. These peddlars may operate illegally, in that they are not licensed by local authorities and much of what they offer may be of dubious quality and legality (Timothy, 1999b; Timothy & Wall, 1997). In most tourist areas, vendors typically sell a variety of products, including hot food, clothing, jewelry, drinks, services (e.g. hair braiding and face painting), and various souvenir items. Table 6.7 demonstrates the range of products sold by street vendors in Yogyakarta, Indonesia. Although vendors may have widespread tourist appeal, they

Table 6.7 Goods for sale by street vendors in Yogyakarta, Indonesia

Product	Frequency	Product	Frequency
Clothing	262	Oil paintings	15
Leather jewelry	131	Cigarette lighters	14
Leather belts	94	Toys	14
Canvas bags / packs	90	Imitation name-brand purses	13
Keychains	87	Cosmetic bags	11
Leather purses	74	Wood whistles	11
Designer jewelry	72	Painted tiles / plates	10
Leather bags / packs	60	Swords	10
Shoes / sandals	50	Socks	9
Wood carvings / toys	50	Brass crafts	8
Candy / snacks	45	Books / magazines	8
Fans	43	Rubber stamps	8
Silverworks	42	Cloth	7
Hot food	40	Brooms	7
Hats	36	Painted animal skins	7
Fresh fruit	33	Ceramic trinkets	6
Sunglasses	31	Islamic emblems	6
Watches	31	Picture frames	6
Wicker products	29	Cigarettes	5
Javanese headwear	27	Place mats	5
Net bags	25	Posters	5
Wayang puppets	21	Scarves	5
Batik cards / paintings	20	Nationalist emblems	4
Drinks	19	Handkerchiefs	3
Masks	15	Watchbands	3

Source: After Timothy & Wall (1997)

often have a propensity to bother customers with persistent, if overbearing, touting (see Chapter 7 for a broader discussion on this).

Vendors may be itinerant, moving from place to place and roaming along beachfronts or main tourist thoroughfares, or they may be stationary, with a small shop or stall near a tourist attraction. In most cases, the peddlars are a part of petty capitalism or the informal employment sector, together with street food-sellers, pedicab drivers, unlicensed guides, prostitutes, and unauthorized guest houses (Cukier & Wall, 1994; Griffith, 1987; Michaud, 1991). The term 'informal sector' was initially used in the early 1970s in the context of dual economic systems in Africa, which were viewed as being polarized into formal and informal sectors. However, subsequent authors have noted that while this categorization may be useful for heuristic reasons, it is an oversimplification of the economic situation in most developing countries (Opperman, 1993; Timothy & Wall, 1997). In some traditional societies, street hawkers are now being recognized and regulated by government officials, they are being enumerated and taxed, and they are receiving official assistance from public agencies in charge of tourism and economic development, leading to a situation where they can nowadays be considered only semi-informal (Timothy & Wall, 1997).

Craft Markets

Several authors have acknowledged the importance of handicraft markets as venues for tourist consumption (e.g. Graburn, 1984; Jules-Rosette, 1984). Craft markets can be an important part of the attraction base in destination communities, particularly in areas where indigenous cultures dominate the tourism landscape. The local colors, styles, products, and people contribute to the appeal of many destinations. Artisan markets give tourists an opportunity to see a variety of products that might be produced locally (although some may also be imported from abroad) and they give local residents an opportunity to earn some much-needed cash by selling their handmade artworks.

Markets are usually laid out physically to optimize visitor use and expenditures. For instance, in his study of a craft market in Guatemala, Hudman (1978) found a tourist-oriented spatial pattern. The market at Chichicastenango was organized spatially to separate tourist items from the items that locals would buy. Tourist merchandise, comprising one-third of the retail space, was located along the outside of the market with booths along the streets leading into the plaza. The central market area was designated more for local consumption with goods such as western-style clothing, prepared foods, and household products. Similar clustering patterns were observed in the main shopping area of Yogyakarta, Indonesia (Timothy & Wall, 1997).

In most less-developed destinations today, there is a complex network of producers, middle people, and sellers of merchandise in craft market places. These networks include producers or contract crafters, far away from the location where their products are sold, who work on small profit margins (Blundell, 1993; Cohen, 2001; Littrell, 1996; Sulaiman, 1992). In many destinations today, crafters have organized themselves into cooperatives as a way of capitalizing on mass purchasing and mass production, as well as a way of mitigating some of the problems that craftspeople and sellers might encounter (Timothy & Wall, 1997; Toops, 1993).

Handicraft markets are a highly gendered space. In some parts of the world, males dominate the market scenes, while in others, women are the dominant vendors (Connelly-Kirch, 1982; Wagner, 1982). Regardless of which gender dominates, working in craft markets and producing handicrafts for sale locally and abroad have become important tools for empowering women socially at the community level and economically at the household level (Swain, 1993). It helps them out of the subordinate role of women in most traditional cultures and negotiates an unusual level of equality in the tourist–resident relationship (Cone, 1995). According to the literature, in most parts of the world, women are the primary producers of tourist handicrafts, because these tend to be based on traditionally-defined women's items, including mats, hats, baskets, shell crafts, purses, tapestries, clothing, and jewelry (Nason, 1984; Swain, 1993). Men tend to be producers of more masculine art forms, such as wood carvings and prints (Wolfe-Keddie, 1993).

Summary

Evidence presented in this chapter suggests that recreationists and tourists will shop anywhere. As a result, even retail establishments that have not been traditionally viewed as having leisure or tourist appeal are beginning to cater to the needs and desires of various sorts of hedonic shoppers.

Souvenir shops abound wherever tourists congregate and they are most typically located near important tourist attractions, often taking on themes and selling products related to the main attraction. Supermarkets and grocers are typically overlooked by tourism scholars even though they are important in tourism, particularly because of their use among visitors who utilize self-catering accommodations (e.g. apartments and timeshares). For many tourists, grocery stores are also appealing because the products on offer are different from those at home. Department stores developed in Britain in the late 1800s in response to the popular need for increased merchandise mixes. They are popular among tourists and recreationists owing primarily to their diversity of products, good value for money, and generally favorable locations.

On a larger scale, one of the most important leisure attractions is the mall, which developed primarily for the upper classes in the late 1800s, although it is now the domain of people across all sectors of society. Malls are typically located on the urban fringe and have become popular hangouts as a result of their tenant variety, recreational facilities, special events, and public services. Similarly, factory outlet centers have become an important component of the leisure retail landscape and have adopted many features of traditional shopping malls, such as massive size, tenant variety, leisure services, and locations in suburban areas near major highways.

Several shopping venues have developed in conjunction with the transportation sector of tourism, the primary one of which is airport retailers. Generally, airport shopping is seen as being either landside (before security and exit formalities) or airside (located beyond security). Travelers and airport employees are able to use airside services, while travelers, employees, and non-flying visitors are typically able to shop in landside establishments. Railway stations provide convenience goods and limited souvenirs. Harbor shops at international ports typically offer souvenirs, clothing, jewelry, and duty-free items for export. Duty-free shops are located at major access points into and out of a country (e.g. borders, harbors, and airports). They typically offer high-quality merchandise at duty-free prices once a person has passed through exit inspections. In a few rare cases, inbound duty-free is allowed. Highway welcome centers are important stops for car-based travelers, offering a range of products from food and drinks to souvenirs and travel-related items (e.g. sunglasses, car adornments, seat cushions, luggage, etc.).

Several other specialized forms of retail cater to the shopping needs of visitors. In museums, it is not uncommon to find shops selling handicrafts and themed souvenirs as a way of supplementing their meager incomes from entrance fees. Similarly, in some well-known wine and whiskey regions, wineries and distilleries have incorporated specialized shops where visitors can sample the product, observe the production process, and make purchases. Special events and theme parks also provide visitors many opportunities to buy food, arts and crafts, and various agricultural products, usually depending on the primary focus of the event or place.

Several communities or villages have also developed as important tourist attractions owing primarily to their shopping appeal. Craft villages in many less-developed countries originated as artisan centers where craft items were made for functional purposes. As tourism grew, however, these communities became exposed to the needs and desires of tourists and shifted their focus to producing art works specifically for tourist consumption. While similar in style and function, tourist shopping villages are small communities, usually located in the developed world near larger towns, where original economic orientations (e.g. agriculture) have been altered to become centers of recreational and tourist shopping. Generally, these villages have more to offer than just retailing opportunities, such as natural sites or historic buildings, but shopping is typically the most important catalyst for their development efforts.

In most developing countries, street vendors provide the most ubiquitous opportunities for tourists to make purchases. They may be itinerant or stationary, but they are typically situated in urban areas where large numbers of tourists congregate or in rural areas adjacent to popular attractions. They generally sell a wide range of souvenirs or other goods and services of interest to tourists. Correspondingly, craft markets exist in many destinations and are appealing venues for most tourists to buy local (or imported) handicrafts.

Chapter 7

Management Issues for Places and People

Introduction

Even though tourists and other leisure consumers have a penchant for shopping, it should not be taken for granted that they will always be interested in every kind of shop, every product on offer, and every location where they congregate. As with all forms of retailing, certain principles apply to leisure and tourist shop management as well. Issues pertaining to store location, design, and merchandise are important elements in creating an atmosphere that appeals to tourists and provokes them to spend (Downs, 1970; Turner & Reisinger, 2001).

In a like manner, destination communities must consider shopping in their tourism planning exercises as a way of enhancing the broader retail landscape and community ambience, and retail managers must not ignore the need for high-quality staff, customer controls, and components of customer satisfaction. Based on this recognition of the importance of retailing management, this chapter takes on a supply-side perspective and highlights many of the primary elements of management from the perspective of tourism- and recreation-oriented shopping. Of particular interest are physical planning and merchandising, shopping destination planning, as well as effective management techniques for the people involved in tourist and leisure retailing to create positive images, increase customer satisfaction, and build patron loyalty.

Location, Location, Location

As the old adage goes, location is everything. It is worth bearing in mind, however, that 'a great location may not guarantee success, [but] a bad location will almost always guarantee failure' (Schroeder, 2002: 23). According to economic and retail geographers and retailing specialists, there are several principles that should guide the site selection process.

First, retail establishments must be located in areas with a large customer base. Depending on the size of the shopping center or individual store and the types of products being sold, a large enough population will need to exist within a reasonable commuting distance (Hathaway & Hughes, 2000; Jones & Simmons, 1987a, 1987b; Killick, 1998; Nelson, 1959; P. Jones, 1991; Salvaneschi, 1996). This is typically known as the shop's 'trade area'. For example, one of the most critical factors in the decision to build several major outlet centers on the Atlantic coast of Connecticut near Interstate Highway 95 was the fact that there was a population base of over ten million people within a two-hour driving radius (i.e. Boston, Providence, Hartford, and New York City). Likewise, in Pennsylvania, the site for Prime Outlets at Grove City was selected because it was located near two interstate highways and had over eight million people living within a 160 km radius (Hathaway & Hughes, 2000). However, population size alone should not determine level of demand for merchandise. Demographic factors, particularly those related to average income levels in the area, age distribution, gender, buying patterns, and ethnic composition, are important variables to consider in the decision-making process (Bearchell, 1975). A needs assessment may also be necessary to learn whether or not the people want or need a new retail establishment.

Pedestrian and vehicle accessibility is another vital consideration in location decision-making (Bearchell, 1975). Proximity to major roads, highways, or pedestrian malls is vital to the success of tourist retailing (Hathaway & Hughes, 2000; Killick, 1998). Most large-scale establishments (e.g. malls and outlet centers) are located near major roads and highways. Smaller shops (e.g. boutiques and specialty shops) are most typically located in urban areas near city streets and car parking. Another important consideration in terms of accessibility is public transportation. The availability of public transportation is important for customers and employees (Schroeder, 2002). The type and degree of public access may determine what position a particular store will hold in the retail hierarchy. For instance, 'destination store' is the title given to specific shops to which shoppers travel to purchase a certain item or items. Most major department stores are destination stores. 'Destination areas' are generally viewed as clusters of related groups of stores, such as jewelers, automobiles, or antiques. 'Traffic generators' are shops or groups of shops, usually in downtown areas, that draw foot and automobile traffic. 'Convenience centers' allow people to dash in to make quick purchases. 'Neighborhood centers' draw consumers from approximately a 3 km radius and can take on various forms from strip malls to shopping centers and individual stores. 'Community stores' generally draw from a 4–7 km area. These stores provide convenience goods and some lines of shopping products.

They are typically located near major roads and highways. 'Regional centers' draw people from longer distances, perhaps upwards of 30 km to a downtown area or major shopping center and are generally accessible by major expressways (Nelson, 1959; Barr & Broudy, 1986).

The local environment should also inform the location decision. This includes elements of the physical environment, including topography and climate, as well as human elements. Public utilities must be available and there should be an adequate buffer between residential and commercial zones (Barr & Broudy, 1986). Areas with high levels of safety and security (Schroeder, 2002), as well as clean surroundings are much more appealing for consumers and employees.

The local competitive retail environment is a major influence on decision-making. A competitor analysis can provide valuable information in understanding what types of similar establishments already exist, what their competitive advantages are, how well their business is succeeding, and what prices they are charging. This type of information can help shop-keepers become and stay competitive, avoid redundancy, and create complementary relationships with other retailers in the neighborhood. Gist (1971) highlighted an additional point. He suggested that, as part of the competitor analysis, managers need to examine how well different types of shops can co-exist in close proximity. In his words,

> certain types of retail operations can live in complete harmony with each other. Certain types of retail stores are antagonistic inasmuch as the presence of the one may actually restrict usage or patronage of the other. Good retail neighbors share their clientele . . . Poor retail neighbors have few, if any, customers in common. (Gist, 1971: 147)

Location analysts refer to a 'trade area' as being a major indicator of location choice in retailing. The term generally refers to the geographic region from which a shop draws its customers, although there are other interpretations as well (Gist, 1971). Trade areas are commonly delineated using vehicle license plate analyses, interviews, questionnaires, and credit card analyses. These approaches allow managers and planners to break trade areas down into general trade zones and smaller areas that encompass more specifically individual shops within larger retail clusters.

Several models have been developed over the years to explain the spatial tendencies of consumption. As noted in Chapter 1, one of the most widely recognized is that of Walter Christaller (1966), who theorized that people will shop at the nearest central place that supplies the item(s) needed, because longer journeys would increase the cost of the merchandise in monetary and temporal terms. As such, each central place is encircled by a complementary region (or hinterland) that is highly dependent on the shopping opportunities in the central place or town. He also noted that stores offering items requiring high levels of purchasing power will succeed only if there is a large market area within a reasonable proximity.

Trade areas may be quite different between utilitarian shopping establishments and those that have more of a tourism orientation. Christaller's model and the notions that most retail specialists put forward do not take into account souvenir shops, museum shops, and other tourism-related retail centers. The trade area of a gift shop in Paris near the Eiffel Tower, for instance, may not include local Parisians at all but instead may be comprised almost entirely of Japanese, North American, and other European visitors. In this case, then, the trade areas of tourist specialty shops can rarely be delineated in the traditional sense and must, therefore, be seen from a different perspective.

Likewise, advances in telecommunications and the Internet have changed the traditional notion of bounded trade areas. With the growth of online and mail-order shopping, trading areas have been expanded to include places far from the traditional spatial hierarchies suggested by retail location authorities. 'There is no need to conceive of the market areas of shopping centres as constituting rigid, discrete, contiguous zones. Consumers favour near rather than distant shopping centres, but the propensity of visiting the nearest centre is probabilistic not deterministic' (Clarke, 1996: 188). Similarly, human mobility and changes in urban structure in North America and, to a lesser extent, in the United Kingdom have brought about a re-locating of commercial businesses from the central business districts, or urban cores, to the outer edges of cities. This postmodern phenomenon has caused a rapid repositioning of shopping centers to the urban fringe along major freeways and adjacent to new suburban development (Garreau, 1991; Law, 1993; Ruston, 1999; Warnaby, 1998; Yeates, 1998). While many interest groups support this change, concerns have been raised that such transformations are causing dereliction in central cities and favors only the more mobile people in society. 'Access for the poor and the elderly [becomes] more difficult. If the new developments do indeed lead to shop closures within existing centres, then the non-car-owning sections of the community will be further disadvantaged' (P. Jones, 1991: 176). These issues must be kept at the fore in the planning and development of leisure-oriented shopping centers and in the choice of retail location.

Shopping Venue Design

The interior and exterior features of shops also may be arranged spatially to enhance the shopping experience, to stimulate the urge to spend within visitors, to assure satisfied customers, and to ensure energy and space efficiency. Shops should be designed functionally and alluringly and, as Broudy and Barr (1995) point out, in a way that augments the perceived value of the merchandise being sold. According to Barr and Broudy (1986), design is one of the most important aspects of retail management because the store itself is, in fact, a functioning selling tool, a promotional device to attract people to buy. The environmental ambience can add value to the shopping experience and the product image in the mind of the buyer.

Shopping is an experience in which people act out their innermost hopes, dreams, aspirations, and desires. A shopping excursion is a personal minidrama for the customer. The merchant is the playwright. The designer supplies the background with furnishings, lighting, spatial relationships, and form to create the mood for buying. (Barr & Broudy, 1986: 2)

Exterior

The exterior of a shop or mall can be an important selling tool through the proper use of lighting, signage, building materials, and windows. The exterior and how it is arranged can function to funnel shoppers into the store (Barr & Broudy, 1986). To do this, the exterior must be attractive, well-designed, and catchy but not overly flamboyant.

The main components of shop exterior planning include size, style, building materials, windows, lighting, signage, doorways and entryways, parking, and physical accessibility. Size, style, and building material may, in some cases, be dictated or regulated by municipal or mall construction codes and ordinances. Shopping malls, by their very size, can be an obstacle to some people shopping in them (Gershman, 1996). According to a study at West Edmonton Mall shortly after its completion, customers complained that it was too large and spread out to shop comfortably (Finn & Woolley-Fisher, 1988). Size selection should be determined by merchandise and customer needs. What is more important than size is how merchandise is arranged and stored (Matheusik, 2001).

Fashionable and tasteful store design can draw tourists and recreationists. Eccentric designs, colors, and construction materials, however, may repel them. Of lavish storefronts and windows, Schroeder (2002: 56) comments, 'most people judge a store's level of exclusivity from its exterior, and won't go inside to see whether the shop's merchandise actually happens to be within their price range'. In selecting materials to be used for storefronts, managers take into consideration issues like weather, neighborhood compatibility, cost, construction time, and ease or difficulty of maintenance

(Barr & Broudy, 1986). Decisions regarding structural items, such as awnings and canopies, which can protect window displays, doorways, and leisure shoppers from inclement weather are very important. The types and sizes of awnings may be restricted by code but, where allowed, they can carry the store's name and create visual harmony between adjacent shops (Diamond & Diamond, 1998).

Windows are an important part of the physical appearance of shops as well. They 'speak' to tourists and recreational shoppers about the goods for sale inside. 'Like a poster outside of a theater or movie house, [a window] gives a small preview of the attractions inside' (Barr & Broudy, 1986: 15).

Effective lighting may enhance windows, entryways, and fronts. If used skillfully and tastefully, it can beautify a store and draw attention to products of particular interest to various market segments (Bell & Turnus, 2001; Diamond & Diamond, 1998). Proper lighting might also assist in confidence building in consumers and staff, because of its potential to contribute to safety and security at entrances and car parks (Barr & Broudy, 1986).

Good signage can help attract customers, relay important messages, and promote recognition (Bell & Turnus, 2001; Diamond & Diamond, 1998). However, too much or of a slapdash quality, signage can detract from the mission of the establishment or the merchandise being sold. Outdoor signage is one of the first elements of physical design that a consumer sees and it is, therefore, as much advertising as identification. According to Barr and Broudy (1986: 138), it provides a way for small shops with small marketing budgets to increase visibility. In common with building style, signage limitations and allowances are often determined by zoning ordinances or by building developers. In the medieval town of Rothenburg-ob-der-Tauber, Germany, for example, stringent building codes restrict the use of signage by tourist retailing establishments to small, lackluster signs that are in accordance with the historic integrity of the town and its architecture. The sizes of signs, how they are hung, and their illumination are crucial considerations for retail managers. Signs are important information sources and, therefore, need to be large enough to be seen at a distance or illuminated sufficiently so that passers-by can see them (Hathaway & Hughes, 2000).

Doorways and entryways provide the welcoming transition from the outside environment to the indoors. While there are clear security concerns related to doorways, including the need for doors to keep some people out, they should provide an inviting and leisure-oriented atmosphere. Entryways are important in bad weather areas as they provide a windproof, weatherproof, and coldproof enclosure for visitors, and they can save considerable amounts of energy (Barr & Broudy, 1986).

It is crucial to provide as much parking as possible; most municipal zoning regulations establish the minimum requirements. If designed properly, parking lots can be an attractive part of the physical layout of the shopping center. Trees, grass, flowers, and shrubs add variety to the asphalt expanses and make the area cooler and greener. Proper lighting helps customers find their cars, see their way around, and feel safe and secure. Providing ample parking for people with disabilities also demonstrates that retailers appreciate, and are aware of, all groups of potential customers.

In many parts of the world, legislation assures the right of access for people with disabilities. The United States' 1992 Americans with Disabilities Act (ADA), for example, is extensive in its treatment of people with disabilities. It deals with many aspects of life, including employment, communications, recreation, and travel. The act states that 'no individual with a disability shall be excluded from participation in or be denied the benefits of services, programs or activities of a public entity or subjected to discrimination of any such entity' (West, 1991: 37). Public in this case refers to public use, not government ownership, which means that in the United States, all businesses, including retail establishments, must provide access to people with disabilities and assure that they have the same opportunities as everyone else.

Interior

The interiors of tourist and leisure retail establishments should possess a pleasant atmosphere that is conducive to browsing, buying, and socializing. It is important for interiors to be designed in a way that maximizes productivity. Once a customer walks through the doorway, the displays and shop layout can influence the course he or she takes through the store. Therefore, it is not prudent or in the store's best interest to 'create a layout that customers can scan quickly. Instead, you want to lead them from one fascinating area to another on a pleasurable voyage of discovery' (Schroeder, 2002: 58). Attractive shop interiors will result in longer stays in the store and, quite simply, as the notion of pleasure shopping suggests, the longer people stay in a store, the more money they will probably spend (Donovan *et al.*, 1994; Sherman *et al.*, 1997; Underhill, 1999). Thus, creating a comfortable and enjoyable indoor environment is fundamental in increasing sales, for 'the amount of time a shopper spends in a store depends on how comfortable and enjoyable the experience is' (Underhill, 1999: 33).

In the context of indoor museums and outdoor living museums, there are some layout patterns that can be useful in managing retailing. The first is controlling the flow of visitors to increase souvenir sales. When flows are directed so that tourists pass through or near the souvenir selling areas, they will be tempted to buy (Prentice, 1993). Second, in large outdoor museums or other tourist attractions, it may be helpful to cluster gift shops together and place them near other important services such as cafeterias, refreshment stands, and rest rooms. Finally, the position of souvenir/gift shops in relation to other services and areas can also influence tourists' buying behavior. Individuals may be more inclined to purchase larger items if the retail center is located adjacent to the exit gate rather than the entrance, as many people will be hesitant to purchase items they have to carry with them all day. This location will also provide visitors a last-chance opportunity to buy something on their way back to the car (Timothy & Boyd, 2003). Smaller items may be placed at various locations throughout the park or museum.

Retail layout involves careful apportionment of space among customers, personnel, and merchandise but, at the same time, it assures that separate spaces are available solely for the use of personnel and the storage of merchandise (Gist, 1971). Observers have long accepted that different types of retail establishments (e.g. groceries, shoes, toys, apparel, etc.) require different layout designs to meet the needs of staff and customers (Broudy & Barr, 1995; Gist, 1971; Schroeder, 2002).

Barr and Broudy (1986; Broudy & Barr, 1995) suggest several guiding principles in the physical layout of retail shops. The following is a selection of their principles that apply best in the tourism and leisure context:

- The interior environment should reflect targeted demographics.
- Store layouts should lead the customer around the selling floor so that all areas are shopped.
- Consider both built-in and movable elements for merchandise display.
- Signs should be integrated into the overall design concept.
- Provide seating where people accompanying the shopper can wait.
- High-turnover and high-profit items should be positioned for impulse buying.
- Shops need to have a bright and upbeat ambience.
- Displays should be configured so that they do not pose a hazard (e.g. avoid sharp corners, protruding objects, exposed electronic outlets, and breakable items).
- Appealing merchandise displays invite customer product examination.
- Provide seating and/or a dressing room for people interesting in purchasing shoes and clothing.
- Provide wide aisles for shopping carts and people confined to wheelchairs.

- Signs are important for offering directions, merchandise identification, and price.
- Be creative with signs.
- Provide automatic teller machines (ATMs) for quick cash.
- Good security systems can prevent shoplifting.
- Put more valuable items in showcases or behind counters, which requires the assistance of service personnel.
- Remember that lighting plays an important role in the nonverbal communication of the sales appeal of some items (e.g. jewelry).
- Create traffic patterns that pull customers to the rear of the store.
- Display units should be appropriately sized for ease of selection.

Interior lighting may be a useful tool in meeting sales objectives. It is one of the most important decorative items in the store. Lighting is 'as important an element in a store as it is in the theater. The quality of lighting can make or break merchandise' (Barr & Broudy, 1986: 80). Lighting fulfills the following purposes in the retail environment:

- It motivates shoppers to buy because an effective lighting setup heightens the sense of excitement. Effective lighting works with the floor layout and background materials to set the tone for the merchandise to attract consumers.
- It illuminates the merchandise so that it can be seen and sold.
- It helps direct customers to the goods for sale.
- It can be used to separate merchandise areas.
- It can help managers de-emphasize structural deficiencies, such as covering up unusual space problems.
- It can provide accurate color renditions to products and flatter customers by enhancing appearances.
- It helps shoppers and staff members feel comfortable and secure. Reduced glare lighting may reduce employee fatigue and allows shoppers to examine goods better.
- It helps break up the monotony of the retail setting (Barr & Broudy, 1986: 81–2).

Interior planning is also concerned with safety and security. The primary security concerns in retail businesses are the sales floor, delivery/merchandise storage area, the building, and money. On the sales floor, visual surveillance can be done via sales staff, security personnel at strategic locations, and video cameras. It can also be accomplished with physical hindrances such as check stations near dressing rooms, locks on fitting room doors, partitions between rooms, safes and vaults, baggage check areas, security buttons, and magnetic tags and shoplifting sensors (Schroeder, 2002). The delivery and merchandise storage areas are best protected by locking delivery areas and implementing electronic surveillance media. The building itself can be safeguarded with alarm systems, laser beams, bullet-proof glass, solid locks on front doors, and appropriate lighting. Finally, one of the primary concerns of merchants is currency protection. Plastic hoods around cash registers and cameras near cash areas are the best ways of preventing currency theft. Another is prohibiting the counting of money openly on the sales floor. Instead, a money-counting area should be included in the manager's office (Barr & Broudy, 1986). Other security measures can be taken to protect the shop after hours, including smoke detectors, fire alarms, and sprinkler systems (Schroeder, 2002).

The primary goal of indoor signage is to help persuade someone to buy a product by telling about it. Its second purpose is to direct shoppers where to go, what is for sale in the area, how to get to other areas, and what is for sale in other parts of the shop (Barr & Field, 1999; Bell & Turnus, 2001). Some marketing specialists refer to signs as 'shelf talkers', because they communicate prices, attributes, and sizes. These types of signs are more factual but there are also signs at the point of purchase that are 'almost conversational in tone, pointing out the virtues of a product and telling the customer something about where the item was made or about the craftsperson or tradition behind the product' (Schroeder, 2002: 70). A store's logo on a sign can provide brand recognition and assist in developing consumer loyalty.

Cleanliness is an important factor that is often excluded from discussions of retail management. Cleanliness and environmental aesthetics are important on the exterior and interior of shopping centers and stores (Page, 1995; Patricios, 1979; Turner & Reisinger, 2001). In fact, according to McIntosh *et al.* (1995), cleanliness is one of the most significant elements of the success of any shopping venue. The leisure shopping experience can be heightened by keeping facilities clean and tidy or ruined by unclean conditions. Clean rest rooms and sales floors, tidy merchandise displays, and orderly environments help create satisfied customers. In tourism communities, cleanliness of the outside environment is equally important.

> If the town is itself attractive and welcoming then visitors are likely to stay longer to enjoy the streets, shops, churches, and museums . . . By staying longer visitors will spend more, thereby bringing economic benefit to the town and its people, creating jobs, raising incomes and the general standard of living. (Parkin *et al.*, 1989: 109)

Merchandise Layout

Just as interior design can be a marketing mechanism, the way merchandise is exhibited can create a competitive advantage and stimulate interest in the products being sold. Displays should draw attention to the unique products being presented and, where appropriate, how they interrelate with other products and attractive settings. This is a result of what retailing specialists call visual merchandising, which may be defined as the use of space and merchandise to form convincing displays that reflect consumer buying habits and expectations (Diamond & Diamond, 1998; Hudson, 1974; Kollat & Willett, 1967; Walters, 1994).

Generally there are two basic ways of exhibiting merchandise: putting large numbers of the item out for self-service, or showcasing a few examples of each product with more in the stock room. Putting as much merchandise as possible on the sales floor can cut back on storage and customer service costs but it is not always the best way to organize all merchandise. Usually, the more expensive an item is, the fewer of them will be put out on the floor (Schroeder, 2002). In high-volume souvenir-type shops, the massing on the floor approach is commonly utilized.

The key to success is to create sales-stimulating merchandise displays. It is ultimately up to store-owners and managers to create displays and visual merchandising that appeal to their particular target markets in the leisure and tourism contexts but a few guidelines and recommendations can be made.

First, regardless of the fixtures managers use to display products (e.g. glass cases, shelves, tables, wall units, pedestals, etc.), the product must remain the principal focus. The display itself should not detract from the core product. The purpose of display items is to show the merchandise in an attractive manner and keep it clean and tidy (Schroeder, 2002: 68).

Second, coordinate the environment with the product's end use. The product layout should not be intimidating. It should establish a comfortable setting for customer investigation (Barr & Broudy, 1986). If the item(s) on display is electronic, power plugs and cords may be provided to allow customers to try out the product, and provide interactive merchandise where appropriate and useful.

Third, related to the previous recommendation is the creation of mini-environments or themes (Matheusik, 2001). These are important in creating a mood and demonstrating how items may be used as they were intended. For example, camping gear might best be displayed in a miniature wilderness area. Cowboy-related products may sell better if set together in a 'Wild West' setting. Many shops utilize furniture to demonstrate their products, creating settings that help buyers imagine how the products might look in their own homes (Schroeder, 2002: 66).

Fourth, perhaps the best counsel is to be creative. Mathèusik (2001: 83) recommends using displays that target the five senses where appropriate, including pieces that stimulate people's senses of vision (e.g. colors and decorations), touch (e.g. allowing shoppers to handle unique merchandise), sound (e.g. tranquil background music), smell, and taste (e.g. baked goods, cheeses, coffee, sauces, and jellies). Barr and Broudy (1986: 53–8) provide several tips on being creative:

- Breathe new life into tried-and-true display methods.
- Review catalogs to start generating refreshing ideas.
- Use eye-catching materials and lighting.
- Use mirrors and fabric.
- Catch the mood of the product and then project it.
- Avoid chaotic backgrounds.
- Assemble and organize merchandise in a sculptural manner using frames and three-dimensional settings.
- Imagine yourself to be the merchandise on display. Ask yourself how you would like to be shown off to your best advantage. Are you classic, elegant, conservative, or avant-garde?
- Set the tone. What mood should shoppers perceive when they walk into the display area? How can visual merchandising give the impression of a below-retail price establishment without talking down to customers?

Schroeder (2002) maintains the importance of avoiding boring layouts in souvenir and specialty shops and makes several design recommendations to assist in this effort. She suggests 'putting up partial partitions perpendicular to the walls forming small display alcoves, or setting up new walls extending out from the existing walls in a zigzag pattern. Freestanding displays can . . . break up a rectangle into smaller spaces that invite shoppers to explore' (Schroeder, 2002: 59).

Fifth, consider the spatial distribution of product types. The sales floor can be arranged into selling zones where similar products are grouped together to create a certain ambiance or level of efficiency. Apparel in a souvenir store (e.g. T-shirts, swimsuits, socks, hats, jackets, and shoes/sandals), for example, sells better when clustered together. Similarly, placing coffee mugs, shot glasses, and beer glasses in a single area can set a tone. Decisions must be made regarding which items can be put out on the floor or in open displays, and which will have to be placed behind lock and key. Generally the more expensive, delicate, and rare items are placed behind glass and can be accessed with the sales-clerk's assistance. Schroeder (2002) also recommends placing some items, such as add-on accessories, treats, or small new items near cash registers for impulse purchases.

Merchandising

The selection of products to sell will depend on many factors, including store location, market demand, profit goals, and merchandise planning. Specialty shops may focus on a fairly narrow range of products, while other leisure and tourism-oriented stores probably have a wider selection. Primary products, or major lines, are the items that best relate directly to the nature of the retail establishment where they are sold. Complementary goods, or minor lines, are goods that 'naturally fit into the customer's purchasing requirements when he[/she] is seeking a major product' (Bearchell, 1975: 107). These supporting articles provide significant additional income with minimal extra effort. For instance, a women's clothing store will probably also sell purses, belts, nylon stockings, and shoes or other accessories that would be desired at the time a dress or pant suit is purchased. In tourist gift shops, it is common to find various souvenirs (major products), as well as complementary goods (e.g. sweets, drinks, stamps, and telephone cards) that support the selling of the main merchandise. Matheusik (2001) uses the example of a ski-resort shop to suggest a similar pattern. He is correct in noting that, in addition to just ski and snowboard items, souvenirs, logo merchandise, and sporting goods, it would be good management to offer a mix of other items including gourmet coffee, specialty foods, and toys, just to name a few.

To achieve profitability and satisfied customers, there are several key issues that need to be considered in making merchandising decisions – all of which should be based on a solid understanding of customer needs, expectations, and desires. While these are multitudinous, six of the most crucial are discussed next.

Width and depth of merchandise

The width and depth of merchandise should be a response to consumer expectations of variety and choice. In most cases, considerable product variety will be necessary to establish a reputation among consumers and credibility in the field. There are some risks associated with merchandising decision-making. For example, even if a wide variety of goods is offered, if it does not meet the needs of consumers and is not relevant to the market, an inappropriate selection can result in alienated shoppers who fail to find what they need from what, at first, seems to be an extensive inventory. It may also result in a loss of confidence by customers who perceive a lack of understanding of the market and its characteristics (Walters, 1994: 45).

Pricing

Another important issue is pricing. Stable and competitive prices are important in attracting and retaining a solid clientele (McIntosh *et al.*, 1995; Turner & Reisinger, 2001). This is what customers expect and will most certainly affect their store selection and purchasing activities. Price is an integral part of merchandise planning because it can direct managers' understanding of sales activity in relation to price points and warehousing costs. Customers typically associate price with quality and sometimes exclusivity, which also needs to be in the forefront as pricing decisions are made (Walters, 1994: 45). Research by Kim and Shin (2001) showed that in the context of airport concessions, pricing was cited as one of the most critical factors of success in passenger satisfaction and retail profitability. Jansen-Verbeke (1987, 1990b) noted similar findings in urban core areas.

Desired profit margins lead most of the decision-making in pricing, although market demand must also play an important part. In most cases, the pricing standard is 100% markup between wholesale and retail (Schroeder, 2002). In high-demand tourist destinations, however, some shops practice a dual pricing system, where goods are priced higher for tourists than for local residents. Hobson (2000) suggested this (EU *versus* non-EU citizens) as a potential way for airport retailers in Europe to recover some of the income lost with the 1999 abolition of EU duty-free sales.

Branding

According to Walters (1994: 44), 'the role of both manufacturer and retailer brands in the customer's store selection and product purchasing decision have significant implications for profit planning'. It goes without saying that the role of brands in consumer decision-making is a crucial factor, for loyalty will cause shoppers to choose the shops that carry their favored brands. Among some groups of tourists (e.g. Japanese), brand is an extremely important consideration in shop and product selection (Foderaro, 1998; Jansen-Verbeke, 1994; Kim & Shin, 2001; Larke, 1994; Mintel International, 1996b; Turner & Reisinger, 2001).

Quality and exclusivity

Decisions on quality relate to customer perceptions of other merchandise characteristics, such as price. Superior quality products are nearly always costlier than lower quality items, owing to specialized labor and material, and they are expensive for the vendor to store and maintain. Consumers' perceptions of quality and expectations are positively correlated (Kim & Shin, 2001; Kinley *et al.*, 2003; Swanson & Horridge, 2002). Quality and exclusivity share a similar relationship because quality may be used to differentiate merchandise offers from those of competitors and, in so doing, to be seen as having a measure of exclusivity (Walters, 1994: 46). The quality of products can tell a great deal about the quality of the shop. High-quality and locally made handicrafts and souvenirs are generally better received among visitors than cheaper souvenirs manufactured abroad to represent the place being visited. The shopping tourists surveyed in Swanson's (1994) study overwhelmingly rated quality as having very high importance in their shopping decision-making. While high quality is important, there is also demand for cheaper and more tawdry items. However, it is important that the tourist offerings are appropriate to the destination and gift shop managers must take care not to allow the range and types of souvenirs to take away from the leisure experience or lessen the aesthetic value of the place (Orbaşli, 2000; Timothy & Boyd, 2003).

Like quality, exclusivity is a common influence in shoppers' decision-making process and may, therefore, be selected as a major element of a retailer's merchandise (Burns & Warren, 1995; Walters, 1994). Today's tourists are attracted more and more by what is sometimes termed 'specialty' retailing – products that are not found everywhere. These are generally not mass-produced but instead are carefully made by artisans (Pysarchik, 1989). Law (1993) suggests that specialty items may be described as luxuries because they are not essential for living. Included in this category are arts and crafts, designer clothes, books, perfumes, and some uncommon household objects. For both customers and merchants, exclusivity has cost repercussions. For retailers, the supply of specialty items is more expensive and so might be its storage, shipment, and packaging. Nonetheless, buyers who want exclusivity are generally willing to pay more and go further afield for it (Burns & Warren, 1995; Walters, 1994).

Availability

Availability is a basic principle of good retail management but, as Walters (1994: 46) notes, it is also an expensive facet of retailing. Assuring availability demands cost at all points in the distribution chain, including shipping, stockholding (i.e. storage and warehousing), distribution, and at the point of sale. Owing to the cost of assuring availability, most shopkeepers are selective and attempt to offer high levels of availability only for competitive reasons (Walters, 1994). Good customer service requires adequate supplies, particularly when specials are being offered. It is frustrating for customers to find an item they like only to be informed that it is out of stock (Heung & Cheng, 2000).

Suppliers

It is crucial today to know as much about retail suppliers as possible. Product quality is often dependent upon supplier behavior and connections with the manufacturer, and liability issues are now a major concern, for it is the seller who is liable for the quality of the products being sold. Level of exclusivity of product, availability, and reputation are three major variables that influence the decision of which supplier to use. Likewise, the number of suppliers will have to be selected and this may depend on the range and exclusivity of the product he or she is supplying.

Management and Planning Principles in Shopping Tourism Communities

While many of the same location issues described earlier are valid in the context of tourist-oriented retail stores, there are some additional recommendations and planning matters that should be addressed at the community level in shopping tourist destinations. As noted in Chapter 6, some small communities, particularly in rural and agricultural regions, have been re-oriented into thriving tourist shopping villages. According to Getz (1993b: 24–6), this usually occurs in one of three ways:

(1) Natural evolution: In this case, tourist-oriented services evolve naturally in response to gradual increases in demand for extant natural and/or heritage attractions. This does not entail any promotional intervention and no single business or individual dominates the tourism development scene. As tourism grows, however, local planning and environmental control measures usually become necessary to reduce the loss of cultural and natural amenities.

(2) Entrepreneur-driven development takes place when an individual or company purposefully leads the development initiative, which then provides a catalyst for others in the community to become involved. Conscious efforts are made to bring visitors to town to shop and enjoy local amenities. As this is an intentional effort, there is plenty of room for heritage and ecological conservation rules to be put into place as tourism develops. The risks of this approach include over-dominance by one or a few individuals and a potential sell-out to non-locals.

(3) The third form is purpose planned development. Within this framework, it is possible to develop a tourist shopping village where none existed before. However, it could also be done by targeting a village where heritage or natural attractions exist. A developer would need to invest in the necessary infrastructure and attractions once a site was selected. The danger in this approach is potential negative reactions

from local residents or loss of local control in the development and planning process.

Regardless of the type of tourism development that occurs in shopping destinations, good planning can help mitigate many of the problems and, at the same time, enhance the positive effects of shopping-based tourism. Discussions on ways to plan and develop tourism to benefit host communities and minimize the negative effects are now widespread and commonplace. Most observers agree that tourism development must be a participatory, collaborative, and incremental process that involves all possible stakeholders and results in grassroots control of tourism, resident involvement in the economic benefits of tourism, and an informed and confident destination community (Bramwell & Sharman, 1999; Hall, 2000; Jamal & Getz, 1995; Scheyvens, 2002; Timothy, 2002a; Timothy & Tosun, 2003; Tosun, 1999; Warnaby, 1998).

Community participation

As noted earlier, residents of tourist shopping communities must be involved in the planning, development, and management processes. Not only should they be involved but it is their right and responsibility to lead the development efforts. Community members should be afforded opportunities to learn about tourism, its benefits, and its consequences. In this way, they will be better prepared to make decisions and to be involved in preparing a local tourism strategy. Getz (1993b: 25–6) suggests several planning guidelines related to community participation that are essential in shopping destinations:

(1) implement an adaptable planning and control process that promotes community-based planning;
(2) undertake a cost–benefit analysis, using long-term sustainability instead of immediate profits, to measure net benefits;
(3) gradually assist local investment and development efforts;
(4) assess the needs of tourists and residents through attitude and behavior research;
(5) avoid large-scale and abrupt changes;
(6) avoid unilateral changes;
(7) plan service sector development to be in accordance with the nature, scale and character of the destination;
(8) address traffic congestion and other negative impacts ahead of time; and
(9) assure that cultural and ecological goals are not undermined when encouraging entrepreneurial activity.

As part of community participation, it is important to bear in mind that this means more than just participation and control of decision-making. It also entails providing opportunities for, and encouraging participation in, the financial benefits of tourism. Encouraging local residents to open shops and other leisure services or to become employed in tourism is crucial to the success of shopping destinations. While there may be a tendency for local retail establishments to be taken over by outside interests in the form of large corporations and foreign investors (Butler, 1980), it is important that local control remains at the core of the retail environment. Tourism planning for shopping areas should emphasize entrepreneurship and assist in finding ways to stimulate local investments. This approach will advance community support for tourism, in general, and decrease financial leakage from the local economy (Getz, 1993b: 23).

Clustering of shops and services

Perhaps the most widely recognized spatial planning principle in urban shopping is clustering (Getz, 1993b; Hall, 1994; Jansen-Verbeke, 1990b, 1991; Mok & Iverson, 2000). Clustering various shops, food services, leisure activities, and tourist attractions together contributes to the area's tourist appeal, keeps visitors longer, and generally results in higher shopping expenditures. Clustering might be done in a single shopping center or by linking various shops and businesses along a major thoroughfare. In large cities, this bunching together of shops and other leisure services is often done around central plazas, parks, and historic buildings and monuments. Getz *et al.* (1994: 14) rightfully argue that dispersed retail establishments in tourist destinations will have more difficulty attracting visitors to leave behind their cars and buses to walk between shops.

Heritage and shopping are good partners

Past research has found that shopping and heritage settings in both rural and urban contexts complement each other well and engender an attractive leisure environment (Blotevogel & Deilmann, 1989; Getz, 1993b; Jansen, 1989; Jansen-Verbeke, 1989, 1990a, 1990b; Law, 1993; Lew, 1988, 1989; Roberts, 1987; Terry, 1977). According to Jansen-Verbeke (1990b), it is the synergy between the two resources (shopping and heritage) that creates the ambience of tourism in most European and North American historic city centers. It is common to find clusters of shops near heritage attractions and in the case of museums, folk-life centers, and some old churches, shopping is available inside the attraction itself. From a sustainable planning and management perspective, however, it is important to assure that the stores, their frontages and signage, and the items for sale do not diminish the heritage value of the city, village, or rural area being visited.

Jansen-Verbeke (1991) argues that, in historic urban areas, pedestrian traffic should receive higher planning priority than vehicular traffic. A planning policy of this nature will enhance the historic ambience of the city and create an atmosphere that is more conducive to shopping. Many cities in Europe have begun implementing pedestrian-only zones in their historic centers since the 1970s. This requires zoning changes that prohibit vehicular traffic in specified areas and land-use planning to provide pedestrian malls.

Pedestrian malls are useful as visitor and traffic management tools because their aim is to reduce the impacts of vehicular traffic in important heritage and shopping districts (Slater, 1984; Timothy & Boyd, 2003). In most cases, merchants view pedestrian-only areas as good business. 'Pedestrianization streets have brought shopping into the leisure realm perhaps more than any other event' (Roberts, 1987: 87). Shopping and other leisure services (e.g. restaurants and entertainment) comprise nearly all of the commercial establishments of pedestrian malls, with shops specializing in shoes, books, bric-a-brac, organic foods, precious stones and jewelry, and music. Orbaşli (2000) notes that urban pedestrian zones should be well designed to provide optimum enjoyment and ease of access among shoppers and heritage tourists. Building façades, signage, street furniture, parks, landscaping, information kiosks, and shops may all contribute to visitors' enjoyment of the heritage-shopping zone (Timothy & Boyd, 2003).

Shopping can enhance urban renewal/gentrification

When leisure and tourism shopping are planned in conjunction with heritage tourism in historic cities, shopping may become a catalyst for re-development of derelict inner cities and historical resources (Ashworth, 2003; Ashworth & Tunbridge, 2000; Cohen, 1996; Whysall, 1995). Of this, Lew (1988: 124) stated:

> older retail districts are often places that have experienced serious decline in economic, social, and visual attractiveness over the years. Tourist-oriented development can be viewed as part of a community's search to find meaning and purpose for its older retail district, and for the local economy in general.

Leisure and tourist shopping (i.e. non-utilitarian) is commonly one of the primary tools used for urban regeneration. Leisure retail development can counteract the forces of suburbanization and bring consumers (tourists and residents) to the central city, particularly in conjunction with other activities and environments.

In both rural and urban environments, tourism/leisure shopping is among the best economic and infrastructural alternatives for declining industries. Many examples exist throughout the world where the functions of old factories, warehouses, harbors, barns, and grain silos are being reinvented and reused for retail outlets and their auxiliary services (e.g. inns, restaurants, bars) (Boulos, 1985; Chase & Pulver, 1983; Jansen-Verbeke, 1991; Kowinski, 1986; Silberberg *et al.*, 1976; Tiesdell *et al.*, 1996). Often as part of tourism-based urban renewal projects, heritage structures are utilized for tourist functions, including retailing. In Orbaşli's (2000: 161) view, this benefits historic quarters by

- restoring historic buildings;
- providing a living function of historic buildings that might otherwise sit empty or be demolished;
- decreasing the number of empty properties, providing a more desirable urban environment, which may lessen violence and crime connected to empty city centers and create more desirable places to live;
- eluding the environmental impacts of shopping being located in newly constructed buildings; and
- creating environments that will help historic towns retain the qualities that make them appealing.

Not unlike central cities, waterfront development has become a major catalyst for shopping tourism growth and leisure shopping over the past 20 years. Many of the world's largest and most fascinating tourist cities are situated on waterfronts owing to the importance of the water in providing energy, transportation, and agriculture at the time of settlement. As part of the wider effort to revitalize urban areas and renew former industrial resources for tourism (e.g. docks, shipyards, factories), many cities have begun upgrading their waterfronts into alluring recreation and tourism resources (Timothy & Boyd, 2003). Among the most famous examples are London, Cape Town, Wellington, Sydney, Liverpool, Toronto, and Baltimore (Brownill, 1994; Craig-Smith, 1995; Kieron, 1992; Page, 1996; Waitt & McGuirk, 1997; Wordon, 1996).

Waterfront development generally focuses on two related tourism attractions: heritage structures and shopping. The heritage element typically revolves around docklands, harbors, factories, and shipbuilding traditions, and the most common modern tourism elements include parks, walkways, museums, gardens, restaurants, snack bars, and shops. Most shops are leisure- and tourism-oriented and include, among others, souvenir shops, clothing stores, bookstores, liquor outlets, bakeries, and sweets shops.

Create an enjoyable leisure shopping environment

As noted in previous chapters and earlier in this chapter, one of the most important factors of success for shopping destinations is an enjoyable shopping environment (Donovan *et al.*, 1994; Heung & Cheng, 2000; Jansen-Verbeke, 1991). Johnson and Howard (1990) addressed this topic and suggested three approaches to creating a pleasant environment to attract shopping tourists. Their first approach is called ambient leisure, which refers to the creation of a pleasant environment for shopping through shopping center design and the spread of specialty shopping in historically unique areas. The second approach is to add various recreational attractions to shopping areas and malls in the way in which West Edmonton Mall and the Mall of America have done. Finally, in common with the previous discussion, they recommend combining heritage experiences with leisure shopping experiences, which will appeal to shoppers and sightseers.

Jansen-Verbeke (1991) presented several criteria for assessing leisure-shopping environments. According to her assessment, the elements of a pleasant shopping environment include a positive image, an attractive design, social affective value, availability during leisure time (e.g. weekends), hospitableness, and liveliness or animation with surprises. Others have suggested cleanliness, beautiful landscaping, special events, street entertainment, quality of food and non-food shops, safety, ethnic character of place, and attractiveness of shop fronts to be important factors (Getz, 1993b; Janiskee & Drews, 1998; Page, 1995; Warnaby, 1998).

Suitable access and parking

Just as important in the context of shops themselves, tourist shopping destinations should also provide plenty of parking and good access to major roadways and other transportation hubs (Jansen-Verbeke, 1991). Good tourism planning will not ignore this important feature of the leisure environment. Traffic and parking in many older and unplanned urban and village shopping areas are a serious problem that might result in negative environmental concerns and create serious problems with resident attitudes and relationships with visitors. In the shopping village of St Jacobs, Ontario, for example, while shopping tourism has created some 400 jobs, improved the local economy, stimulated village beautification projects, and helped restore historic buildings, it has resulted in vehicular and pedestrian traffic congestion, parking problems, litter, and disrespect for private property (Mitchell *et al.*, 1998). Directing the heaviest traffic away from the main shopping zones ought to be a clear priority. In villages, rural areas and town centers that receive considerable bus traffic in their shopping areas, special access and parking arrangements will usually be required (Getz, 1993b; Mitchell *et al.*, 1998).

Managing People in Tourist and Leisure Shopping

So far this chapter has emphasized the most prominent management issues related to the places associated with shopping. Equally important, however, are the principles and concerns affiliated with the people of tourist and leisure shopping, including store staff, other service providers, and the customers themselves. These will be examined from a retail management perspective in the sections that follow.

Personnel and other service providers

Retailing is one of the most labor-intensive and largest sectors of the service economy, employing millions of people throughout the world. Retailing is also one of the most important services involved in the tourism industry and millions of people are employed directly in the tourist and leisure shopping sector. One of the main keys to a successful tourist/leisure shopping business is high-quality employees who are committed to strict standards of customer service. Personnel can make or break a business.

Many authors have focused considerable attention on the staffing issues specifically in the context of recreation and tourism by drawing on the general human resource management body of knowledge (e.g. Edginton *et al.*, 2001; Middleton, 1994; Newman & Hodgetts, 1998). Most of the concerns of staff management in the service industries generally, and tourism in particular, are closely aligned with those in the retail sector. For example, all human resource managers face common issues in hiring, training, and retaining, regardless of whichever service sector they work in. Therefore, discussions of staff issues in tourism are plentiful in published textbooks and empirical studies and will not be addressed in depth here. Instead, this section aims to examine some of the matters that are most relevant to shopping service staff in the leisure and tourism context.

Retail establishments in leisure settings and at tourist destinations are primarily owned and operated by private sector interests. However, in some cases, such as national parks and historic sites, commercial centers may be operated by public agencies. Each form of ownership faces unique personnel problems. In the private sector, tourism-oriented establishments face the following human resource problems (Swarbrooke, 1995: 227):

- High employee turnover occurs in all areas of the service economy but seems to be particularly prevalent in the retail sector. This is generally viewed as a result of relatively low wages, the droning nature of sales-related employment, and long hours.

- A lack of career ladders creates few opportunities for the most diligent and highly motivated staff.
- Retail positions in tourism are time and energy intensive and employees are expected to be service oriented and in good spirits at all times. Finding personnel who can perform well in stressful retail work environments is difficult.
- All tourist destinations have some level of seasonal variation in demand. Seasonal changes mean that jobs in tourist and leisure retailing are temporary and uncertain. This may result in lower levels of commitment by staff members and restricts time available for training.
- Throughout the developed world, tourism and retail jobs have a comparatively poor status and, as previously mentioned, lower pay scales. This condition makes hiring and retaining trustworthy and assiduous staff a difficult challenge.

In the public sector, several problems can also be identified (Swarbrooke, 1995: 228):

- Opposed to the problem in the private sector, public sector retailing tends to have a low turnover rate. Stronger job security (in some cases) keeps many on staff far longer than they should be. Likewise, tight budgets and the resultant lack of opportunities to create new positions means that fewer people with fresh ideas and new experiences can be hired.
- Public-sector wages are usually fixed at various levels based on time served rather than on productivity.
- Recruitment procedures and disciplinary actions are standardized and not necessarily established with retail services in mind, which often results in their being inappropriate to the specific retail situation.
- Public-sector labor practices tend to be rather inflexible – a characteristic that is not always well-suited to operating in the leisure and tourism industries. For example, it is not uncommon for shops in popular destinations to be closed on Sundays and holidays, which is when many tourists and leisure consumers prefer to shop.

Maintaining high-quality staff is a crucial part of leisure retail management. Ensuring that new employees are well grounded in the organization and that they grasp clearly the nature and role of their jobs can help in this important task. Offering attractive incentives, such as financial rewards (e.g. bonuses and commissions), public recognition, and prizes, will go a long way in making the shop a better place to work. Periodical staff evaluations are vital, because they allow managers to monitor individual performance and tender awards or disciplinary actions when they are deserved (Timothy & Boyd, 2003). Providing positive feedback when deserved will also help retain valuable staff members. In some cases, particularly in small-scale shopping establishments, personnel may have to be trained in multiple tasks, such as merchandise ordering, stocking shelves, operating the cash register, answering telephones, providing information, and assisting customers with their purchasing decisions. Generally, in larger shops, there is a larger budget (and need) available to hire workers who specialize in certain facets of the operation.

On the rare occasion that there are volunteer workers on staff, it is important that they too are treated with respect and are valued on a par with paid employees. Most tourist and leisure shops do not utilize volunteer staff, although they are commonly found in museum and heritage-site gift shops. Recruiting volunteers is an important task, because their characteristics and behaviors may also contribute to the success or failure of a retail business. There is a common, but flawed, view among tourism managers that, because they cannot afford to be too choosy, no volunteer should be turned down. However, according to Jago and Deery (2001: 205), this erroneous notion can be very detrimental to the institution. In their words, this perception 'greatly increases the likelihood of taking on volunteers who are totally unsuitable for the organisation and the tasks at hand'. Putting volunteers through the same rigorous hiring process as paid staff is important because it will allow managers to weed out those who may pose a real threat to the success of the business. According to Jago and Deery, like bad paid staff, bad volunteers can ruin a business. Likewise, each volunteer is different. Many may be highly talented in retail work with existing knowledge and skills, while others may have to undergo intensive training to become effective workers.

Whether a person works in a volunteer or paid, private or public capacity, good personality, creativity, a cheerful disposition, a keen sense of service, good communications skills, diligent work habits, knowledge of the merchandise for sale, and knowledge of the importance of the tourist resources in the area where the shop is located are characteristics of good-quality retail personnel (Newman & Hodgetts, 1998; Swanson, 1994; Timothy & Boyd, 2003).

There is a tendency among shopkeepers and their employees in many tourist destinations to take advantage of tourists by being dishonest and misleading in their sales techniques and in the products they sell. Very often false information is offered in order to sell a product, goods are sold with pieces missing, shopkeepers refuse to exchange damaged goods, inferior quality is offered as superior quality, or fake items are sold as originals (Hoare, 1998; McIntosh *et al.*, 1995). Many retailers feel they can get away with this form of manipulation because tourists are only in town temporarily and are not inclined to return to the destination to sort out the problem. This has reached problematic levels in some places and empirical research shows that it has become a major irritation among tourists, resulting in a tarnished destination image. In a study of Hong Kong shopping, Heung and Cheng (2000) found this to be one of the most crucial factors in creating negative experiences among visitors.

Similarly, there is some argument that Korean inbound tour operators in Australia are taking advantage of Korean tourists by replacing valuable sightseeing time and famous attractions with too much shopping. It is not atypical for operators to take their tourists to shopping centers more than twice a day, while ignoring interesting attractions, as a way of earning commissions from retailers. For many Korean tourists, this is seen as excessive and ruins the travel experience. In fact, recent research shows that the excessive efforts by operators to get their clients to buy has resulted in shopping being rated among the lowest (39th out of 43) preferred activities undertaken in Australia by Koreans who travel via a Korean inbound operator (Ko, 1999: 74). This problem is compounded further because Korean shopping centers in Australia generally pay a higher rate of commission compared to other shopping centers. So, Korean tourists are usually taken to the shops that pay the highest fees, neglecting other stores that might offer merchandise of interest to the travelers (Ko, 1999: 76).

> The need for Korean inbound operators to maximise their potential revenue from the tours, means that all too often Korean tourists are being taken through a never ending series of shops as part of their tour. Although they came to see Australia, the comment by one Korean tourist was that, 'all we saw was the inside of every Korean shop in Sydney and on the Gold Cost'. (Hobson, 1996: 241)

Ultimately, Hobson (1996: 242) believes this practice will hurt Korean tourism to Australia, because it is not in the best interest of the tourist.

According to a study by Mak *et al.* (1999), many Taiwanese tourists who visit Hong Kong are put off by the city's high prices, low service quality, and most importantly for this discussion, the dishonesty of shopkeepers. This led many study participants to evaluate their Hong Kong experience negatively. While this is clearly the exception rather than the rule in Hong Kong, the issue has received considerable media attention in recent years (Ko, 1999; Tanzer & Tucker, 1996), leading Mak *et al.* (1999: 196) to warn that a bad word-of-mouth reputation on this matter will 'adversely affect Hong Kong's image of a shopper's paradise'.

These unethical approaches should be strongly discouraged by retail managers and employees must be trained not to utilize these devices to win sales. Not only does this hurt the individual business, it may also damage the entire destination. For this reason, McIntosh *et al.* (1995) argue that shopkeepers who employ these fraudulent tactics should be prosecuted to the full extent of the law.

As noted in Chapter 6, street and market vendors are one of the most omnipresent retailers in tourist destinations throughout the world. As the hawkers are part of the tourist experience, many tourists view them as entertaining and bringing character to destinations. By the same token, however, most tourists see them as a nuisance with their persistent calling and invitations to browse through their merchandise (de Albuquerque & McElroy, 2001). Tactics utilized by street-sellers and vendors can be broken into two styles. The first is a passive approach wherein traders wait until tourists approach them. They usually offer a greeting, such as 'good morning' or remain silent until the tourist begins a conversation. The second method is active or aggressive, where the seller yells to the tourists to attract their attention and may even try to coerce them to buy something (Connelly-Kirch, 1982: 394). Connelly-Kirch found the first approach to be the most common in Tonga, owing to many sellers' difficulties in conversing in English and because being passive is considered the most respectful strategy.

The second method is usually viewed by tourists as bothersome or even harassment, although this may be culturally conditioned. When people are not used to this form of loud and sometimes overbearing behavior, misinterpretations ensue. Insistent hawkers calling out loudly to potential customers is a normal part of everyday life in the Caribbean but, for first-time visitors, it might be viewed as persecution or at the very least a nuisance. Repeat visitors tend not to be as bothered by it (de Albuquerque & McElroy, 2001), although some forms of harassment include actual verbal and physical abuse which can occur at any time to any visitor. Table 7.1 shows the various types of harassment reported by tourists in Barbados and the percentage of tourists reporting them. Data from exit surveys in the Caribbean show that one of the most frequently identified negative experience for tourists on many of the islands is harassment by craft vendors. In Barbados, for instance, harassment on the beaches and in the streets consistently tops the list of what visitors liked least about their trip. Similar problems exist in Jamaica (Deveny, 1998). In Barbados, over half of North Americans and Europeans report experiencing some degree of harassment. Nearly 70% of British visitors report undergoing higher levels of

Table 7.1 Types of harassment against tourists in Barbados

Type of harassment	Average % of non-Caribbean vsitors reporting this form of harassment	Percentage of non-Caribbean visitors reporting not having experienced this form of harassment
Persistence of vendors	78	18
Peddling drugs	28	68
Verbal abuse	14	82
Sexual abuse	9	87
Physical abuse	2	92

Source: Adapted from de Albuquerque and McElroy (2001)

harassment, which is probably a result of the fact that they stay a week longer on average than North Americans and, therefore, have more exposure to harassment. Visitors from other Caribbean islands report the least degree of harassment, because they tend to blend in more and the vendors often mistake them for locals (de Albuquerque & McElroy, 2001: 480).

Official responses to this problem have been quite intense. In 1998 in Jamaica, harassment of cruise passengers became so severe in places like Ocho Rios and Montego Bay that plain-clothes police officers and military soldiers were deployed to patrol tourist zones (Deveny, 1998). That same year, in an effort to keep tourists happy and quell bad publicity, the government raised fines for peddlars by more than six times for 'aggressive selling' to US$500 and plans were being made to raise the penalty to US$2800 the following year (Clark, 1998). In Barbados, beach wardens and police have been positioned at places where tourists typically assemble. Additionally, vendors have been restricted to booths and portable kiosks and unlicensed vendors have been threatened with arrest. De Albuquerque and McElroy (2001) tell of one case where a major cruise company threatened to cancel its stops in Grenada owing to incessant harassment of its passengers.

In some countries, vendor nuisance has become so severe that governments have begun to criminalize it. In 1995, proposed legislation in Barbados started the process of defining tourist harassment by aiming to create three new legal offences: annoying, threatening, and harassing. Huge fines were endorsed for annoying and harassing (US$1250) and for threatening (US$2500). Jail terms of between two and three years were proposed. Public outcry and political influence brought about a revoking of the new legislation, in favor of milder penalties and clearer definitions of annoying, harassing, and threatening (de Abuquerque & McElroy, 2001). The position of the tourists and government leaders is clear, but what of the vendors' perspective? Many vendors, taxi-drivers, hair-braiders, and beach masseurs hardly consider their persistence as harassment. To make a sale, one must be assertive and, furthermore, the normative culture of sales in the Caribbean includes calling out to potential customers, praising the caliber of one's product, and following prospective buyers if necessary. Secondly, shouting sales pitches on the street is not an annoyance, because streets in the Caribbean have always been a regular place to buy and sell various products. Likewise, beaches are public space and they have every right to be there. Hawkers also have difficulty understanding why they cannot earn a little money from the 'wealthy tourists'. After all, tourists think nothing of paying ridiculous prices for food and drinks at their hotels – surely they could afford an inexpensive T-shirt, a souvenir, or a massage. Vendors are usually very polite to tourists, starting a conversation with 'greetings' or 'good morning, sir'. But, when they are ignored or waved away, the tourists are the rude ones, so vendors sometimes amplify their sales efforts. Much of this is based on cultural differences, because in Europe and North America, people do not usually respond to greetings or approaches by unfamiliar persons in public. On the islands, however, people are much more sociable in public arenas. Finally, vendors often see legislators as bullies who stoop to pressure from foreign-owned tourism companies and try to take away their livelihoods and treat them as criminals (de Albuquerque & McElroy, 2001: 488–9).

Managing tourist and leisure shoppers

From a destination perspective, visitor management models and practices tend to focus on ways to reduce the negative physical impacts of overcrowding, raise interest and awareness among visitors of a place's eco-logical or heritage value, and educate visitors on appropriate behavior (Moscardo, 1999; Shackley, 1998). From the retailing literature and from the perspective of individual shops, the majority of writing focuses on various ways to get people to spend (Broudy & Barr, 1995; Schroeder, 2002; Walters, 1994). These are briefly examined in this section in the context of tourist and leisure shopping.

As previously noted, using interior design mechanisms and structural layouts in shops can guide customers through the store past merchandise that might pique their interest. When consumers are directed so they pass near certain items, they will be tempted to buy and many will make unex-pected purchases. It is also important to implement design mechanisms, such as multiple cashier stations and more than one entry and exit portal, to ease congestion during peak hours. Overcrowding in shopping centers and individual stores results in cranky customers and unpleasant shopping experiences. It also provides shoplifters with more opportunities to steal.

At the level of community or destination, it is important that tourism officials remember the notion of carrying capacity, which is simply a threshold that, when exceeded, something negative begins to occur. While determining carrying capacity is not an exact science, and indeed capacity varies from one location to another, crowd management is an important consideration in tourism planning in shopping destinations. Large crowds have a tendency to diminish the leisure nature of shopping, so it is important for planners and managers to understand the goals of sustainable tourism management, which are, in the shopping context, to maximize consumers' appreciation and enjoyment of the experience while minimizing the harmful effects that large crowds can cause (e.g. ecological damage, antagonism between residents and tourists, negative cultural change, etc.). While masses of tourists can bring about negative impacts, it is important to remember that too many shops and the wrong kinds of shops can also become excessive and contribute to an uninviting tourist environment.

Vehicular traffic congestion in urban shopping areas can be reduced by steering vehicles in a pattern that avoids town centers and areas of high heritage value. Enacting and enforcing lower speed limits, creating efficient and user-friendly urban transportation systems, and forming park-and-ride programs and facilities outside the urban core, can soothe the situation (Page, 1992).

While methods of getting people to spend and taking into account carrying capacity issues are important components of managing shoppers, perhaps the most important management practice is creating satisfied customers through quality customer service. Satisfied customers will become repeat customers and they will spread positive feedback to other potential customers at home.

Customer service

Customer service is viewed here as a combination of customer and personnel management. In common with the lodging and catering sectors of tourism, quality customer service is central to success in retailing. This is even more the case for shopping than for tourist attractions, because people will always desire to visit famous attractions and destinations but, once there, they will have the option of selecting alternative lodging or a food service establishment that provides them with the best service. In Schroeder's (2002: 204) words, stores that offer service beyond the usual and expected show an eagerness to please customers that sets them apart from the crowd. A unique service will also be something customers will talk about, and that positive word of mouth is worth more than any paid advertising.

The four most important factors that lead leisure and tourist shoppers to select a particular store and which improves their satisfaction levels are: reasonable prices and good values; high-quality and wide-ranging merchandise; location; and high levels of customer service (Department of the Arts, Sport, the Environment, Tourism and Territories, 1988; Haigh, 1994). As good value, merchandising, and location have already been addressed, customer service is the focus of the remainder of this chapter. The following sections discuss several ways of catering to the needs of consumers that will enhance the value of customer service in shops and shopping destinations (Kim & Shin, 2001). First and foremost, however, is understanding the customers and their likes, dislikes, desires, and cultural backgrounds (Whysell, 1989).

Provide customer comforts

Whether customers spend all day shopping or whether it is a matter of minutes, providing basic comforts is essential to the success of retail establishments. A common condition among people who shop for long, continuous periods of time is 'shopping fatigue'. This term is known also as 'museum fatigue', which according to Schouten (1995b: 260), is when people begin to feel exhausted, their heads begin to swim, and their feet become sore and tired when they have spent a lot of time on their feet at a tourist attraction. As a result of this condition, the longer people are in a museum or, in this case, a mall or individual store, the faster they move toward the exit; or the longer they stay in the shop, the less attention they pay to the merchandise. If the shopper does not experience shopping fatigue, it is likely that someone in the same party will. Providing places for shoppers and their associates to sit down and rest will ease some of the symptoms of shopping fatigue. Likewise, providing cool water to drink or warm beverages in cold weather can go a long way in winning the loyalty of consumers (Lichfield, 1990; Schroeder, 2002).

Public access to bathrooms is another important ingredient in providing customer comforts. All too often, for various reasons (worries about crowds, cleaning responsibilities, etc.) retail establishments close access to their toilets. While this may appear to be a sound management decision, it rarely is, except in extraordinary circumstances, because it will have a tendency to turn people off by promoting a 'you're not worthy of our commode' attitude. Having a rest room available to customers when the store just down the street does not may, in combination with price and products, mean the difference between winning or losing a sale.

Areas specifically devoted to children may also be an important offering for potential customers who are traveling with kids. Playgrounds or entertainment areas for children while parents shop is a popular feature of some large malls and shopping centers. This type of service allows parents to concentrate on buying items or to stroll along at a leisurely pace. Bathrooms with changing tables or nursing lounges are also an important design issue that demonstrates to shoppers that they are wanted. These services are especially important in places such as malls and other large shopping centers, where shopping may take hours or an entire day.

Additionally, Schroeder (2002: 203) advises shop managers to look at the store from the perspective of someone who might have trouble getting around. The store should be compatible with consumers who are elderly or who have physical disabilities: (1) aisles must be wide enough for wheelchair, walker, and stroller traffic; (2) signage needs to be large enough to be readable by people with visual problems; (3) unnecessary steps should be eliminated; and (4) baskets or carts should be provided for customers to carry their selections.

Staff interaction with customers

As part of personnel training and management, it is essential to emphasize courteous behavior, good use of language, and knowledge about the store and its products. Good communications skills are necessary to get along well with customers. A warm welcome can set a relaxing mood and being offered assistance without being too aggressive is generally welcomed by shoppers. Swanson's (1994) study found that one of the most important service quality items was salespeople who allow customers to browse, knowledgeable staff, and friendly salespeople who initiate pleasant conversations. In addition, good telephone manners and a pleasant personality are essential (Schroeder, 2002).

Special services

Offering special services can be an effective tool in creating a competitive advantage in leisure shopping environments. Schroeder (2002) lists several types of services that stores can offer to tourists and recreational shoppers. These include but are certainly not limited to the following services:

• antique appraisals,
• cleaning and repairs,
• book signings by authors,

- hands-on craft demonstrations,
- cooking classes or food sampling,
- giving small gifts with larger purchases,
- free recipe cards,
- gift wrapping,
- personalization or custom orders,
- senior and child discounts,
- matching prices with competitors,
- tourist information,
- shipping services to tourists' home countries or regions, and
- free refreshments.

Managing retail for foreign visitors

With increased globalization and higher levels of international travel, it is important for retail managers everywhere to accommodate the needs of foreign visitors. Such efforts show international tourists that their patronage is valued and demonstrates the commitment of the retail establishment to diversify its market base. This will result in increased sales by making an impression on current shoppers, which will lead to satisfied customers and positive feedback at home. It can also result in a repeat clientele if tour operators realize that a good shopping experience can reflect well on them too.

The most common ways of catering to the needs of international visitors include using the language(s) of the primary markets, providing currency conversion services, and being sensitive to the specific cultural norms and customs of foreign visitors. This will, of course, require at least some level of research and training to understand who the primary markets are and their tastes and expectations.

Foreign languages: Foreign languages can be used in the retail situation in at least three ways. The first is staff's speaking proficiency. Managers need to be aware of the native languages spoken by a shop's largest market segments. Sawgrass Mills Mall in Florida is one of the largest shopping centers in the United States and is especially popular among visitors from Central and South America. Many people from Brazil, Mexico, Argentina, Chile, and other Latin American countries visit this mall each year, sometimes in conjunction with a visit to Disney World. Sawgrass has seen considerable success owing to its careful treatment of Latino shoppers. Each week dozens of busloads of Spanish- and Portuguese-speaking tourists arrive, spending upwards of US$300 per person per visit. Visitors are greeted by tri-lingual hosts, who hand out complementary shopping bags. Such efforts, according to management, makes these international

Table 7.2 Did language problems prevent a purchase?

	Country of residence		
	Japan	Other Asia	Continental Europe
Yes	38.6%	8.9%	18.2%
No	60.4%	90.1%	79.6%
Don't know	1.0%	1.0%	2.2%

Source: Bureau of Tourism Research (1990)

visitors feel particularly welcome, which results in higher levels of spending (International Council of Shopping Centers, 2000; Painton, 1994). The second use of foreign languages is signage. Bi-lingual signs can help direct foreign visitors to special items that they might appreciate, can assist in managing crowds, and are useful marketing tools, especially when special deals are being offered.

Conversely, not being able to cater to the linguistic needs of foreign visitors can create problems and result in loss of sales. For instance, according to a study by the Bureau of Tourism Research (1990) of Australia, this is a major problem in that country (Table 7.2). When asked if the language problem prevented the purchase of a gift or souvenir during their stay in Australia, 39% of tourists from Japan said that it did. Likewise, over 18% of the visitors from Continental Europe had the same experience. Overall, some 11% of all visitors to Australia said that language problems prevented their purchase of a gift item. Understandably, most visitors to Australia from New Zealand and North America did not find language a major issue. However, given the large size of the Japanese, European, and Korean tourist markets in Australia, the number of shops that missed out on sales to visitors because of language constraints is high.

Providing foreign currency exchange: One competitive advantage that can easily be adopted by retail managers is foreign currency exchange or accepting foreign currency in lieu of local money. It is not uncommon for visitors to run out of local currency while shopping – a situation that can obviously curtail their spending. Providing money exchange counters in large shopping centers or complexes, or individual shops being willing to accept foreign currency will be seen as going the extra mile in their efforts to cater to the needs of tourists. Many visitors, as in the case of Sawgrass Mills Mall and several other malls throughout North America, arrive directly from the plane with their backpacks and luggage, ready to shop. Sawgrass provides a currency exchange booth by its main entrances, where visitors can exchange Mexican pesos, Brazilian reals, and several other currencies (Elliot, 2001; Painton, 1994). Many shops on both sides of the US–Canada and US–Mexico borders have found success in accepting the currencies of visitors from across the divide.

Catering to specific cultural norms. Culture is something learned and every society has different cultural norms. Collective social behaviors and traditions dictate what appropriate or inappropriate behavior is. Cultural differences are most notable in the tourism setting when people of the destination encounter visitors from abroad. This situation often results in difficulties in communication and providing adequate services to foreign visitors. It is incumbent on shop managers to understand and teach their employees about various cultural differences and how these affect expectations, desires and behaviors among visitors (Alexander, 1997).

Because the Japanese are one of the most ubiquitous tourist groups in the world and have especially well-developed and well-known cultural norms that affect their shopping preferences and behaviors (see Chapter 4), it is vital that store managers, owners, and sales clerks at major shopping destinations understand the unique cultural and socioeconomic reasons that drive Japanese tourists' shopping activities and treat potential shoppers as they expect to be treated (Larke, 1994). One outlet center near New York City, which attracts thousands of Japanese tourists each year, regularly holds workshops for employees to provide tips on how best to serve Japanese customers. They are taught specific cultural behaviors like bowing, that it is wrong to approach the shopper aggressively, and to place change on a tray rather than in the customer's hand. The center also has at least one Japanese-speaking employee and distributes size-conversion charts in Japanese, as well as a list of stores that carry clothes small enough for Japanese women (Foderaro, 1998: 4). Likewise, BAA has found success in catering to its foreign travelers by monitoring traffic flows at various times of the day. For instance, knowing that typical Japanese travelers prefer to buy whisky as a present, whereas Chinese travelers typically prefer brandy, would contribute a great deal to customer satisfaction. Knowing when flights to Japan or China are leaving means that in-store product displays can be changed, staff with specific language skills can be scheduled to work, and foreign language signs can be replaced (Hobson, 2000: 176). The following are retail- and culture-related issues that tourist shop managers and staff need to consider when dealing with the high-spending and fastidious Japanese visitor (Rob Tonge & Associates, 1995).

- In most cases, imported products are not well appreciated by Japanese consumers because they are not considered good-quality souvenirs. Managers and staff need to understand the meaning of *omiyage* and make every effort to stock 'genuine' souvenirs for their Japanese shoppers (Nishiyama, 1996).

- Status is very important in Japanese society. Rank, face, and status are engrained in all facets of daily life, which results in high levels of respect and humility. Likewise, using correct titles is of paramount importance (Nishiyama, 1996; Rob Tonge & Associates, 1995).
- In Japan, the old truism, 'the customer is king' is taken very seriously in the retail setting. The Japanese are a very service-oriented society, where courtesy and politeness reign (Rob Tonge & Associates, 1995). Service orientation is an important element in the retail sector of Japan and sales people must be polite in speech and behavior. Japanese sales staff members are trained to be extraordinarily courteous and sensitive to the needs of shoppers. Proper greetings are also important in the Japanese retail setting (Larke, 1994). Nishiyama (1996) recommends that shop employees should have an 'attitude of gratitude' toward shoppers, because it is only natural that they should expect high levels of service quality outside Japan as well (Rob Tonge & Associates, 1995).
- Japanese shoppers are keen on special services, such as gift wrapping and post-sales service. Also, according to Nishiyama (1996), shopkeepers should be ready and willing to adopt a flexible pricing policy, because Japanese shoppers are attracted to special deals for special people. These extra amenities will make Japanese visitors feel more at home and, as a result, they will probably be more willing to spend and return. The Japanese are especially fond of outward appearances (*teisai*), so gift wrapping should be done in a decorative and fancy yet tasteful way. According to Nishiyama, it is not uncommon for the packaging of gift items in Japan to be more expensive than the item itself.
- Most Japanese shoppers abroad would also appreciate having the store clerk show them the price equivalent of what they are purchasing in Japanese yen. Retail personnel should be trained to know how to calculate local prices into yen, so that shoppers can see and understand better how much they are paying (Nishiyama, 1996). Some shops have found success in marking prices in both local currency and its equivalent in Japanese yen (Hobson & Christensen, 2001).

Summary

Good location in relation to other services, transportation routes, and attractions is vital to the success of leisure and tourist retailing. Additionally, venue design and physical elements of design, style, color, and layout can create aesthetically pleasing environments that encourage browsing, impulse buying, and other forms of purchasing. As well, the width and depth of merchandise, pricing, branding, quality and exclusivity, and product availability have been shown to contribute to a leisure-oriented retail environment that keeps people longer and encourages them to spend.

In addition to the physical layout and design of shopping establishments, several planning principles and paradigms exist at the destination community level that are important in the successful development of shopping tourism. These include community participation in retail endeavors and decision-making, prime physical locations and clustering of shops, pleasant community environments, and partnerships between shopping and heritage, or other forms of tourism. Such efforts and approaches are useful tools for renewing declining and derelict urban centers.

Finally, from the people perspective, high-quality and knowledgeable sales personnel are an important asset in any retail establishment; the research shows that this is especially important in the leisure context, as sales people can make or break the recreational experience. Shoppers themselves can also be managed in ways that encourage them to browse and buy and have the least negative impacts on the retail venue. Customer service is perhaps the most important part of retail service provision and can be done best by offering customer comforts, special services, and high-quality staff interactions. If a retail establishment hopes to draw foreign tourists, several provisions will have to be made: foreign language staff and signage, accepting foreign currencies or providing money exchange services, offering merchandise that appeals to specific groups of people, and being sensitive to foreign cultures and shopping expectations will go a long way in securing foreign patronage.

Chapter 8

Conclusion

As noted in the introductory chapter, shopping is a complex phenomenon that is laden with sociocultural, political, economic, and spatial meaning. While several observers have written about shopping as a generic form of modern-day mass consumption, with the exception of marketing and retail specialists, few scholars have made shopping a serious area of study. Furthermore, it is only in the past 20 years or so that it has been picked up as a topic of considerable scholarship in the context of leisure and tourism, although the leisure side of shopping has received more attention in the literature than the tourism-specific relationships.

Inharmoniously with traditional views, sociologists and consumer psychologists have, in the past 25 years or so, begun to debunk the notion of shopping as a simple, rational, and set process consumers proceed through to make logical purchasing decisions. The recent acknowledgement of non-utilitarian forms of shopping (e.g. leisure and tourism) is a direct indication of this paradigmatic shift. With recent trends in modernization and technological growth, people have begun to view shopping from new perspectives. To this end, in the developed world at least, shopping has become more of a leisure, or hedonic, pursuit than a functional need, even in the context of buying groceries and household products. In the tourism setting, shopping takes on even a deeper hedonic role as the number one activity common to almost all categories of tourism and all types of destinations. Kowinski's (1985) famous volume, *The Malling of America*, describes the development of the shopping mall phenomenon in North America as a direct result of shopping's leisure function in a modern consumer society. The malling of America has now spread to become the 'malling of the world, for, in the past decade, consumerism and materialism have touched the far reaches of the earth, resulting in the proliferation of shopping malls and outlet centers everywhere, including the developing world (Erkip, 2003; *Far Eastern Economic Review*, 2003; Fiorenza, 1994; Li *et al.*, 2003; Lin, 2002; Wasserman, 1996).

Even though an increasing number of researchers have started conducting basic research on the demographics and motivations of tourist and leisure shopping, there are still many things in the realm of social relationships, economics, and culture we do not understand about recreational and tourist shoppers (Miller *et al.*, 1998). Some of these are highlighted here.

Shopping traditionally has been seen as a female activity, stemming from the customary role of women, as housewives, in purchasing groceries, clothing, and other household items, as well as the elitist, gendered space of shopping centers associated with the upper class 'ladies' of the late 19th and early 20th centuries (Rappaport, 2000). As a result, general research on shopping from a gendered perspective has heretofore focused almost solely on the role of women in purchase decision-making, the social meaning of shopping in their lives, and their stereotyped predispositions to shop (Campbell, 1997; Fischer & Gainer, 1991; Kowaleski-Wallace, 1997; Moore, 1991; Nava, 1997; Reeves, 1996; Stone, 1954; Terry, 1977; Underhill, 1999). According to most observers, men detest it but women love it. The leisure literature related to gender and shopping deals primarily with gendered spaces in malls and the effects of familial and friendship relations on the shopping experience. In the ambit of tourism, most research conducted until now focuses on women as buyers of souvenirs (Anderson & Littrell, 1995, 1996; Jansen-Verbeke, 1987) and producers and sellers of handicrafts for tourist consumption (Cone, 1995; Connelly-Kirch, 1982; Swain, 1993; Wagner, 1982).

Several areas touching on the gendered dynamics of leisure and tourist shopping have yet to be addressed adequately by researchers. Primary on the list are the socially prescribed meanings assigned to gender roles and the expectations that come with them. There is also a need to understand the role of men in the domain of shopping. Little, if any, research has been conducted specifically on the leisure place of shopping for men, the types of consumption involved, and the product, place and people characteristics that appeal to males. While most studies have found that women shop more than men, even on vacation, it would be interesting to understand how the changes in traditional gender roles and family structure are affecting, if they are, the popularity of shopping among women and men. As men have become more active in taking care of the home and children, there may be some attitudinal changes toward shopping among men as well, particularly in the realm of grocery shopping, and other forms of buying for household necessities. McCormick (2001) and Mintel International (1996b) found in their studies that while women are still the primary shoppers on vacation trips, interest among men for shopping while on holiday is on the rise. The reasons for this change and the conditions that promote it would be a valuable topic of research for understanding why men are less likely to shop at home (even in leisure contexts) but more inclined to shop away from home.

Miller (2001) argues that racism and class distinctions bear considerable weight when it comes to shop ownership, patronage, and store location. In some places, owing to racial profiling and harassment, some people are targeted for scrutiny when they shop. Obviously this treatment may render shopping a non-leisure experience. As was demonstrated in several places in this book, culture, nationality, and ethnicity have a significant bearing on the types of products people buy, the activities they undertake, and the types of shops they frequent. Cultural traditions and national social mores commonly determine shopping behavior, which merchants must consider in their retail planning exercises. Nonetheless, for the most part, ethnicity and race have not received adequate attention in the consumption-related literature (Zikmund, 1977). There is a general acceptance that race and ethnicity are relevant to decision-making processes related to leisure and travel behavior but little has been written on the role of these variables in leisure shopping behavior and in decisions to shop while on vacation. What has been written focuses almost entirely on the demand side of leisure and tourism. What of the supply side? How do the characteristics of various cultural groups influence what they buy and where they shop as tourists? Are there ethnic, cultural, or racial predispositions to destination preferences or to product characteristics? Do different destination cultures have dissimilar ways of producing and selling souvenirs and handicrafts to tourists? If they are, in what ways are leisure- and tourism-related retail management procedures affected by culture and destination norms? This is only a small sample of questions that might be answered through additional work on the cultural and ethnic effects of shopping behavior.

Although age was noted as a personal variable that influences consumer behavior, it is still not well understood as a factor in tourist and leisure shopping. It is known that age and the life cycle have an effect on where people choose to holiday and the types of activities they undertake. It is not clear, however, how tourist and leisure shopping at various stages of the life cycle play out, although Maynard (1990) did note that as people age, they generally become less interested in buying material items than they are in spending money on family associations and quality experiences. Answers to such questions as, 'Does age affect shopping behavior during holiday trips?', could provide valuable scientific knowledge as well as practical information for managers and destinations.

New and emerging types of locations and venues also open up many research questions. Ever more destinations are being developed on the world periphery. Venues, such as supermarkets and department stores that traditionally were not viewed as tourist services, now have to be considered in the leisure planning realm as well. Retailers also have to cater, through human resource, merchandising, and physical planning, to the needs and expectations of tourists and local recreationists.

Similarly, new manifestations of leisure and tourist shopping are becoming commonplace. Internet shopping, for instance, is now one of the fastest growing forms of retailing, which very often has a leisure motive at its core. Online auctions have many characteristics of gambling and, for many people, this may become an addiction. Future research needs to address this issue, including the extent to which this might replace traditional shopping activities and the health, social, and economic implications this will have.

Additionally, Coles (2003, 2004) discusses a growing trend in car sales, wherein customers become tourists by visiting automobile assembly plants to see the production of the cars they will buy. This is a growing trend outside the automobile industry as well. As part of the shopping experience, tourists are beginning to go beyond the point of sale, retailer, and distributor to include site visits to manufacturing plants as part of the purchasing process. Additional research could be fruitful in building an understanding of backward and forward linkages between the consumers (i.e. tourists) and the producers and other suppliers in the supply chain.

Another prospective area of research that could provide important management and theoretical knowledge is the existing and potential relationships between shopping and various specialized forms of tourism. The discussion in this book has touched upon the close ties between heritage tourism and shopping but it would be of considerable interest to learn how other types of tourism, such as nature-based, sport, literary, religious, and visiting friends and relatives, might interact with retail establishments and travelers' desire to shop. As each type obviously has different expectations and motivations for tourism, do they also have specialized motives and needs for shopping?

In conclusion, it is clear from the discussion in this book that tourists will shop anywhere and that the general population is in a constant quest for leisure opportunities to shop closer to home. As researchers, however, we are only beginning to understand the multitudinous dimensions of shopping and leisure tourism that deserve additional research attention in the realms of venue design, merchandising, motivations, experiences, perceptions, supply systems, impacts, sociocultural and demographic influences on decision-making, and many more. The goal of this book was to consolidate the main ideas, concepts and issues that exist in the realm of shopping from a tourism and leisure point of view into a useable framework for leisure and tourist shopping studies. While it is certainly not a completely comprehensive discourse on all that has been said or could be said, its aim is to establish a foundation from which other examinations of shopping may go forward.

References

Agarwal, V.B. and Yochum, G.R. (2000) Determinants of tourist spending. In A.G. Woodside, G.I. Crouch, J.A. Mazanec, M. Oppermann and M.Y. Sakai (eds) *Consumer Psychology of Tourism, Hospitality and Leisure* (pp. 311–30). Wallingford: CAB International.

Ahmed, Z.U. (1996) An international marketing perspective of Canadian tourists' shopping behaviour: Minot (North Dakota). *Journal of Vacation Marketing* 2 (3), 207–14.

Ahmed, Z.U. and Corrigan, F. (1995) An international marketing perspective of Canadian tourists' shopping behavior: Minot (North Dakota) a case in point. In Z.U. Ahmed (ed.) *The Business of International Tourism* (pp. 196–23). Minot, ND: Institute for International Business, Minot State University.

Ahmed, Z.U. and Krohn, F.B. (1992) Understanding the unique consumer behavior of Japanese tourists. *Journal of Travel and Tourism Marketing* 1 (3), 73–86.

Ahn, J.Y. and Jeong, G.H. (1996) Behavioural characteristics of Korean outbound travel market: Marketing implications for Indo-China's tourism industry. In K.S. Chon (ed.) *Proceedings of the conference on Tourism in Indo-China: Opportunities for Investment, Development and Marketing* (pp. 54–64). Houston: University of Houston.

Akau'ola, L., Ilaiu, L. and Samate, A. (1980) The social and cultural impact of tourism in Tonga. In F. Rajotte (ed.) *Pacific Tourism: As Islanders See It* (pp. 17–23). Suva: Institute of Pacific Studies, University of the South Pacific.

Alexander, N. (1997) *International Retailing*. Oxford: Blackwell.

Anderson, L. and Littrell, M.A. (1995) Souvenir-purchase behavior of women tourists. *Annals of Tourism Research* 22 (2), 328–48.

Anderson, L. and Littrell, M.A. (1996) Group profiles of women as tourists and purchasers of souvenirs. *Family and Consumer Sciences Research Journal* 25 (1), 28–56.

Andruss, P.L. (2000) How malls tap rich vein of foreign tourists. *Marketing News* (4 December), 6–7.

Angle, T. (1974) *Shopping Malls: A Place to Go*. Kent, OH: Kent State University.

Anthony, J. (1992) Is duty-free really a bargain? *National Geographic Traveler* 9 (1), 117–19.

Anthony, K.H. (1985) The shopping mall: A teenage hangout. *Adolescence* 20, 307–12.

Appleby, J. (1993) Consumption in early modern thought. In J. Brewer and R. Porter (eds) *Consumption and the World of Goods* (pp. 162–73). London: Routledge.

Arizona Office of Tourism (2001) *Shop and Play Arizona*. Phoenix: Arizona Office of Tourism.

Arizona Republic (2001) Shopping drives choice of destination. (10 June), T2.

Arizona Shopping and Attraction Consortium (2000) Arizona Shopping and Attraction Consortium Fills Tourism Niche (unpublished report). Phoenix: AZSAC.

Arreola, D.D. (1999) Across the street is Mexico: Invention and persistence of the border town curio landscape. *Yearbook of the Association of Pacific Coast Geographers* 61, 9–41.

Arreola, D.D. and Curtis, J.R. (1993) *The Mexican Border Cities: Landscape Anatomy and Place Personality*. Tucson: University of Arizona Press.

Arreola, D.D. and Madsen, K. (1999) Variability of tourist attraction on an international boundary: Sonora, Mexico border towns. *Visions in Leisure and Business* 17 (4), 19–32.

Asgary, N., de Los Santos, G., Vincent, V. and Davila, V. (1997) The determinants of expenditures by Mexican visitors to the border cities of Texas. *Tourism Economics* 3 (4), 319–28.

Ashworth, G.J. (2003) Heritage, identity and places: For tourists and host communities. In S. Singh, D.J. Timothy and R.K. Dowling (eds) *Tourism in Destination Communities* (pp. 79–97). Wallingford: CAB International.

Ashworth, G.J. and Tunbridge, J.E. (2000) *The Tourist-Historic City: Retrospect and Prospect of Managing the Heritage City*. New York: Pergamon.

Asplet, M. and Cooper, M. (2000) Cultural designs in New Zealand souvenir clothing: The question of authenticity. *Tourism Management* 21 (3), 307–12.

Babin, B.J., Darden, W.R. and Griffin, M. (1994) Work and/or fun: Measuring hedonic and utilitarian shopping value. *Journal of Consumer Research* 20 (4), 644–56.

Bachvarov, M. (1997) End of the model? Tourism in post-communist Bulgaria. *Tourism Management* 18, 43–50.

Bacon, R.W. (1991) Consumer shopping and equilibrium market areas in the present of demands for nonshopping goods and for leisure. *Environment and Planning A* 23 (9), 1361–74.

Bacon, R.W. (1992) The travel to shop behaviour of consumers in equilibrium market areas. *Journal of Transport Economics and Policy* 26, 283–98.

Bacon, R.W. (1993) A model of travelling to shop with congestion costs. *Journal of Transport Economics and Policy* 27, 277–89.

Baker, A. (2000) *Serious Shopping: Psychotherapy and Consumerism*. London: Free Association Books.

Balabanis, G. and Vassileiou, S. (1999) Some attitudinal predictors of home shopping through the Internet. *Journal of Marketing Management* 15 (5), 361–85.

Balkan, E.M. and Rutz, H.J. (1999) Development and the consumption of leisure. *Scandinavian Journal of Development Alternatives* 18 (2/3), 229–51.

Balke, F. and Rausch, R. (1990) Erlebniswelt Shopping Center. In S. Agricola, A. Haag and M. Stoffers (eds) *Freizeitwirtschaft: Märkte und Konsumwelten* (pp. 188–93). Erkrath: Deutsche Gesellschaft für Freizeit.

Banks, L.W. (1998) Viva Algodones! Sonora, Mexico welcomes Yuma's snowbirds. *Arizona Highways* 74 (8), 35–7.

Barnett, L.A. (1995) *Research about Leisure: Past, Present and Future*. Champaign, IL: Sagamore.

Barr, V. and Broudy, C.E. (1986) *Designing to Sell: A Complete Guide to Retail Store Planning and Design*. New York: McGraw-Hill.

Barr, V. and Field, K. (1999) *Stores: Retail Display and Design*. Glen Cove, NY: PBC International.

Barron's (1998) There's nothing run-of-the-mill about this retailing concept. 78 (18), 12.

Bartlett, T. (2000) Glendale thrives as state's antique capital. *Travel Weekly* (04 December), 51–2.

Baudrillard, J. (1988) The system of objects. *Art Monthly* 115, 5–8.

Bearchell, C.A. (1975) *Retailing: A Professional Approach*. New York: Harcourt.

Beck, R. (1998) Forget the beach, travelers opt for the mall on vacations. *Sentinel Tribune* (Bowling Green), 30 July.

Becker, K. (2000) Visitors flock to giant malls. *Globe and Mail* (Toronto) (5 January), T5.

Beddingfield, K. (1999) Mall tourists. *National Geographic Traveler* (May), 32.

Begley, L. (1999) Shopping: London, cheaper and chicer. *Travel & Leisure* 29 (2), 42–51.

Bell, J. and Turnus, K. (2001) *Silent Selling: Best Practices and Effective Strategies in Visual Merchandising*. New York: Fairchild.

Bellenger, D.N. and Korgaonkar, P.K. (1980) Profiling the recreational shopper. *Journal of Retailing* 56 (3), 77–92.

Bellenger, D.N., Robertson, D.H. and Greenberg, B.A. (1977) Shopping centre patronage motives. *Journal of Retailing* 53 (2), 29–38.

Bellenger, D.N., Robertson, D.H. and Hirschman, E.C. (1978) Impulse buying varies by product. *Journal of Advertising Research* 18 (6), 15–18.

Belsky, G. (1992) Watch out, Disneyland! *Money* 21 (10), 213–22.

Bentor, Y. (1993) Tibetan tourist thangkas in the Kathmandu Valley. *Annals of Tourism Research* 20 (1), 107–37.

Bergadaa, M., Faure, C. and Perrien, J. (1995) Enduring involvement with shopping. *Journal of Social Psychology* 135 (1), 17–25.

Bia, Y. (1996) The international duty free market. *Travel and Tourism Analyst* 6, 37–63.

Birnbaum, D. (1996) Monaco, C'est Magnifique! *New Woman* 26 (7), 26.

Blake, C. (1996) Shop around the clock. *Internet World* 7 (1), 70–1.

Bloch, P.H., Ridgway, N.M. and Dawson, S.A. (1994) The shopping mall as consumer habitat. *Journal of Retailing* 70 (1), 23–42.

Bloch, P.H., Ridgway, N.M. and Nelson, J.E. (1991) Leisure and the shopping mall. *Advances in Consumer Research* 18, 445–52.

Bloch, P.H., Ridgway, N.M. and Sherrell, D.L. (1989) Extending the concept of shopping: An investigation of browsing activity. *Journal of the Academy of Marketing Science* 17, 13–21.

Blotevogel, H.H. and Deilmann, B. (1989) World Tourist Center Oberhausen: aufstieg und Fall der Planung eines Megazentrums. *Geographische Rundschau* 41 (11), 640–5.

Blundell, V. (1993) Aboriginal empowerment and souvenir trade in Canada. *Annals of Tourism Research* 20 (1), 64–87.

Bly, L. (1998) Driven by discounts: outlet malls offer day-trippers bargains they can't refuse. *USA Today* (14 August), 4.

Bocock, R. (1993) *Consumption*. London: Routledge.

Bolabola, C.A.B. (1980) The impact of tourism on Fijian woodcarving. In F. Rajotte (ed.) *Pacific Tourism: As Islanders See It* (pp. 93–7). Suva: Institute of Pacific Studies, University of the South Pacific.

Boniface, P. and Fowler, P.J. (1993) *Heritage and Tourism in 'The Global Village'*. London: Routledge.

Borden, T. (2001) U.S. seniors fear Mexico tax. *Arizona Republic* (18 April), A1.

Borrus, K.S. (1988) Marketing crafts through museum shops. *Museums* 157, 22–7.

Boudreau, G.R. (1983) Shopping for recreation. *Recreation Canada* 41 (4), 13–15.

Boulos, L. (1985) Needs and opportunities for improving tourism-related facilities in downtown and harbourfront areas: Shopping facilities. In *Improving Tourism Related Facilities in Downtown and Harbourfront Areas: Final Report of the OAS Regional Workshop* (pp. 36–41). Washington, DC: Organization of American States.

Bourdieu, P. (1984) *Distinction: A Social Critique of the Judgement of Taste.* London: Routledge.

Bowlby, R. (2001) *Carried Away: The Invention of Modern Shopping.* New York: Columbia University Press.

Bowman, G. (1996) Passion, power and politics in a Palestinian tourist market. In T. Selwyn (ed.) *The Tourist Image: Myths and Myth Making in Tourism* (pp. 83–103). Chichester: Wiley.

Boyd, S.W. (1999) North-South divide: The role of the border in tourism to Northern Ireland. *Visions in Leisure and Business* 17 (4), 50–71.

Boydell, M. (1987) Tour operators cash in on affluent Taiwanese. *Asian Business* 23 (11), 78–81.

Bramwell, B. and Sharman, A. (1999) Collaboration in local tourism policy-making. *Annals of Tourism Research* 26, 392–415.

Brennan, D.M. (1984) Bloomingdale's boutique concepts. *Restaurant Business* 83 (9), 179–94, 198.

Bromley, R.D.F. and Thomas, C.J. (1993) Retail change and the issues. In R.D.F. Bromley and C.J. Thomas (eds) *Retail Change: Contemporary Issues* (pp. 2–14). London: University College London Press.

Broudy, C.E. and Barr, V. (1995) *Time-Saver Details for Store Planning and Design.* New York: McGraw-Hill.

Brown, A. (1995) Shopping: Siamese spree. *Travel & Leisure* 25 (11), 88–92.

Brown, D. (1996) Genuine fakes. In T. Selwyn (ed.) *The Tourist Image: Myths and Myth Making in Tourism* (pp. 33–48). Chichester: Wiley.

Brown, G. (1992) Tourism and symbolic consumption. In P. Johnson and B. Thomas (eds) *Choice and Demand in Tourism* (pp. 57–71). London: Mansell.

Brown, T.C. (1997) The fourth member of NAFTA: the U.S.-Mexico border. *Annals of the American Academy of Political and Social Science* 550, 105–21.

Brownill, S. (1994) Selling the inner city: Regeneration and place marketing in London's Docklands. In J.R. Gold and S.V. Ward (eds) *Place Promotion: The Use of Publicity and Marketing to Sell Towns and Regions* (pp. 133–52). Chichester: Wiley.

Bruner, E.M. (1994) Abraham Lincoln as authentic reproduction: A critique of postmodernism. *American Anthropologist* 96 (2), 290–304.

Bunn, S. (2000) Stealing souls for souvenirs: Or why tourists want 'the real thing'. In M. Hitchcock and K. Teague (eds) *Souvenirs: The Material Culture of Tourism* (pp. 166–93). Aldershot: Ashgate.

Bureau of Tourism Research (1990) *Tourism Shopping Survey, October to December 1989* (Occasional Paper No. 7). Canberra: Bureau of Tourism Research.

Bureau of Transport Economics (1979) *Inwards Duty-free Shopping at Australian International Air Terminals: An Economic Evaluation.* Canberra: Bureau of Transport Economics.

Burns, D.J. and Warren H.B. (1995) Need for uniqueness: Shopping mall preference and choice of activity. *International Journal of Retail & Distribution Management, 23* (12): 4–12.

The Business Times (1998) Good fortune for local handicraft. (18 September), 18.

Bussey, K. (1987) Leisure + shopping =? *Leisure Management 7* (9), 22–6.

Butcher-Younghans, S. (1993) *Historic House Museums: A Practical Handbooks for Their Care, Preservation, and Management.* New York: Oxford University Press.

Butler, R.W. (1980) The concept of a tourist area cycle of evolution and implications for management of resources. *Canadian Geographer 24* (1), 5–12.

Butler, R.W. (1991) West Edmonton Mall as a tourist attraction. *Canadian Geographer 35* (3), 287–95.

Butler, R.W. (1996) The role of tourism in cultural transformation in developing countries. In W. Nuryanti (ed.) *Tourism and Culture: Global Civilization in Change* (pp. 91–101). Yogyakarta: Gadjah Mada University Press.

Butler, W. (1998) To market, to market. *Southern Living 33* (5), 32.

Bygvrå, S. (1990) Border shopping between Denmark and West Germany. *Contemporary Drug Problems 17* (4), 595–611.

Bygvrå, S. (1992) *Purchasing Flows Across the German-Danish Border.* Aabenraa, Denmark: Danish Institute of Border Region Studies.

Bygvrå, S. (1997) *Der deutsch-dänische Grenzhandel in den ersten Jahren des europäischen Binnenmarktes.* Aabenraa, Denmark: Institut for Grænseregionsforskning.

Bygvrå, S. (1998) The road to the Single European Market as seen through the Danish retail trade: cross-border shopping between Denmark and Germany. *International Review of Retail, Distribution and Consumer Research 8* (2), 147–64.

Bygvrå, S. (1999) Einkaufsfahrten der Dänen über die Grenze: Ergebnisse einer Umfrage. *Grenzfriedenshefte 1,* 30–6.

Bygvrå, S. (2000) Retail trade at European borders. *European Retail Digest 27,* 39–40.

Cahill, R. (1987) *Border Towns of the Southwest: Shopping, Dining, Fun and Adventure from Tijuana to Juarez.* Boulder, CO: Pruett.

Campbell, C. (1991) To have possessions: A handbook on ownership and property. *Journal of Social Behavior and Personality 6,* 57–75.

Campbell, C. (1994) Capitalism, consumption and the problem of motives. In J. Friedman (ed.) *Consumption and Identity* (pp. 23–46). Chur, Switzerland: Harwood.

Campbell, C. (1997) Shopping, pleasure and the sex war. In P. Falk and C. Campbell (eds) *The Shopping Experience* (pp. 166–76). London: Sage.

Canadian Chamber of Commerce (1992) *The Cross Border Shopping Issue.* Ottawa: Canadian Chamber of Commerce.

Carr, J. (1990) The social aspects of shopping: Pleasure or chore? The consumer perspective. *Royal Society of Arts Journal 138,* 189–97.

Caviedes, C.N. (1994) Argentine-Chilean cooperation and disagreement along the southern Patagonian border. In W.A. Gallusser (ed.) *Political Boundaries and Coexistence* (pp. 135–43). Bern: Peter Lang.

Chadee, D. and Mieczkowski, Z. (1987) An empirical analysis of the effects of the exchange rate on Canadian tourism. *Journal of Travel Research 26* (1), 13–17.

Chain Store Age Executive (1989) Aloha, big spenders: Ala Moana upscales to meet affluent market. 65 (11), 174–5.

Chamberlain, L. (1991) *Small Business Ontario Report No. 44: Cross Border Shopping.* Toronto: Ministry of Industry, Trade and Technology.

Chaney, D. (1983) The department store as a cultural form. *Theory, Culture & Society* 1 (3), 22–31.

Charin, L. (1999) Bargain shopping on the Internet. *McCall's* (1 October), 126–8.

Charney, A.H. and Pavlakovich-Kochi, V.K. (2002) *The Economic Impacts of Mexican Visitors to Arizona: 2001.* Tucson: Tucson-Mexico Trade Office.

Chase, R.A. and Pulver, G.C. (1983) The impact of shopping center development on downtowns of small nonmetropolitan communities. *Journal of the Community Development Society* 14 (2), 51–66.

Chatterjee, A. (1991) Cross-border shopping: searching for a solution. *Canadian Business Review* 18, 26–31.

Chen, X. (1997) Shopping experiences of tourists. Unpublished master's thesis, Utah State University, Logan, Utah.

Cheng, M. (1999) Walk on the wild side. *Asian Business* 35 (6), 24–5.

Chubb, M. and Chubb, H.R. (1981) *One Third of Our Time? An Introduction to Recreation Behavior and Resources.* New York: Wiley.

Christaller, W. (1966) *Central Places in Southern Germany.* Englewood Cliffs, NJ: Prentice-Hall.

Christiansen, T. and Snepenger, D.J. (2002) Is it the mood or the mall that encourages tourists to shop? *Journal of Shopping Center Research* 9 (1), 7–26.

Clark, J. (1998) Easier-going vendors prove to be hard sell. *USA Today* (13 November), 2.

Clark, T. (1994) National boundaries, border zones, and marketing strategy: A conceptual framework and theoretical model of secondary boundary effects. *Journal of Marketing* 58, 67–80.

Clarke, D.B. (1996) The limits to retail capital. In N. Wrigley and M. Lowe (eds) *Retailing, Consumption and Capital: Towards the New Retail Geography* (pp. 284–301). Harlow: Longman.

Cochise College (1998) *Border Survey Results.* Douglas, AZ: Cochise College, Center for Economic Research.

Cockerham, P.W. (1994) Safe shopping. *Stores Magazine* (June), 38–9.

Cohen, E. (1988a) Authenticity and commoditization in tourism. *Annals of Tourism Research* 15, 371–86.

Cohen, E. (1988b) From tribal costume to pop fashion: The 'boutiquisation' of the textiles of the Hill Tribes of northern Thailand. *Studies in Popular Culture* 11 (2), 49–59.

Cohen, E. (1989a) International politics and the transformation of folk crafts: The Hmong (Meo) of Thailand and Laos. *Journal of the Siam Society* 77 (1), 69–82.

Cohen, E. (1989b) The commercialization of ethnic crafts. *Journal of Design History* 2 (2), 161–8.

Cohen, E. (1990) Hmong (Meo) commercialized refugee art: From ornament to picture. In D. Eban (ed.) *Art as a Means of Communication in Pre-literate Societies* (pp. 51–95). Jerusalem: Wright International Symposium.

Cohen, E. (1992) Tourist arts. *Progress in Tourism, Recreation and Hospitality Management* 4, 3–32.

Cohen, E. (1993a) Introduction: Investigating tourist art. *Annals of Tourism Research* 20 (1), 1–8.

Cohen, E. (1993b) The heterogeneization of a tourist art. *Annals of Tourism Research* 20 (1), 138–63.

Cohen, E. (1995a) The representation of Arabs and Jews on postcards in Israel. *History of Photography* 19 (3), 210–20.

Cohen, E. (1995b) Touristic craft ribbon development in Thailand. *Tourism Management* 16 (3), 225–35.

Cohen, J.H. (2001) Textile, tourism and community development. *Annals of Tourism Research* 28 (2), 378–98.

Cohen, L. (1996) From town center to shopping center: the reconfiguration of community marketplaces in postwar America. *American Historical Review* 101 (4), 1050–81.

Coles, T. (1999a) Competition, contested retail space and the rise of the department store in Imperial Germany. *International Review of Retail, Distribution and Consumer Research* 9 (3), 275–89.

Coles, T. (1999b) Department stores as innovations in retail marketing: Some observations on marketing practice and perception in Wilhelmine, Germany. *Journal of Macromarketing* 19 (1), 34–47.

Coles, T. (2003) The car's the star: Exploring the conceptual links between tourism and retailing through the case of an international car business. Unpublished conference paper, Australia-New Zealand International Business Academy Meeting, Dunedin, New Zealand, 7–8 November.

Coles, T. (2004) Tourism, shopping and retailing: An axiomatic relationship? In A. Lew, C.M. Hall and A.M. Williams (eds) *A Companion to Tourism* (pp. 360–73). Oxford: Blackwell.

Cone, C.A. (1995) Crafting selves: The lives of two Mayan women. *Annals of Tourism Research* 22 (2), 314–27.

Connelly-Kirch, D. (1982) Economic and social correlates of handicraft selling in Tonga. *Annals of Tourism Research* 9 (3), 383–402.

Consumers Digest (1997) Holiday shopping online: Your guide to hot Web sites. 36 (6), 29–31.

Craig-Smith, S.J. (1995) The role of tourism in inner-harbor redevelopment. In S.J. Craig-Smith and M. Fagence (eds) *Recreation and Tourism as a Catalyst for Urban Waterfront Redevelopment* (pp. 15–35). Westport, CT: Praeger.

Cramer, J. (1995) Best sellers. *Leisure Management* 15 (11), 62–3.

Creno, G. (2001) Mutant malls: Boxy shopping centers give way to bizarre bazaars. *Arizona Republic* (4 February), D1, D11.

Crippen, K. (2000) The threads that tie textiles to tourism. In M. Hitchcock and W. Nuryanti (eds) *Building on Batik: The Globalization of a Craft Community* (pp. 271–84). Aldershot: Ashgate.

Crompton, J.L. (1979) Motivations for pleasure vacation. *Annals of Tourism Research* 6 (4), 408–24.

Crozier, B. (2000) From earliest contacts: An examination of Inuit and Aleut art in Scottish collections. In M. Hitchcock and K. Teague (eds) *Souvenirs: The Material Cultuer of Tourism* (pp. 52–71). Aldershot: Avebury.

Csikszentmihalyi, M. (1981). Leisure and socialization. *Social Forces* 60, 332–40.

Cukier, J. and Wall, G. (1994) Informal tourism employment: Vendors in Bali, Indonesia. *Tourism Management* 15, 464–7.

Cuneen, J. (2000) Sports collectibles as commodities: Assessing worth for sports memorabilia from personal meaning to cultural merit to market value. Paper presented at the annual meeting of the North American Society for Sport Management, Colorado Springs, Colorado.

Curtis, A. (2001) Shopping mall will take center stage on Strip in 2002. *Arizona Republic* (8 April), T8.

Dahms, F. (1991a) Economic revitalization in St. Jacobs, Ontario: Ingredients for transforming a dying village into a thriving tourist destination. *Small Town* 21 (6), 12–18.

Dahms, F. (1991b) St. Jacobs, Ontario: From declining village to thriving tourist community. *Ontario Geography* 36, 1–13.

Davis, D. (1966a) *A History of Shopping*. London: Routledge and Kegan Paul.

Davis, D. (1966b) *Fairs, Shops, and Supermarkets: A History of English Shopping.* Toronto: University of Toronto Press.

de Albuquerque, K. and McElroy, J.L. (2001) Tourist harassment: Barbados survey results. *Annals of Tourism Research* 28 (2), 477–92.

de Los Santos, G. and Vincent, V. (1993) Tex-Mex tourism. *Business Mexico* 3 (3), 27–9.

de Vidas, A.A. (1995) Textiles, memory and the souvenir industry in the Andes. In M. Lanfant, J.B. Allcock and E.M. Bruner (eds) *International Tourism: Identity and Change* (pp. 67–83). London: Sage.

Department of Environment, Housing and Community Development (1978) *The Shopping Centre as a Community Leisure Resource*. Canberra: Australian Government Publishing Service.

Department of Hotel and Tourism Management (2001) Carry on shopping. *Horizons: HTM Magazine* 1 (2), 4–7.

Department of the Arts, Sport, the Environment, Tourism and Territories (1988) *Tourism Shopping in Australia: Report of the Committee of Inquiry*. Canberra: Government of Australia.

Deveny, P.J. (1998) Jamaica aims to calm tourist fears. *The Wall Street Journal* (7 May), A16.

Dhaliwal, R. (1998) A not-so-great Singapore sale? *The Straits Times* (26 March).

Di Matteo, L. (1993) Determinants of cross-border trips and spending by Canadians in the United States: 1979–1991. *Canadian Business Economics* 1 (3), 51–61.

Di Matteo, L. (1999) Cross-border trips by Canadians and Americans and the differential impact of the border. *Visions in Leisure and Business* 17 (4), 72–92.

Di Matteo, L. and Di Matteo, R. (1993) The determinants of expenditures by Canadian visitors to the United States. *Journal of Travel Research* 31 (4), 34–42.

Di Matteo, L. and Di Matteo, R. (1996) An analysis of Canadian cross-border travel. *Annals of Tourism Research* 23 (1), 103–22.

Diamond, J. and Diamond, E. (1998) *Contemporary Visual Merchandising*. Paramus, NJ: Prentice Hall.

Diehl, P.N. (1983) The effects of the peso devaluation on Texas border cities. *Texas Business Review* 57, 120–5.

Dimanche, F. (2003) The Louisiana tax free shopping program for international visitors: A case study. *Journal of Travel Research* 41 (3), 311–14.

Dimanche, F. and Samdahl, D. (1994) Leisure as symbolic consumption: a conceptualization and prospectus for future research. *Leisure Sciences* 16, 119–29.

Donovan, R.J., Rossiter, J.R., Marcoolyn, G., and Nesdale, A. (1994) Store atmosphere and purchasing behavior. *Journal of Retailing* 79 (3), 283–94.

Dooher, D. (1997) Mall of America. *Mpls. St Paul* 25 (11), 80.

Douglas, M. (1997) In defense of shopping. In P. Falk and C. Campbell (eds) *The Shopping Experience* (pp. 15–30). London: Sage.

Dougoud, R.C. (2000) Souvenirs from Kambot (Papua New Guinea): The sacred search for authenticity. In M. Hitchcock and K. Teague (eds) *Souvenirs: The Material Culture of Tourism* (pp. 223–37). Aldershot: Ashgate.

Dowling, R.K. and Getz, D. (2000) Wine tourism futures. In B. Faulkner, G. Moscardo and E. Laws (eds) *Tourism in the Twenty-First Century: Reflections on Experience* (pp. 49–66). London: Continuum.

Downs, R.M. (1970) The cognitive structure of an urban shopping center. *Environment and Behavior* 2 (2), 13–39.

Dubai Tourism (2003) Events in Dubai (online). www.dubaitourism.co.ac/www/events/events.asp, accessed November 20, 2003

Dudding, V. and Ryan, C. (2000) The impacts of tourism on a rural retail sector: A New Zealand case study. *Tourism Economics* 6 (4), 301–19.

Duncan, H.H., Travis, S.S. and McAuley, W.J. (1994) The meaning of and motivation for mall walking among older adults. *Activities, Adaptation & Aging* 19 (1), 37–52.

Dunnan, N. (1998) A good neighbor offers good deals. *New Choices* 38 (9), 10.

Edgington, C.R., Hudson, S.D. and Lankford, S.V. (2001) *Managing Recreation, Parks, and Leisure Services: An Introduction.* Champaign, Ill: Sagamore.

Edwards, E. (1996) Postcards–greetings from another world. In T. Selwyn (ed.) *The Tourist Image: Myths and Myth Making in Tourism* (pp. 197–221). Chicheser: Wiley.

Edwards, J.A. (1989) Historic sites and their local environments. In D.T. Herbert, R.C. Prentice and C.J. Thomas (eds) *Heritage Sites: Strategies for Marketing and Development* (pp. 272–93). Aldershot: Avebury.

Edwards, T. (2000) *Contradictions of Consumption: Concepts, Practices and Politics in Consumer Society.* Buckingham: Open University Press.

Elliot, A. (2001) South Florida megamall lures the Americas. *Miami Herald* (14 January), 10–11.

Emerson, C. (1993) State of shopping: retail recreation amid thrills and tills. *Nevada* 3 (3), 29.

Erkip, F. (2003) The shopping mall as an emergent public space in Turkey. *Environment and Planning A* 35 (6), 1073–94.

Evans, G. (1998) Mementoes to take home: the ancient trade in souvenirs. In J.M. Fladmark (ed.) *In Search of Heritage: As Pilgrim or Tourist?* (pp. 105–26). Shaftesbury: Donhead.

Evans, G. (2000) Contemporary crafts as souvenirs, artefacts and functional goods and their role in local economic diversification and cultural development. In M. Hitchcock and K. Teague (eds) *Souvenirs: The Material Culture of Tourism* (pp. 127–46). Aldershot: Ashgate.

Evans-Pritchard, D. (1993) Ancient art in modern context. *Annals of Tourism Research* 20 (1), 9–31.

Fairbairn, K.J. (1991) West Edmonton Mall: Entrepreneurial innovation and consumer response. *Canadian Geographer* 35 (3), 261–8.

Far Eastern Economic Review (2003) Malaysia's monster mall. 166 (29), 44–9.

Far Eastern Economic Review (1997) A short-term bargain. 160 (49), 46.

Feest, C.F. (1992) *Native Arts of North America.* London: Thames and Hudson.

Feinberg, R.A., Sheffler, B., Meoli, J. and Rummel, A. (1989) There's something social happening at the mall. *Journal of Business and Psychology* 4 (1), 49–63.

Field, D. (1999) Collectors grab at chances to hunt treasure. *USA Today* (18 May), 5E.

Fine, B. and Leopold, E. (1993) *The World of Consumption.* London: Routledge.

Finn, A. and Erdem, T. (1995) The economic impact of a mega-multi-mall: estimation issues in the case of West Edmonton Mall. *Tourism Management* 16 (5), 367–73.

Finn, A., McQuity, S. and Rigby, J. (1994) Residents' acceptance and use of a mega-multi-mall: West Edmonton Mall evidence. *International Journal of Research in Marketing* 11, 127–44.

Finn, A. and Rigby, J. (1987) *Edmonton Area Residents' Views on and Use of West Edmonton Mall*. Edmonton: Faculty of Business, University of Alberta.

Finn, A. and Rigby, J. (1992) West Edmonton Mall: Consumer combined-purpose trips and the birth of the mega-multi-mall. *Canadian Journal of Administrative Sciences* 9 (2), 134–45.

Finn, A. and Woolley-Fisher, P. (1988) *West Edmonton Mall and Shopping in the Edmonton Area: Results of a 1988 Survey of Area Residents*. Edmonton: Faculty of Business, University of Alberta.

Fiorenza, D. (1994) Shopping malls in Argentina. *Spazio E Societa – Space and Society* 17 (68), 9–14.

Fischer, E. and Gainer, B. (1991) I shop therefore I am: The role of shopping in the social construction of women's identities. In J.A. Costa (ed.) *Gender and Consumer Behavior* (pp. 350–7). Salt Lake City: Association for Consumer Research.

Fisher, S. (1996) Outlet store packs them in over holiday. *New Britain Herald* (7 September).

Fiske, J. (1989) Shopping for pleasure. In J. Fiske (ed.) *Reading Popular Culture* (pp. 13–42). London: Unwin Hyman.

Fitzgerald, J.D., Quinn, T.P., Whelan, B.J. and Williams, J.A. (1988) *An Analysis of Cross-Border Shopping*. Dublin: The Economic and Social Research Institute.

Fitzgerald, K. (2000) Maui comes to mall. *Advertising Age* 71 (6), 30–2.

Flannery, P. (2001) Security pinching border business. *Arizona Republic* (2 October), A1–2.

Fletcher, S. and Macauley, C. (1983) The shopping mall as a therapeutic arena. *Geriatric Nursing* 4 (2), 105–6.

Foderaro, L.W. (1998) A universal quest for bargains: Japanese flock to outlet center in the Hudson Valley. *The New York Times* (18 June), 15.

Fox, J. (1995) Weak Canadian dollar chills cross-border trips. *Discount Store News* 34 (8), 1, 74.

Fox, W.F. (1986) Tax structure and the location of economic activity along state borders. *National Tax Journal* 39 (4), 387–401.

Fram, E.H. and Ajami, R. (1994) Globalization of markets and shopping stress: cross-country comparisons. *Business Horizons* 37 (1), 17–23.

Freathy, P. and O'Connell, F. (1999) A typology of European airport retailing. *Service Industries Journal* 19 (3), 119–34.

Friedman, J. (1994) Introduction. In J. Friedman (ed.) *Consumption and Identity* (pp. 1–22). Chur, Switzerland: Harwood.

Ganslmayr, H. (1988) Museums and crafts. *Museums* 157, 2–8.

Garnsey, E. (1999) Attention, bargain shoppers. *Travel & Leisure* 29 (12), 184–8.

Garreau, J. (1991) *Edge City: Life on the New Frontier*. London: Doubleday.

Gershman, S. (1996) Mall of the Gods. *Travel Holiday* 179 (8), 82–9.

Getz, D. (1993a) Planning for tourism business districts. *Annals of Tourism Research* 20 (3), 583–600.

Getz, D. (1993b) Tourist shopping villages: Development and planning strategies. *Tourism Management* 14 (1), 15–26.

Getz, D., Joncas, D. and Kelly, M. (1994) Tourist shopping villages in the Calgary region. *Journal of Tourism Studies* 5 (1), 2–15.

Giddens, A. (1991) *Modernity and Self-Identity: Self and Society in the Late-Modern Age*. Cambridge: Polity Press.

Gibbons, J.D. and Fish, M. (1987) Market sensitivity of U.S. and Mexican border travel. *Journal of Travel Research* 26 (1), 2–6.

Gilpin, E. (1952) *Tour and Shop*. Philadelphia: Livingston.

Gindon, R. (1984) A taste of America in Kansas City. *Restaurant Business* 83 (6) 259–62.

Gist, R.R. (1971) *Basic Retailing: Text and Cases*. New York: Wiley.

Glennie, P. and Thrift, N. (1996) Consumption, shopping and gender. In N. Wrigley and M. Lowe (eds) *Retailing, Consumption and Capital: Towards the New Retail Geography* (pp. 221–37). Harlow: Longman.

Gołembski, G. (1990) Tourism in the economy of shortage. *Annals of Tourism Research* 17 (1), 55–68.

Goodman and Carr Consulting (1992) *Sunday Shopping–Tourism Exemption in Metropolitan Toronto: Background and Implications for Retailers*. Toronto: Goodman and Carr/National Library of Canada.

Goodman, L.R. (1992) A working paper on crossborder shopping: The Canadian impact on North Dakota. In H.J. Selwood and J.C. Lehr (eds) *Reflections from the Prairies: Geographical Essays* (pp. 80–9). Winnipeg: Department of Geography, University of Winnipeg.

Gordon, B. (1986) The souvenir: messenger of the extraordinary. *Journal of Popular Culture* 20 (3), 135–46.

Gormsen, E. (1990) Kunsthandwerk in der dritten Welt unter dem Einfluss des Tourismus. *Geographische Rundschau* 42 (1), 42–7.

Goss, J. (1992) Modernity and post-modernity in the retail landscape. In K. Anderson and F. Gale (eds), *Inventing Places: Studies in Cultural Geography*, pp. 159–177. London: Longman.

Goss, J. (1993) 'The magic of the mall': an analysis of form, function, and meaning in the contemporary retail built environment. *Annals of the Association of American Geographers* 83 (1), 18–47.

Goss, J. (1999) Once-upon-a-time in the commodity world: An unofficial guide to Mall of America. *Annals of the Association of American Geographers* 89 (1), 45–75.

Government of New Brunswick (1992) *A Discussion Paper on Cross Border Shopping*. Fredericton: Department of Economic Development and Tourism.

Government of Ontario (1991) *Report on Cross-Border Shopping*. Toronto: Standing Committee on Finance and Economic Affairs.

Graburn, N.H.H. (ed.) (1976) *Ethnic and Tourist Arts: Cultural Expressions from the Fourth World*. Berkeley: University of California Press.

Graburn, N.H.H. (1984) The evolution of tourist arts. *Annals of Tourism Research* 11 (3), 393–419.

Graburn, N.H.H. (2000a) Foreword. In M. Hitchcock and K. Teague (eds) *Souvenirs: The Material Culture of Tourism* (pp. xii-xvii). Aldershot: Ashgate.

Graburn, N.H.H. (2000b) Traditions, tourism and textiles: Creativity at the cutting edge. In M. Hitchcock and W. Nuryanti (eds) *Building on Batik: The Globalization of a Craft Community* (pp. 338–53). Aldershot: Ashgate.

Graham, A. (2001) *Managing Airports: An International Perspective*. Oxford: Butterworth Heinemann.

Graham, D.F., Graham, I. and MacLean, M.J. (1991) Going to the mall: A leisure activity of urban elderly people. *Canadian Journal on Aging* 10 (4), 345–58.

Gratton, C. and Taylor, P. (1987) Leisure and shopping: The doomsday experience. *Leisure Management* 7 (3), 29–30.

Grieco, M. (2000) Kente connections: The role of the Internet in developing an economic base for Ghana. In M. Hitchcock and K. Teague (eds) *Souvenirs: The Material Culture of Tourism* (pp. 246–52). Aldershot: Ashgate.

Griffith, H.D. (1987) Beach operations: Their contributions to tourism in Barbados. *Caribbean Finance and Management* 3, 55–65.

Guy, C.M. (1998) Classifications of retail stores and shopping centres: Some methodological issues. *GeoJournal* 45 (4), 255–64.

Haigh, R. (1994) *Holidays in Store: Shopping Patterns of International Tourists.* Canberra: Bureau of Tourism Research.

Hajdú, Z. (1994) Cities in the frontier regions of the Hungarian state: Changing borders, changing political systems, new evaluated contacts. In W.A. Gallusser (ed.) *Political Boundaries and Coexistence* (pp. 209–18). Bern: Peter Lang.

Halewood, C. and Hannam, K. (2001) Viking heritage tourism: Authenticity and commodification. *Annals of Tourism Research* 28, 565–80.

Hall, C.M. (1994) Tourism and retail shopping development. *Leisure Options: Australian Journal of Leisure and Recreation* 4 (3), 5–17.

Hall, C.M. (2000) *Tourism Planning: Policies, Processes and Relationships.* Harlow: Prentice Hall.

Hall, C.M. and Macionis, N. (1998) Wine tourism in Australia and New Zealand. In R.W. Butler, C.M. Hall and J. Jenkins (eds) *Tourism and Recreation in Rural Areas* (pp. 197–224). Chichester: Wiley.

Hall, D.R. (1991) Evolutionary pattern of tourism development in Eastern Europe and the Soviet Union. In D.R. Hall (ed.) *Tourism and Economic Development in Eastern Europe and the Soviet Union* (pp. 79–115). London: Belhaven Press.

Hall, D.R. (1995) Tourism change in Central and Eastern Europe. In A. Montanari and A.M. Williams (eds) *European Tourism: Regions, Spaces and Restructuring* (pp. 221–44). Chichester: Wiley.

Hallsworth, A. (1988) West Edmonton Mall: Canada's shopping fantasy-land. *Retail and Distribution Management* 16 (1), 26–9.

Hanefors, M. and Selwyn, T. (2000) Dalecarlian masques: One souvenir's many voices. In M. Hitchcock and K. Teague (eds) *Souvenirs: The Material Culture of Tourism* (pp. 253–83). Aldershot: Ashgate.

Harvey, D. (1989) *The Condition of Postmodernity.* Oxford: Basil Blackwell.

Hathaway, J.T. and Hughes, J.C. (2000) Factory outlet malls: The example of Prime Outlets at Grove City. In K.J. Patrick and J.L. Scarpaci (eds) *A Geographic Perspective of Pittsburgh and the Alleghenies: From Precambrian to Post-Industrial* (pp. 189–95). Washington, DC: Association of American Geographers.

Hein, K. (1996) Shop like a New Yorker. *Incentive* 170 (9), 91.

Helsingin Sanomat (2002) New record for Christmas tourism in Finnish Lapland. (18 December). English version on WWW at http://www.helsinki-hs.net/news.asp.

Henrici, J. (1999) Trading culture: tourism and tourist art in Pisac, Peru. In M. Robinson and P. Boniface (eds) *Tourism and Cultural Conflicts* (pp. 161–80). Wallingford: CAB International.

Henry, G.M. (1986) Welcome to the Pleasure Dome. *Time* (27 October), 75.

Heung, V.C.S. and Cheng, E. (2000) Assessing tourists' satisfaction with shopping in the Hong Kong Special Administrative Region of China. *Journal of Travel Research* 38 (4), 396–404.

Heung, V.C.S. and Qu H. (1998) Tourism shopping and its contributions to Hong Kong. _Tourism Management_ 19 (4), 383–6.

Hinch, T. and Butler, R. (1988) The rejuvenation of a tourism centre: Port Stanley, Ontario. _Ontario Geography_ 32, 29–52.

Hirschman, E.C. (1980) Innovativenss, novelty seeking, and consumer creativity. _Journal of Consumer Research_ 7, 283–95.

Hirschman, E.C. (1984) Experience seeking: a subjectivist perspective of consumption. _Journal of Business Research_ 12, 115–36.

Hirschman, E.C. (1986) The effect of verbal and pictorial advertising stimuli on aesthetic, utilitarian and familiarity perceptions. _Journal of Advertising_ 15 (2), 27–34.

Hirschman, E.C. and Holbrook, M.B. (1982) Hedonic consumption: Emerging concepts, methods and propositions. _Journal of Marketing_ 46 (3), 92–101.

Hirschman, E.C. and Solomon, M.R. (1984) Utilitarian, aesthetic, and familiarity responses to verbal versus visual advertisements. _Advances in Consumer Research_ 11, 426–31.

Hitchcock, M. (2000) Introduction. In M. Hitchcock and K. Teague (eds) _Souvenirs: The Material Culture of Tourism_ (pp. 1–17). Aldershot: Ashgate.

Hitchcock, M. and Nuryanti, W. (2000) Conclusions. In M. Hitchcock and W. Nuryanti (eds) _Building on Batik: The Globalization of a Craft Community_ (pp. 355–60). Aldershot: Ashgate.

Hoare, A. (1998) Bringing home the gifts. _Russian Life_ 41 (3), 45–6.

Hobson, J.S.P. (1996) Leisure shopping and tourism: The case of the South Korean market to Australia. _Turizam_ 44 (9/10), 228–44.

Hobson, J.S.P. (2000) Tourist shopping in transit: The case of BAAPK. _Journal of Vacation Marketing_ 6 (2), 170–83.

Hobson, J.S.P. and Christensen, M. (2001) Cultural and structural issues affecting Japanese tourist shopping behaviour. _Asia Pacific Journal of Tourism Research_ 6 (1), 37–45.

Holbrook, B. and Jackson, P. (1996) The social milieux of two North London shopping centres. _Geoforum_ 27 (2), 193–204.

Holbrook, M.B. and Hirschman, E.C. (1982) The experiential aspects of consumption: consumer fantasies, feelings, and fun. _Journal of Consumer Research_ 9, 132–40.

Holder, J. (1989) Tourism and the future of Caribbean handicraft. _Tourism Management_ 10 (4), 310–14.

Hopkins, J. (1991) West Edmonton Mall as a centre for social interaction. _Canadian Geographer_ 35 (3), 268–79.

Horner, A.E. (1993) Tourist arts in Africa before tourism. _Annals of Tourism Research_ 20 (1), 52–63.

Horoi, S.R. (1980) Tourism and Solomon handicrafts. In F. Rajotte (ed.) _Pacific Tourism: As Islanders See It_ (pp. 111–14). Suva: Institute of Pacific Studies, University of the South Pacific.

Hotel Online Special Report (1998) Correlation between cultural tourism and shopping. (31 December).

Houlihan, M. (2000) Souvenirs with soul: 800 years of pilgrimage to Santiago de Compostela. In M. Hitchcock and K. Teague (eds) _Souvenirs: The Material Culture of Tourism_ (pp. 18–24). Aldershot: Ashgate.

Houston-Montgomery, B. (1994) Shopping: Going over the top in Manhattan's East Village. _Travel & Leisure_ 24 (2), 48–52.

Hovinen, G.R. (1995) Heritage issues in urban tourism: An assessment of new trends in Lancaster County. *Tourism Management* 16 (5), 381–8.

Howard, E. (1990a) Conclusion. In E. Howard (ed.) *Leisure and Retailing* (pp. 59–62). Harlow: Longman.

Howard, E. (1990b) Development of ideas about leisure and shopping. In E. Howard (ed.) *Leisure and Retailing* (pp. 7–15). Harlow: Longman.

Hoyer, W.D. and Ridgway, N.M. (1984) Variety seeking as an explanation for exploratory purchase behavior: A theoretical model. *Advances in Consumer Research* 11, 114–19.

Hudman, L.E. (1978) Tourist impacts: the need for planning. *Annals of Tourism Research* 5 (1), 112–25.

Hudman, L.E. and Hawkins, D.E. (1989) *Tourism in Contemporary Society*. Englewood Cliffs, NJ: Prentice Hall.

Hudson, R. (1974) Images of the retailing environment: An example of the use of the repertory grid methodology. *Environment and Behavior* 6 (4), 470–94.

Humphrey, K. (1998) *Shelf Life: Supermarkets and the Changing Cultures of Consumption*. Cambridge: Cambridge University Press.

Humphreys, J.M. (1991) *Buy Greater Athens: The Economic Costs of Consumer Outshopping and the Potential Benefits of Reducing Outshopping Expenditures*. Athens, GA: University of Georgia.

Hunt, C. (2001) Dubai: A shopper's Mecca. *Travel Weekly* 60 (17), 5.

Hutchinson, B. (1994) Trouble in big mall country. *Canadian Business* 67 (9), 68–76.

International Council of Shopping Centers (2000) *Attracting Tourists to Shopping Centers*. New York: International Council of Shopping Centers.

Irwin, R.L., Wang, P. and Sutton, W.A. (1996) Comparative analysis of diaries and projected spending to assess patron expenditure behavior at short-term sporting events. *Festival Management and Event Tourism* 4 (1/2), 29–37.

Iso-Ahola, S.E. (1980) *The Social Psychology of Leisure and Recreation*. Dubuque, IA: William C. Brown.

Iverson, T.J. (1997) Japanese visitors to Guam: Lessons from experience. *Journal of Travel and Tourism Marketing* 6 (1), 41–54.

Iyer, E.S. (1989) Unplanned purchasing: knowledge of shopping environment and time pressure. *Journal of Retailing* 65 (1), 40–57.

Jackson, E.L. (1991) Shopping and leisure: Implications of West Edmonton Mall for leisure and for leisure research. *Canadian Geographer* 35 (3), 280–7.

Jackson, E.L. and Burton, T.L. (eds) (1999) *Leisure Studies: Prospects for the Twenty-First Century*. State College, PA: Venture.

Jackson, E.L. and Johnson, D.B. (1991) Geographic implications of mega-malls with special reference to West Edmonton Mall. *Canadian Geographer* 35 (3), 226–32.

Jackson, K.T. (1996) All the world's a mall: Reflections on the social and economic consequences of the American shopping center. *American Historical Review* 101 (4), 1111–1121.

Jackson, P. and Holbrook, B. (1995) Multiple meanings: Shopping and the cultural politics of identity. *Environment and Planning A* 27 (12), 1913–30.

Jacobs, J. (1985) *The Mall: An Attempted Escape from Everyday Life*. Prospect Heights, IL: Waveland Press.

Jago, L.K. and Deery, M.A. (2001) Managing volunteers. In S. Drummond and I. Yeoman (eds) *Quality Issues in Heritage Visitor Attractions* (pp. 194–216). Oxford: Butterworth Heinemann.

Jamal, T.B. and Getz, D. (1995) Collaboration theory and tourism planning. *Annals of Tourism Research* 22, 186–204.

Jamison, D.J. (1999) Masks without meaning: Notes on the processes of production, consumption, and exchange in the context of first world-third world tourism. *Journal of Macromarketing* 19 (1), 8–19.

Janiskee, R.L. and Drews, P.L. (1998) Rural festivals and community reimaging. In R.W. Butler, C.M. Hall and J. Jenkins (eds), *Tourism and Recreation in Rural Areas* (pp. 157–75). Chichester: Wiley.

Jansen, A.C.M. (1989) 'Funshopping' as a geographical notion, or the attraction of the inner city of Amsterdam as a shopping area. *Tijdschrift voor Economische en Sociale Geografie* 80 (3), 171–83.

Jansen-Verbeke, M. (1987) Women, shopping and leisure. *Leisure Studies*, 6 (1): 71–86.

Jansen-Verbeke, M. (1989) Inner cities and urban tourism resources in the Netherlands: New challenges for local authorities. In P. Bramham (ed.) *Leisure and Urban Processes: Critical Studies of Leisure Policy in West European Cities* (pp. 213–53). London: Routledge.

Jansen-Verbeke, M. (1990a) From leisure shopping to shopping tourism. In *Proceedings of the ISA Congress, Madrid* (pp. 1–17). Madrid: ISA.

Jansen-Verbeke, M. (1990b) Leisure + shopping = tourism product mix. In G. Ashworth and B. Goodall (eds) *Marketing Tourism Places* (pp. 128–37). London: Routledge.

Jansen-Verbeke, M. (1991) Leisure shopping: A magic concept for the tourism industry? *Tourism Management* 12, 9–14.

Jansen-Verbeke, M. (1994) The synergism between shopping and tourism: The Japanese experience. In W. F. Theobold (ed.) *Global Tourism: The Next Decade* (pp. 347–62). Oxford: Butterworth-Heinemann.

Jansen-Verbeke, M. (1998) The synergism between shopping and tourism. In W.F. Theobold (ed.) *Global Tourism* (2nd edn) (pp. 428–46). Oxford: Butterworth-Heinemann.

Janssen, P. (1996) Shopping till they drop. *Asian Business* 32 (5), 14.

Jarboe, G.R. and McDaniel, C.D. (1987) A profile of browsers in regional shopping malls. *Journal of the Academy of Marketing Science* 15 (1), 46–53.

Jenner, P. and Smith, C. (1993) Europe's microstates: Andorra, Monaco, Liechtenstein, and San Marino. *EIU International Tourism Reports* 1, 69–89.

Jensen, O.G. (2000) Water pots from East Greenland. *Suluk* 3, 45.

Johnson, D.B. (1987) The West Edmonton Mall: From super-regional to mega-regional shopping centre. *International Journal of Retailing* 2 (2), 53–69.

Johnson, D.B. (1991) Structural features of West Edmonton Mall. *Canadian Geographer* 35 (3), 249–61.

Johnson, R. (1992) Small town bed and breakfasts: St. Jacobs, Ontario, tries an alternative form of tourist accommodation. *Small Town* 22 (6), 20–5.

Johnson, R.C.A. and Mannell, R.C. (1983) The relationship of crowd density and environmental amenities to perceptions of malls as leisure and shopping environments. *Recreation Research Review* 10 (4), 18–23.

Johnson, S. (1990) Behavioural analysis. In E. Howard (ed.) *Leisure and Retailing* (pp. 43–50). Harlow: Longman.

Johnson, S. and Howard, E. (1990) The leisure market: Consumer choice and consumer activity. In E. Howard (ed.) *Leisure and Retailing* (pp. 25–42). Harlow: Longman.

Jones, J.M. (1998) Rural outshopping behavior: Another look at orientation and social influences. *Developments in Marketing Science* 21, 499–500.

Jones, J.M. and Vijayasarathy, L.R. (1998) Internet consumer catalog shopping: Findings from an exploratory study and directions for future research. *Internet Research* 8 (4), 322–30.

Jones, K. (1991) Mega-chaining, corporate concentration and the mega-mall. *Canadian Geographer* 35 (3), 241–9.

Jones, K. and Simmons, J. (1987a) *Location, Location, Location: Analyzing the Retail Environment*. Toronto: Methuen.

Jones, K. and Simmons, J. (1987b) *The Retail Environment*. London: Routledge.

Jones, M.A. (1999) Entertaining shopping experiences: An exploratory investigation. *Journal of Retailing and Consumer Services* 6, 129–39.

Jones, P. (1991) Regional shopping centres: The planning issues. *Service Industries Journal* 11 (2), 171–8.

Judd, D.R. (1995) Promoting tourism in US cities. *Tourism Management* 16 (3), 175–87.

Jules-Rosette, B. (1984) *The Messages of Tourist Art: An African Semiotic System in Comparative Perspective*. New York: Plenum Press.

Just Travel (2003) The Dubai Shopping Festival. On WWW at http://www.justtravel.com/au/tours/Dubai/Dubai.html. Accessed 20 November 2003.

Kamphorst, T.J. (1991) The leisure goods market and fun shopping in the Netherlands. *World Leisure & Recreation* 33 (1), 36–42.

Kaplan, J.E. (1987) Attitude toward shopping and store patronage: An exploratory study. Unpublished master's thesis, The University of Texas at Austin.

Kemp, K. (1992) Cross-border shopping: Trends and measurement issues. *Canadian Economic Observer* 5, 1–13.

Kent, R.L. (1989) The role of mystery in preferences for shopping malls. *Landscape Journal* 8, 28–35.

Kent, W.E., Shock, P.J. and Snow, R.E. (1983) Shopping: tourism's unsung hero(ine). *Journal of Travel Research* 21 (4), 2–4.

Keown, C.F. (1989) A model of tourists' propensity to buy: The case of Japanese visitors to Hawaii. *Journal of Travel Research* 27 (3), 31–4.

Kieron, S. (ed.) (1992) *Regeneration: Toronto's Waterfront and the Sustainable City*. Toronto: Royal Commission on the Future of the Toronto Waterfront.

Killick, S. (1998) Designer destination. *Property Week* 63 (28), 38–9.

Kim, H. and Shin, J. (2001) A contextual investigation of the operation and management of airport concessions. *Tourism Management* 23, 149–55.

Kim, S. and Littrell, M.A. (1999) Predicting souvenir purchase intentions. *Journal of Travel Research* 38 (2), 153–62.

Kim, S. and Littrell, M.A. (2001) Souvenir buying intentions for self versus others. *Annals of Tourism Research* 28 (3), 638–57.

Kincade, D. and Woodard, G. (2001) Shopping for souvenir clothing. *Pacific Tourism Review* 5 (3/4), 159–65.

Kinley, T.R., Josiam, B.M. and Kim, Y. (2003) Why and where tourists shop: Motivations of tourist-shoppers and their preferred shopping center attributes. *Journal of Shopping Center Research* 10 (1), 7–28.

Knickerbocker, P. (1995) Shopping: the soul of Mexico. *Travel & Leisure* 25 (2), 96–100.

Knight, M.B. (1999) America's tourist attractions. *Chain Store Age* 75 (3), 64–6.

Ko, T.G. (1999) The issues and implications of escorted shopping tours in a tourist destination region: The case study of Korean package tourists in Australia. *Journal of Travel and Tourism Marketing* 8 (3), 71–80.

Koeppel, D. (1999) Prescriptions to go. *Travel Holiday* 182 (1), 35–9.

Kollat, D.T. and Willett, R.P. (1967) Customer impulse purchasing behavior. *Journal of Marketing Research* 4, 21–31.

Kovács, Z. (1989) Border changes and their effect on the structure of Hungarian society. *Political Geography Quarterly* 8 (1), 79–86.

Kowaleski-Wallace, E. (1997) *Consuming Subjects: Women, Shopping, and Business in the Eighteenth Century*. New York: Columbia University Press.

Kowinski, W.S. (1985) *The Malling of America: An Inside Look at the Great Consumer Paradise*. New York: William Morrow.

Kowinski, W.S. (1986) Endless summer at the world's biggest shopping wonderland. *Smithsonian* 17 (9), 35–43.

Kozak, M. (2001) Comparative assessment of tourist satisfaction with destinations across two nationalities. *Tourism Management* 22, 391–401.

Kreck, L.A. (1985) The effect of the across-the-border commerce of Canadian tourists on the city of Spokane. *Journal of Travel Research* 24 (1), 27–31.

Kreiner, J. (1996) Piccadilly is the place to get royaled up about shopping. *Insight* 12 (2), 42–3.

Lambert, E. (1996) Shopping in Venice: Exploring Italian design with John Stefanidis. *Architecture Digest* 53 (9), 74–86.

Larke, R. (1994) *Japanese Retailing*. London: Routlege.

Lash, S. and Friedman, J. (eds) (1992) *Modernity and Identity*. Oxford: Blackwell.

Law, C.M. (1993) *Urban Tourism: Attracting Visitors to Large Cities*. London: Mansell.

Law, R. and Au, N. (2000) Relationship modeling in tourism shopping: A decision rules induction approach. *Tourism Management* 21 (3), 241–9.

Lederman, E. (1995) Bargains, with honor: Today's thrifty Japanese work their capital. *Conde Nast Traveler* 30 (3), 88–90.

Lee, S.L. (1993a) Overview of recent developments and policies on retail planning in Singapore. In S.L. Lee and S. Choo (eds) *The Changing Face of Retail Development and Planning in Singapore* (pp. 3–16). Singapore: School of Building and Estate Management, National University of Singapore.

Lee, S.L. (1993b) SME retailers in the HDB towns: Retail mix and business performance. In S.L. Lee and S. Choo (eds) *The Changing Face of Retail Development and Planning in Singapore* (pp. 62–79). Singapore: School of Building and Estate Management, National University of Singapore.

Lee, S.L. and Boon, Y.L. (1993) The changing face of the Singapore shopper. In S.L. Lee and S. Choo (eds) *The Changing Face of Retail Development and Planning in Singapore* (pp. 17–61). Singapore: School of Building and Estate Management, National University of Singapore.

Lehtonen, T.K. (1994) Shoppailu sosiaalisena muotona. *Sosiologia* 31 (3), 192–203.

Leimgruber, W. (1981) Political boundaries as a factor in regional integration: Examples from Basle and Ticino. *Regio Basiliensis* 22, 192–201.

Leimgruber, W. (1988) Border trade: The boundary as an incentive and an obstacle to shopping trips. *Nordia* 22 (1), 53–60.

Leimgruber, W. (1991) Boundary, values and identity: The Swiss-Italian transborder region. In D. Rumley and J.V. Minghi (eds) *The Geography of Border Landscapes* (pp. 43–62). London: Routledge.

Lengfelder, J. and Timothy, D.J. (2000) Leisure time in the 1990s and beyond: Cherished friend or incessant foe? *Visions in Leisure and Business* 19 (1), 13–26.

Lesser, J.A. and Hughes, M.A. (1986) Towards a typology of shoppers. *Business Horizons* 29 (6), 56–62.

Levell, N. (2000) Reproducing India: International exhibitions and Victorian tourism. In M. Hitchcock and K. Teague (eds) *Souvenirs: The Material Culture of Tourism* (pp. 36–51). Aldershot: Avebury.

Levy, S.J. (1959) Symbols for sale. *Harvard Business Review* 37, 117–19.

Lew, A.A. (1988) Tourism and place studies: An example of older retail districts in Oregon. *Journal of Geography* 87 (4), 122–6.

Lew, A.A. (1989) Authenticity and sense of place in the tourism development experience of older retail districts. *Journal of Travel Research* 27 (2), 15–22.

Lewis, G.H. (1989) Rats and bunnies: Core kids in an American mall. *Adolescence* 24, 881–9.

Lewis, G.H. (1990) Community through exclusion and illusion: The creation of social worlds in an American shopping mall. *Journal of Popular Culture* 24, 121–36.

Li, F., Nicholls, J.A.F., Zhou, N., Mandokovic, T. and Zhuang, G. (2003) A Pacific Rim debut: Shoppers in China and Chile. *Asia Pacific Journal of Marketing and Logistics* 15 (1/2), 115–31.

Lichfield, D. (1990) From combination to integration. In E. Howard (ed.) *Leisure and Retailing* (pp. 51–8). Harlow: Longman.

Lin, L. (2002) Indoor city and quasi-public space: A study of the shopping mall system in Hong Kong. *China Perspectives* 39, 46–52.

Littrell, M.A. (1990) Symbolic significance of textile crafts for tourists. *Annals of Tourism Research* 17 (2), 228–45.

Littrell, M.A. (1996) Shopping experiences and marketing of culture to tourists. In M. Robinson, N. Evans and P. Callaghan (eds) *Tourism and Culture: Image, Identity and Marketing* (pp. 107–20). Newcastle: University of Northumbria.

Littrell, M.A. and Dickson, M.A. (1999) *Social Responsibility in the Global Market: Fair Trade of Cultural Products*. Thousand Oaks, CA: Sage.

Littrell, M.A., Anderson, L.F. and Brown, P.J. (1993) What makes a craft souvenir authentic? *Annals of Tourism Research* 20 (1), 197–215.

Littrell, M.A., Baizerman, S., Kean, R., Gahring, S., Niemeyer, S., Reilly, R. and Stout, J. (1994) Souvenirs and tourism styles. *Journal of Travel Research* 32 (3), 3–11.

Lodging Hospitality (1999) Like culture, will shop, survey finds. 55 (9), 17.

Love, L.L. and Sheldon, P.S. (1998) Souvenirs: messengers of meaning. *Advances in Consumer Research* 25, 170–5.

Lowe, M. and Wrigley, N. (1996) Towards the new retail geography. In N. Wrigley and M. Lowe (eds) *Retailing, Consumption and Capital: Towards the New Retail Geography* (pp. 3–30). Harlow: Longman.

Lowe, W. (1998) Bagging a real deal on your next vacation. *New Choices* 38 (4), 98–9.

Lundberg, D.E. (1990) *The Tourist Business*. New York: Van Nostrand Reinhold.

Lyons, J. (1991) Border merchants. *Forbes* (19 August), 56–7.

MacCannell, D. (1973) Staged authenticity: Arrangements of social space in tourist settings. *American Journal of Sociology* 79 (3), 589–603.

MacCannell, D. (1976) *The Tourist: A New Theory of the Leisure Class*. New York: Schocken.

Mak, B.L.M., Tsang, N.K.F. and Cheung, I.C.Y. (1999) Taiwanese tourists' shopping preferences. *Journal of Vacation Marketing* 5 (2), 190–8.

Mall of America (2002) Welcome to the Mall of America. On WWW at http//: www.mallofamerica.com. Accessed 30 December 2003.

Mannell, R.C. and Kleiber, D.A. (1997) *A Social Psychology of Leisure*. State College, PA: Venture.

Marjanen, H. (1995) Longitudinal study on consumer spatial shopping behaviour with special reference to out-of-town shopping. *Journal of Retailing and Consumer Service* 2 (3), 163–74.

Markwick, M.C. (2001) Tourism and the development of handicraft production in the Maltese islands. *Tourism Geographies* 3 (1), 29–51.

Mars, G. and Mars, V. (2000) 'Souvenir-gifts' as tokens of filial esteem: The meanings of Blackpool souvenirs. In M. Hitchcock and K. Teague (eds) *Souvenirs: The Material Culture of Tourism* (pp. 91–111). Aldershot: Avebury.

Marsh, R. (1991) Selling heritage. *Leisure Management* 11 (10), 38–40.

Martin, B. and Mason, S. (1987) Current trends in leisure: leisure and shopping. *Leisure Studies* 6 (1), 93–7.

Mata, F. and Stanley, D. (1995) *Analysis of Potential Markets for the Parks Canada Product Lines*. Hull, Quebec: Department of Canadian Heritage, Strategic Research and Analysis.

Matheusik, M. (2001) When in doubt, shop. *Ski Area Management* 40 (1), 66–7, 83.

Matley, I.M. (1976) *The Geography of International Tourism*. Washington, DC: Association of American Geographers.

Maynard, P. (1990) The perfect couple? *Leisure Management* 10 (4), 34–8.

McBoyle, G. (1996) Green tourism and Scottish distilleries. *Tourism Management* 17, 255–63.

McCormick, R.R. (2001) Shopping. Paper presented at the Travel Industry Association of America Marketing Outlook Forum, 1–4 October.

McCracken, G. (1986) Culture and consumption: A theoretical account of the structure and movement of the cultural meaning of consumer goods. *Journal of Consumer Research* 13 (1), 71–84.

McCracken, G. (1987) The history of consumption: A literature review and consumer guide. *Journal of Consumer Policy* 10, 139–66.

McGoldrick, P.J. and Thompson, M.G. (1991) *Regional Shopping Centres*. Aldershot: Avebury.

McIntosh, R.W., Goeldner, C.R. and Ritchie, J.R.B. (1995) *Tourism: Principles, Practices, Philosophies* (7th edn). New York: Wiley.

Meldman, M. (1995) Four faces of Mexico: Along the U.S. border, boundless bargains. *The Washington Post* (24 September), E1.

Michael, E. (2002) Antiques and tourism in Australia. *Tourism Management* 23, 117–25.

Michaud, J. (1991) A social anthropology of tourism in Ladakh, India. *Annals of Tourism Research* 18, 605–21.

Michalkó, G. (2002) Országkép és kiskereskedelem a külföldi turisták sza badidős vásárlásai a magyarországi idegen vezetők szemével. *Turizmus Bulletin* 6 (3), 22–9.

Michalkó, G. and Timothy, D.J. (2001) Cross-border shopping in Hungary: Causes and effects. *Visions in Leisure and Business* 20 (1), 4–22.

Michman, R.D. and Greco, A.J. (1995) *Retailing Triumphs and Blunders: Victims of Competition in the New Age of Marketing Management*. Westport, CT: Quorum Books.

Middleton, V.T.C. (1994) *Marketing in Travel and Tourism*. Oxford: Butterworth Heinemann.

Mikesell, J.L. (1971) Sales taxation and the border county problem. *Quarterly Review of Economics and Business* 11 (1), 23–9.

Mikus, W. (1994) Research methods in border studies: Results for Latin America. In W.A. Gallusser (ed.) *Political Boundaries and Coexistence* (pp. 441–9). Bern: Peter Lang.

Miller, D. (1987) *Material Culture and Mass Consumption*. Oxford: Blackwell.

Miller, D. (1998) *A Theory of Shopping*. Ithaca, NY: Cornell University Press.

Miller, D. (2001) *The Dialectics of Shopping*. Chicago: University of Chicago Press.

Miller, D., Jackson, P., Thrift, N., Holbrook, B. and Rowlands, M. (1998) *Shopping, Place and Identity*. London: Routledge.

Minghi, J.V. (1994) The impact of Slovenian independence on the Italo-Slovene borderland: An assessment of the first three years. In W.A. Gallusser (ed.) *Political Boundaries and Coexistence* (pp. 88–94). Bern: Peter Lang.

Minghi, J.V. (1999) Borderland 'day tourists' from the East: Trieste's transitory shopping fair. *Visions in Leisure and Business* 17 (4), 32–49.

Mintel International (1996a) *Leisure Shopping*. London: Mintel International.

Mintel International (1996b) *Travel Shopping–Retailer Opportunities*. London: Mintel International.

Mitchell, C.J.A. (1998) Entrepreneurialism, commodification and creative destruction: A model of post-modern community development. *Journal of Rural Studies* 14 (3),273–86.

Mitchell, C.J.A., Parkin, T. and Hanley, S. (1998) Are tourists a blessing or bane? Resident attitudes towards tourism in the village of St. Jacobs, Ontario. *Small Town* 28 (6), 18–23.

Moeran, B. (1983) The language of Japanese tourism. *Annals of Tourism Research* 10, 93–108.

Mok, C. and Iverson, T.J. (2000) Expenditure-based segmentation: Taiwanese tourists to Guam. *Tourism Management*, 21 (3), 299–305.

Mok, C. and Lam, T. (1997) A model of tourists' shopping propensity: A case of Taiwanese visitors to Hong Kong. *Pacific Tourism Review* 1 (2), 137–45.

Moore, S. (1991) *Looking for Trouble: On Shopping, Gender and the Cinema*. London: Serpent's Tail.

Morbello, M. (1996) Zoo veneers: Animals and ethnic crafts at the San Diego Zoo. *Communication Review* 1 (4), 521–43.

Moreno, J.M. and Littrell, M.A. (1996) Marketing culture to tourists: interpreting and translating textile traditions in Antigua, Guatemala. In M. Robinson, N. Evans and P. Callaghan (eds) *Tourism and Culture: Image, Identity and Marketing* (pp. 137–45). Newcastle: University of Northumbria.

Moreno, J.M. and Littrell, M.A. (2001) Negotiating tradition: tourism retailers in Guatemala. *Annals of Tourism Research* 28 (3), 659–85.

Morgan, G. (1990) The changing nature of shopping centres. In E. Howard (ed.) *Leisure and Retailing* (pp. 17–24). Harlow: Longman.

Moscardo, G. (1999) *Making Visitors Mindful*. Champaign, Ill: Sagamore.

Murphy, P.E. (1985) *Tourism: A Community Approach*. London: Methuen.

Nason, J.D. (1984) Tourism, handicrafts, and ethnic identity in Micronesia. *Annals of Tourism Research* 11 (3), 421–49.

Nava, M. (1997) Modernity's disavowal: Women, the city and the department store. In P. Falk and C. Campbell (eds) *The Shopping Experience* (pp. 56–91). London: Sage.

Naylor, L.A. (1992) Mega malls: beyond shopping. *Better Homes and Gardens* 70 (11), 213–20.

Nelson, E. (1998) *Mall of America: Reflections of a Virtual Community*. Lakeville, MN: Galde Press.

Nelson, R.L. (1959) *The Selection of Retail Locations*. New York: F.W. Dodge.

Newby, P. (1993) Shopping as leisure. In R.D.F. Bromley and C.J. Thomas (eds) *Retail Change: Contemporary Issues* (pp. 208–28). London: University College London Press.

Newman, D.R. and Hodgetts, R.M. (1998) *Human Resource Management: A Customer-Oriented Approach*. Upper Saddle River, NJ: Prentice Hall.

News for You (1996) Outlet malls attract tourists. 44 (31), 3.

Ngamsom, B. (1998) Shopping tourism: A case study of Thailand. In K.S. Chon (ed.) *Proceedings, Tourism and Hotel Industry in Indo-China and Southeast Asia: Development, Marketing, and Sustainability Conference* (pp. 112–28). Houston, TX: University of Houston.

Nielson, S.B. (2002) Cross-border shopping from small to large countries. *Economics Letters* 77, 309–13.

Nieminen, M. (2000) Santa Claus Theme Park: A work in progress. *Helsingin Sanomat* (online English version) On WWW at http://helsinki-hs.net/news.asp. Accessed on 19 December 2000.

Nin, C.Y. (1994) Trade at the Sino-Kazakhstani Border: A visit to Korgas and Yining. *China Tourism* 167, 60–5.

Nishiyama, K. (1996) *Welcoming the Japanese Visitor: Insights, Tips, Tactics*. Honolulu: University of Hawai'i Press.

Obeyesekere, S.V. (1988) The role of a craft museum in marketing/promoting crafts, and the Lakpahana experience. *Museums* 157, 10–17.

O'Connor, P. (1999) *Electronic Information Distribution in Tourism and Hospitality*. Wallingford: CAB International.

Oliver, R.L. (1980) A cognitive model of the antecedents and consequences of satisfaction decisions. *Journal of Marketing Research* 17, 460–9.

Olshavsky, R.W. and Granbois, D.H. (1979) Consumer decision making – fact or fiction? *Journal of Consumer Research* 6, 93–100.

O'Meara, K. (2000) Adventure tourism's future: Keeping it real. *Travel Weekly* 59 (77), 44.

Onderwater, L., Richards, G. and Stam, S. (2000) Why tourists buy textile souvenirs: European evidence. *Tourism, Culture & Communication* 2 (1), 39–48.

O'Neill, M.J. and Jasper, C.R. (1992) An evaluation of models of consumer spatial behavior using the environment-behavior paradigm. *Environment and Behavior* 24 (4), 411–40.

Opperman, M. (1993) Tourism space in developing countries. *Annals of Tourism Research* 20, 535–56.

Orbaşli, A. (2002) *Tourists in Historic Towns: Urban Conservation and Heritage Management*. London: E & FN Spon.

Outletbound (2002) Outletbound: Guide to the Nation's Best Outlets. On WWW at http://:www.outletbound.com. Accessed 29 November 2002.

Page, S.J. (1992) Managing tourism in a small historic city. *Town & Country Planning* 61 (7/8), 208–11.

Page, S.J. (1995) *Urban Tourism*. London: Routledge.

Page, S.J. (1996) Wellington. *Cities* 13 (2), 125–34.

Paige, R.C. and Littrell, M.A. (2003) Tourism activities and shopping preferences. *Journal of Shopping Center Research* 10 (2), 7–26.

Painton, F. (1994) Shopping spoken here. *Time* (5 September), 58.

Pál, Á. and Nagy, I. (1999) Socio-economic processes in the Hungarian-Yugoslavian border zone. In H. Eskelinen, I. Liikanen and J. Oksa (eds) *Curtains of Iron and Gold: Reconstructing Borders and Scales of Interaction* (pp. 229–41). Aldershot: Ashgate.

Papadopoulos, N.G. (1980) Consumer outshopping research: Review and extension. *Journal of Retailing* 56 (4), 41–58.

Park, M.K. (2000) Social and cultural factors influencing tourists' souvenir-purchasing behavior: A comparative study on Japanese 'omiyage' and Korean 'sunmul'. *Journal of Travel and Tourism Marketing* 9 (1/2), 81–91.

Parkin, I., Middleton, P. and Beswick, V. (1989) Managing the town and city for visitors and local people. In D.L. Uzzell (ed.) *Heritage Interpretation, Vol. 2: The Visitor Experience* (pp. 108–14). London: Belhaven.

Parnwell, M.J.G. (1993) Tourism and rural handicrafts in Thailand. In M. Hitchcock, V.T. King and M.J.G. Parnwell (eds) *Tourism in South-East Asia* (pp. 234–57). London: Routledge.

Patricios, N.N. (1979) Human aspects of planning shopping centers. *Environment and Behavior* 11 (4), 511–38.

Patrick, J.M. and Renforth, W. (1996) The effects of the peso devaluation on cross-border retailing. *Journal of Borderlands Studies* 11 (1), 25–41.

Patton, S.G. (1986) Factory outlets and travel industry development: The case of Reading, Pennsylvania. *Journal of Travel Research* 25 (1), 10–13.

Pavlakovic, V.K. and Kim, H.H. (1990) Outshopping by maquila employees: Implications for Arizona's border communities. *Arizona Review* (Spring), 9–16.

Pearce, D.G. (1984) Planning for tourism in Belize. *Geographical Review* 74 (3), 291–303.

Pearce, D.G. (1989) *Tourist Development*. London: Longman.

Pearce, D.G. (1998) Tourist districts in Paris: Structure and functions. *Tourism Management* 19 (1), 49–65.

Pearce, D.G. (1999) Tourism in Paris: studies at the microscale. *Annals of Tourism Research* 26 (1), 77–97.

Pearce, P.L., Moscardo, G.M. and Ross, G. (1996) *Tourism Community Relationships*. Oxford: Pergamon.

Peberdy, S. (2000) Border crossings: Small entrepreneurs and cross-border trade between South Africa and Mozambique. *Tijdschrift voor Economische en Sociale Geografie* 91 (4), 361–78.

Pesmen, S. (1994) It's a mall world after all. *Advertising Age* 65 (53), 3, 9.

Piron, F. (2002) International outshopping and ethnocentrism. *European Journal of Marketing* 36 (1/2), 189–210.

Plog, S. (1973) Why destination areas rise and fall in popularity. *Cornell Hotel and Restaurant Administration Quarterly* 14 (3), 13–16.

Popelka, C.A. and Littrell, M.A. (1991) Influence of tourism on handcraft evolution. *Annals of Tourism Research* 18 (3), 392–413.

Prentice, R.C. (1992) 'Out-shopping' and the externalization of the Isle of Man retailing economy. _Scottish Geographical Magazine_ 108 (1), 17–21.

Prentice, R.C. (1993) _Tourism and Heritage Attractions_. London: Routledge.

Preteceille, E. and Terrail, J.P. (1985) _Capitalism, Consumption and Needs_. Oxford: Blackwell.

Pretes, M. (1996) Postmodern tourism: The Santa Claus industry. _Annals of Tourism Research_ 22 (1), 1–15.

Prideaux, B. and Kim, S.M. (1999) Trends in Korean tourism: The Australian connection. In K. Pookong and B. King (eds) _Asia-Pacific Tourism: Regional Cooperation, Planning and Development_ (pp. 197–209). Melbourne: Hospitality Press.

Princen, T., Maniates, M. and Conca, K. (eds) (2002) _Confronting Consumption_. Cambridge, MA: MIT Press.

Prock, J. (1983) The peso devaluations and their effect on Texas border economies. _Inter-American Economic Affairs_ 37 (3), 83–92.

Prus, R. and Dawson, L. (1991) Shop 'til you drop: Shopping as recreational and laborious activity. _Canadian Journal of Sociology_ 16 (2), 145–64.

Pysarchik, D.T. (1989) Tourism retailing. In S. Witt and L. Moutinho (eds) _Tourism Marketing and Management Handbook_ (pp. 553–56). New York: Prentice Hall.

Rappaport, E.D. (2000) _Shopping for Pleasure: Women in the Making of London's West End_. Princeton: Princeton University Press.

Rathbun, R.D. (1986) _Shopping Centers and Malls_. New York: Retail Reporting Corporation.

Reeves, D. (1996) Women shopping. In C. Booth, J. Darke and S.J. Yeandle (eds) _Changing Places: Women's Live in the City_ (pp. 128–41). London: Paul Chapman.

Reid, T.R. (2000) It's all downhill in Andorra. _Sky_ (February), 19–22.

Reisinger, Y. and Turner, L.W. (2002) The determination of shopping satisfaction of Japanese tourists visiting Hawaii and the Gold Coast compared. _Journal of Travel Research_ 41 (2), 167–76.

Reynolds, J. (1993) The proliferation of the planned shopping centre. In R.D.F. Bromley and C.J. Thomas (eds) _Retail Change: Contemporary Issues_ (pp. 70–87). London: University College London Press.

Riegler, S. (1999) The new capital of cutting edge. _Travel & Leisure_ 29 (6), 142–6.

Riehle, H. (1987) Convenience store update. _Restaurants USA_ 8 (2), 40–4.

Ritchie, K.D. (1993) A spatial analysis of cross-border shopping in Southern Ontario. Unpublished BA Honors Thesis, Department of Geography, University of Waterloo.

Ritzer, G. and Liska, A. (1997) 'McDisneyization' and 'post-tourism': Complementary perspectives on contemporary tourism. In C. Rojek and J. Urry (eds) _Touring Cultures: Transformations of Travel and Theory_ (pp. 96–208). London: Routledge.

Rob Tonge and Associates (1995) _How to Do Business with the Japanese Visitor Market: A Guide for Small Tourist Businesses_, 5th edn. Coolum Beach, Qld: Gull Publishing.

Roberts, J. (1987) Buying leisure. _Leisure Studies_ 6 (1), 87–91.

Rosa, T. (2001) Md. mall offers more than shopping. _Travel Weekly_ 60 (26), 34.

Rowley, J. and Slack, F. (1999) The retail experience in airport departure lounges: Reaching for timelessness and placelessness. _International Marketing Review_ 16 (4/5), 363–375.

Roy, A. (1994) Correlates of mall visit frequency. _Journal of Retailing_ 70 (2), 139–61.

Rucker, M., Kaiser, S., Barry, M., Brummett, D., Freeman, C. and Peters, A. (1986) The imported export market: An investigation of foreign visitors' gift and personal purchase. In N.K. Malhotra and J.M. Hawes (eds) *Developments in Marketing Science* (pp. 120–4). Greenvale, NY: Academy of Marketing Science.

Ruston, P. (1999) *Out of Town Shopping: The Future of Retailing.* London: The British Library.

Ryan, C. (1991) *Recreational Tourism: A Social Science Perspective.* London: Routledge.

Ryan, C. and Crotts, J. (1997) Carving and tourism: A Maori perspective. *Annals of Tourism Research* 24, 898–918.

Ryan, C. and Huyton, J. (1998) Dispositions to buy postcards with Aboriginal designs at Uluru-Kata Tjuta National Park. *Journal of Sustainable Tourism* 6 (3), 254–9.

Sack, R. (1988) The consumers' world: Place as context. *Annals of the Association of American Geographers* 78, 642–64.

Sack, R. (1992) *Place, Modernity, and the Consumer's World: A Relational Framework for Geographical Analysis.* Baltimore, MD: The Johns Hopkins University Press.

Salvaneschi, L. (1996) *Location, Location, Location: How to Select the Best Site for Your Business.* Grants Pass, OR: Oasis Press.

Sándor, J. (1990) A nyugati határszél idegenforgalma a vonzás és a keresletkinálat tükrében. *Idegenforgalmi Közlemények* 1, 25–34.

Sargent, P. (1985) Leisure and shopping. *Leisure Management* 5 (7), 11–13.

Sargent, P. (1988) The leisureplex and the dinosaurs: Developments in shopping and leisure. *Leisure Management* 8 (5), 20–4.

Sargent, P. (2002) Big is beautiful. *Leisure Management* 22 (2), 46–8.

Satterthwaite, A. (2001) *Going Shopping: Consumer Choices and Community Conse-quences.* New Haven, CT: Yale University Press.

Scanian, D. (1991) The recession: Canadian dollars helping Massena ride it out. *Ottawa Citizen* (18 May).

Scarce, J. (2000) Tourism and material culture in Turkey. In M. Hitchcock and K. Teague (eds) *Souvenirs: The Material Culture of Tourism* (pp. 25–35). Aldershot: Avebury.

Schädler, K.F. (1979) African arts and crafts in a world of changing values. In J.A. Kryden (ed.) *Tourism and Development* (pp. 146–56). Cambridge: Cambridge University Press.

Scheyvens, R. (2002) *Tourism for Development.* Harlow: Prentice Hall.

Schouten, F.F.J. (1995a) Heritage as historical reality. In D.T. Herbert (ed.) *Heritage, Tourism and Society* (pp. 21–31). London: Mansell.

Schouten, F.F.J. (1995b) Improving visitor care in heritage attractions. *Tourism Man-agement* 16 (4), 259–61.

Schroeder, C.L. (2002) *Specialty Shop Retailing: How to Run Your Own Store.* New York: Wiley.

Shackley, M. (1997) Tourism and the management of cultural resources in the Pays Dogon, Mali. *International Journal of Heritage Studies* 3 (1), 17–27.

Shackley, M. (1998) *Visitor Management: Case Studies from World Heritage Sites.* Oxford: Butterworth Heinemann.

Shackley, M. (2001) *Managing Sacred Sites: Service Provision and Visitor Experience.* London: Continuum.

Shenhav-Keller, S. (1993) The Israeli souvenir: its text and context. *Annals of Tourism Research* 20 (1), 182–96.

Shenhav-Keller, S. (1995) The Jewish pilgrim and the purchase of a souvenir in Israel. In M. Lanfant, J.B. Allcock and E.M. Bruner (eds) *International Tourism: Identity and Change* (pp. 143–58). London: Sage.

Sherman, E., Mathur, A. and Smith, R.B. (1997) Store environment and consumer purchase behavior: mediating role of consumer emotions. *Psychology and Marketing* 14 (4), 361–78.

Sherry, J.F. (1990) A sociocultural analysis of a Midwestern American flea market. *Journal of Consumer Research* 17, 13–30.

Shields, R. (1989) Social spatialization and the built environment: The case of the West Edmonton Mall. *Environment and Planning D* 7 (2), 147–64.

Shields, R. (1992) The individual, consumption cultures and the fate of community. In R. Shields (ed.) *Lifestyle Shopping: The Subject of Consumption* (pp. 99–113). London: Routledge.

Shokeir, M.A. (1991) Japanese travelers' propensity for shopping in American airport shops. Unpublished Master's Thesis, University of Wisconsin-Stout.

Shop America Alliance (2001a) *Annual Report, 2001*. Phoenix: Shop America Alliance.

Shop America Alliance (2001b) *Where to Shop in the USA, 2001*. Phoenix: Shop America Alliance.

Silberberg, T. (1995) Cultural tourism and business opportunities for museums and heritage sites. *Tourism Management* 16, 361–5.

Silberberg, T., Garrett, D., Lall, F., Bernstein, J., Firsten, R. and Silberberg, H. (1976) *A Guide for the Revitalization of Retail Districts*. Toronto: Ontario Ministry of Industry and Tourism.

Simmons, J. (1991) The regional mall in Canada. *Canadian Geographer* 35 (3), 232–40.

Simms, E.A. and Narine, M. (1994) A survey of shopping behaviour of consumers in Trinidad and Tobago: The case of grocery shopping. *Social and Economic Studies* 43 (2), 107–37.

Simons, M. (2000) Aboriginal heritage art and moral rights. *Annals of Tourism Research* 27, 412–31.

Slater, T.R. (1984) Preservation, conservation and planning in historic towns. *The Geographical Journal* 150 (3), 322–34.

Slivka, J. (2001) Vendors trail fires and sell T-shirts. *Arizona Republic* (3 September), A13.

Smith, R.K. and Olson, L.S. (2001) Tourist shopping activities and development of travel sophistication. *Visions in Leisure and Business* 20 (1), 23–33.

Smith, S. (1989) Funding our heritage. In D.L. Uzzell (ed.) *Heritage Interpretation, Vol 2, The Visitor Experience* (pp. 23–8). London: Belhaven.

Smith, V.L. (1996) Indigenous tourism: The four Hs. In R. Butler and T. Hinch (eds) *Tourism and Indigenous Peoples* (pp. 283–307). London: International Thomson Business Press.

Snepenger, D.J. (1987) Segmenting the vacation market by novelty-seeking role. *Journal of Travel Research* 26 (2), 8–14.

Snepenger, D.J., Murphy, L., O'Connell, R. and Gregg, E. (2003) Tourists and residents use of a shopping space. *Annals of Tourism Research* 39 (3), 567–80.

Solomon, M.R. (1992) *Consumer Behavior: Buying, Having and Being*. Needham Heights, MA: Allyn and Bacon.

Stanley, N. (2000) Souvenirs, ethics and aesthetics: Some contemporary dilemmas in the South Pacific. In M. Hitchcock and K. Teague (eds) *Souvenirs: The Material Culture of Tourism* (pp. 238–45). Aldershot: Ashgate.

Stansfield, C.A. (1971) The nature of seafront development and social status of seaside resorts. *Loisir et Société/Society and Leisure* 4, 117–46.

Stansfield, C.A. (1972) The development of modern seaside resorts. *Parks and Recreation* 5: 14–17, 43–6.

Starkey, M. (1989) *Born to Shop*. Eastbourne: Monarch.

Stefano, F. (1976) *Pictorial Souvenirs and Commemoratives of North America*. New York: E.P. Dutton.

Stephenson, R.P. and Willett, R.P. (1969) Analysis of consumer retail patronage strategies. In P.R. McDonald (ed.) *Marketing Involvement in Society and the Economy* (pp. 31–322). Chicago: American Marketing Association.

Stern, H. (1962) The significance of impulse buying today. *Journal of Marketing* 26 (2), 59–62.

Stevenson, D. (1991) Cross-border dispute. *Canadian Consumer* 21 (7), 8–15.

Stoltman, J.J., Gentry, J.W., Anglin, K.A., and Burns, A.C. (1990) Situational influences on the consumer decision sequence. *Journal of Business Research* 21 (3), 195–207.

Stone, G.P. (1954) City shoppers and urban identification: Observations on the social psychology of city life. *American Journal of Sociology* 60 (1), 36–45.

Stryjakiewicz, T. (1998) The changing role of border zones in the transforming economies of East-Central Europe: The case of Poland. *GeoJournal* 44 (3), 203–13.

Sulaiman, S. (1992) *The Role of Handicraft in Cultural Tourism Development* (Activity Report No. 7.2). Yogyakarta: UNESCO/Directorate General of Tourism.

Sun, L. (1998) A comparison study of the shopping behavior of business and leisure travelers in the Minneapolis/St. Paul International Airport. Unpublished master's thesis, University of Wisconsin-Stout.

Swain, M.B. (1993) Women producers of ethnic arts. *Annals of Tourism Research* 20 (1), 32–51.

Swanson, K.K. (1994) Souvenir marketing in tourism retailing: Shopper and retailer perceptions. Unpublished doctoral dissertation, Texas Tech University.

Swanson, K.K. and Horridge, P. (2002) Tourists' souvenir purchase behavior and retailers' awareness of tourists' purchase behavior in the Southwest. *Clothing and Textiles Research Journal* 20 (2), 62–76.

Swarbrooke, J. (1995) *The Development and Management of Visitor Attractions*. Oxford: Butterworth Heinemann.

Szabo, J. (1996) Bonanza on the border: A loco buying spree along the Tex-Mex Trail. *Travel & Leisure* 26 (11), 58–64.

Taillefer, F. (1991) Le paradoxe Andorran. *Revue Geographique des Pyrenees et du Sud-Ouest* 62 (2), 117–38.

Tanzer, A. (1996) Spoiled Hong Kong. *Forbes* 157 (4), 148–9.

Tanzer, A. and Tucker, A. (1996) All of the best and none of the worst of Hong Kong. *Forbes* (FYI Supplement, 23 September), 174–82.

Tauber, E.M. (1972) Why do people shop? *Journal of Marketing* 36, 46–59.

Tauber, E.M. (1995) Why do people shop? *Marketing Management* 4 (2), 58–60.

Teague, K. (2000) Tourist markets and Himalayan craftsmen. In M. Hitchcock and K. Teague (eds) *Souvenirs: The Material Culture of Tourism* (pp. 194–208). Aldershot: Ashgate.

Telfer, D.J. (2001) Strategic alliances along the Niagara Wine Route. *Tourism Management* 22 (1), 21–30.

Terry, C.F. (1977) The shopping center as a setting for leisure behavior, an Australian example: Implications for urban recreational planning. Unpublished master's thesis, University of Texas at Austin.

The Economist (1992) Decline and mall. (29 August), 25.

The Economist (1996) Heathrow, shopping mall. (27 July), 52.

Thomas, C.J. (1989) The roles of historic sites and reasons for visiting. In D.T. Herbert, R.C. Prentice and C.J. Thomas (eds) *Heritage Sites: Strategies for Marketing and Development* (pp. 62–93). Aldershot: Avebury.

Thompson, C. and Cutler, E. (1997) The effect of nationality on tourist arts: The case of The Gambia, West Africa. *International Journal of Hospitality Management* 16 (2), 225–9.

Thompson, J.R. (1971) Characteristics and behavior of out-shopping consumers. *Journal of Retailing* 47 (1), 70–80.

Thorpe, D. (1994) The Mall of America. *Parabola* 19 (2), 25–9.

Tiesdell, S., Oc, T. and Heath, T. (1996) *Revitalizing Historic Urban Quarters*. Oxford: Architectural Press.

Timothy, D.J. (1995) Political boundaries and tourism: Borders as tourist attractions. *Tourism Management* 16, 525–32.

Timothy, D.J. (1998) Collecting places: Geodetic lines in tourist space. *Journal of Travel and Tourism Marketing* 7 (4), 123–9.

Timothy, D.J. (1999a) Cross-border shopping: Tourism in the Canada–United States borderlands. *Visions in Leisure and Business* 17 (4), 4–18.

Timothy, D.J. (1999b) Tourism and street vendors. *International Institute for Asian Studies Newsletter* 19, 12.

Timothy, D.J. (2001) *Tourism and Political Boundaries*. London: Routledge.

Timothy, D.J. (2002a) Tourism and community development issues. In R. Sharpley and D.J. Telfer (eds) *Tourism and Development: Concepts and Issues* (pp. 149–64). Clevedon: Channel View Publications.

Timothy, D.J. (2002b) Tourism in borderlands: Competition, complementarity, and cross-frontier cooperation. In S. Krakover and Y. Gradus (eds) *Tourism in Frontier Areas* (pp. 233–58). Lanham, MD: Lexington Books.

Timothy, D.J. and Boyd, S.W. (2003) *Heritage Tourism*. Harlow: Prentice Hall.

Timothy, D.J. and Butler, R.W. (1995) Cross-border shopping: A North American perspective. *Annals of Tourism Research* 22 (1), 16–34.

Timothy, D.J. and Tosun, C. (2003) Appropriate planning for tourism in destination communities: Participation, incremental growth and collaboration. In S. Singh, D.J. Timothy and R.K. Dowling (eds) *Tourism in Destination Communities* (pp. 181–204). Wallingford: CAB International.

Timothy, D.J. and Wall, G. (1995) Tourist accommodation in an Asian historic city. *Journal of Tourism Studies* 6 (2), 63–73.

Timothy, D.J. and Wall, G. (1997) Selling to tourists: Indonesian street vendors. *Annals of Tourism Research* 24 (2), 322–40.

Toops, S.W. (1993) Xinjiang's handicraft industry. *Annals of Tourism Research* 20 (1), 88–106.

Toops, S.W. (1995) Tourism in Xinjiang: practice and place. In A.A. Lew and L. Yu (eds) *Tourism in China: Geographic, Political, and Economic Perspectives* (pp. 179–202). Boulder, CO: Westview Press.

Tosun, C. (1999) Towards a typology of community participation in the tourism development process. *Anatolia* 10 (2), 113–34.

Tourism Shopping Implementation Committee (1990) *Tourism Shopping in the Nineties*. Canberra: Australian Government Publishing Service.

Travel and Tourism Executive Report (1997) Hong Kong tourism seeks cure for handover hangover. 18 (5), 1–6.

Travel Industry Association of America (2000) Shopping, shopping, shopping! *TIA Press Release*, 14 November.

Travel Industry Association of America (2001) *The Shopping Traveler*. Washington, DC: Travel Industry Association of America.

Travel Weekly (2000a) Plan features Paris shopping. 59 (74), 20.

Travel Weekly (2000b) Select Italy offers Florence shopping. 59 (95), E9.

Travel Weekly (2001) LVCVA fashions program with shoppers in mind. 60 (67), 32.

Turner, L.W. and Reisinger, Y. (2001) Shopping satisfaction for domestic tourists. *Journal of Retailing and Consumer Services* 8, 15–27.

Tythacott, L. (2000) Exotic souvenirs of the travelling surrealists. In M. Hitchcock and K. Teague (eds) *Souvenirs: The Material Culture of Tourism* (pp. 72–8). Aldershot: Ashgate.

Underhill, P. (1999) *Why We Buy: The Science of Shopping*. New York: Simon and Schuster.

Underwood, E. (1994) Mall busters, like crime, a boon for home shopping. *Brandweek* (17 January), 18.

Urry, J. (1995) *Consuming Places*. London: Routledge.

US Department of Commerce (1999) *Shopping and Cultural/Heritage Tourism: A Special Study of Overseas Travelers to the United States*. Washington, DC: US Department of Commerce.

Uzzell, D.L. (1995) The myth of the indoor city. *Journal of Environmental Psychology* 15, 299–310.

Valdez, A. and Sifanek, S.J. (1997) Drug tourists and drug policy on the U.S.–Mexican border: An ethnographic investigation of the acquisition of prescription drugs. *Journal of Drug Issues* 27 (4), 879–97.

Veblen, T. (1934) *The Theory of the Leisure Class: An Economic Study of Institutions*. New York: The Modern Library.

Verlini, J. (2000) Awaji Ningyo: Its changing role within a local, national and international community. In M. Hitchcock and K. Teague (eds) *Souvenirs: The Material Culture of Tourism* (pp. 157–65). Aldershot: Ashgate.

Vester, H.G. (1996) The shopping mall: A tourist destination of postmodernity. *Gruppendynamik* 27 (1), 57–66.

Vincent, V.C. and de los Santos, G. (1990) Winter Texans: Two segments of the senior travel market. *Journal of Travel Research* 29 (1), 9–12.

Vogel, R.J. (1995) Crossing the border for health care: An exploratory analysis of consumer choice. *Journal of Borderlands Studies* 10 (1), 19–44.

Vogt, C.A. and Fesenmaier, D.R. (1998) Expanding the functional information search model. *Annals of Tourism Research* 25 (3), 551–78.

Vukonić, B. (2002) Religion, tourism and economics: A convenient symbiosis. *Tourism Recreation Research* 27 (2), 59–64.

Wade, B. (1985) From lifeline to leisure. *Town & Country Planning* 54 (7/8), 215–16.

Wagner, U. (1982) *Catching the Tourist: Women Handicraft Traders in the Gambia*. Stockholm: Department of Social Anthropology, University of Stockholm.

Waitt, G. and McGuirk, P.M. (1997) Selling waterfront heritage: A critique of Millers Point, Sydney. *Tijdschrift voor Economische en Sociale Geografie* 88 (4), 342–52.

Wakabayashi, G. (1995) I'll take Hong Kong. *Travel & Leisure* 25 (9), 132–43.

Wakefield, K.L. and Baker, J. (1998) Excitement at the mall: Determinants and effects on shopping response. _Journal of Retailing_ 74 (4), 515–39.

Wall, G. and Hohol, F. (1989) Tourism in small towns: Elora, Elmira and St. Jacobs. In J.G. Nelson, J.A. Carruthers and A.R. Howarth (eds) _Urban Heritage: Preserving, Planning and Managing Historical Heritage in Communities_ (pp. 61–7). Waterloo: Heritage Resources Centre, University of Waterloo.

Wallendorf, M. and Arnould, E.J. (1988) My favourite things: A cross-cultural inquiry into object attachment, possessiveness, and social linkage. _Journal of Consumer Research_ 14, 531–47.

Walters, D. (1994) _Retailing Management: Analysis, Planning and Control._ London: Macmillan.

Walvin, J. (1992) Selling the sun: Tourism and material consumption. _Revista Interamericana_ 22 (1/2), 208–25.

Wang, Z.H. and Ryan, C. (1998) New Zealand retailers' perceptions of some tourists' negotiating styles for souvenir purchases. _Tourism, Culture and Communication_ 1 (2), 139–52.

Warnaby, G. (1998) Marketing UK cities as shopping destinations: Problems and prospects. _Journal of Retailing and Consumer Services_ 5 (1), 55–8.

Wasserman, D. (1996) The borderlands mall: Form and function of an imported landscape. _Journal of Borderlands Studies_ 11 (2), 69–88.

Weigand, K. (1990) Drei Jahrzehnte Einkaufstourismus über die deutsch-dänische Grenze. _Geographische Rundschau_ 42 (5), 286–90.

Weller, A. (1997) Bahamas' best buys. _National Geographic Traveler_ 14 (1), 24–8.

West, I. (2000) The 'Whimsey': A part of American and Canadian Victoriana. In M. Hitchcock and K. Teague (eds) _Souvenirs: The Material Culture of Tourism_ (pp. 284–7). Aldershot: Ashgate.

West, J. (1991) _The Americans with Disabilities Act: From Policy to Practice._ New York: Milbank Memorial Fund.

West Edmonton Mall (2002) West Edmonton Mall: The World's Largest Entertainment and Shopping Centre. On WWW at http//:www.westedmall.com. Accessed 30 December 2003.

Westbrook, R.A. and Black, W.C. (1985) A motivation-based shopper typology. _Journal of Retailing_ 61 (1), 78–103.

Westover, T.N. (1976) The suburban shopping mall as a leisure environment. Unpublished master's thesis, University of California, Davis.

Whysall, P. (1995) Regenerating inner city shopping centres: The British experience. _Journal of Retailing and Consumer Services_ 2 (1), 3–13.

Wieffering, E. (1994) What has the Mall of America done to Minneapolis? _American Demographics_ 16 (2), 13–16.

Wilkinson, J. (2000) Tourism and Ainu identity, Hokkaido, Northern Japan. In M. Hitchcock and K. Teague (eds) _Souvenirs: The Material Culture of Tourism_ (pp. 147–56). Aldershot: Ashgate.

Williams, A.M. and Baláž, V. (2000) _Tourism in Transition: Economic Change in Central Europe._ London: I.B. Tauris.

Wolfe-Keddie, J. (1993) Tourism in the Eastern Arctic: Coping with 'Dangerous Children'. _Journal of Applied Recreation Research_ 18 (2), 143–62.

Wondoamiseno, R. and Basuki, S.S. (1986) _Kotagede between Two Gates._ Yogyakarta: Department of Architecture, Gadjah Mada University.

Wong, H. (1980) Recreation-shopping centre: Recreation facility for the passive majority. _Recreation Canada_ 38 (2), 6–13.

Wong, J. and Law, R. (2003) Difference in shopping satisfaction levels: A study of tourists in Hong Kong. *Tourism Management* 24, 401–10.

Worden, N. (1996) Contested heritage at the Cape Town Waterfront. *International Journal of Heritage Studies* 1 (1/2), 59–75.

Yamamoto, D. and Gill, A.M. (2002) Issues of globalization and reflexivity in the Japanese tourism production system: The case of Whistler, British Columbia. *The Professional Geographer* 54 (1), 83–93.

Yeates, M. (1998) *The North American City* (5th edn). New York: Longman.

Yenckel, J.T. (1995) Big bargains across the borders: Deals abound in Mexico and Canada as currencies plunge. *The Washington Post* (15 January), E2.

Yogerst, J. (1993) Best bargains on that Asian shopping trip: Hong Kong and Singapore offer the mostest. *Conde Nast Traveler* 28 (9), 40.

Zalatan, A. (1998) Wives' involvement in tourism decision processes. *Annals of Tourism Research* 25 (4), 890–903.

Zhao, X. (1994) Barter tourism along the China-Russia border. *Annals of Tourism Research* 21 (2), 401–03.

Zhenge, P. (1993) Trade at the Sino-Russian border. *China Tourism* 159, 70–3.

Zikmund, W.G. (1977) A taxonomy of black shopping behavior. *Journal of Retailing* 53 (2), 61–72.

Index